BOSS

MEGAN VOLPERT

BROAD

MIGVEL:

Thanks for your service!

♡

Boss Broad
Copyright © 2019 by Megan Volpert
Cover design by Seth Pennington
Author photograph on front cover by Chrisoula Baikos

Sibling Rivalry Press, LLC
PO Box 26147
Little Rock, AR 72221
info@siblingrivalrypress.com
www.siblingrivalrypress.com

ISBN: 978-1-943977-63-5
Library of Congress Control No. 2019933542

This title is housed permanently in the Rare Books and Special Collections Vault of the Library of Congress.

First Sibling Rivalry Press Edition, June 2019

BOSS

MEGAN VOLPERT

BROAD

SIBLING RIVALRY PRESS
DISTURB / ENRAPTURE
LITTLE ROCK / ARKANSAS

FOR PASTOR ABBY NORMAN

DEVOTIONALS

HYMNAL

We're all born into this coffin
That's bound to keep us grounded
It was all I could do
To punch one hole through
And run some guitar strings around it
But it turns out you can't just display it
You got to pick it up often and play it

CHAPTER ONE

WHY AM I ALWAYS SITTING ON THE UPPER DECK OF A BUS, high on something legal, hurtling toward the Thanksgiving holiday when I am beginning work on a major new project? This time I am carrying along back issues of *GQ* and I've just caught up through September, with Stephen Colbert on the cover.

Colbert is about fifty episodes deep into his run now and *GQ*'s story is a preview profile, asking the important question of who he will be, given that he has to set down his *Colbert Report* character. I identify with this problem, having just completed a project shot through with the voice of a parallel type of jackass. One of the best things about *The Late Show* is Colbert offering up the possibility of some type of more authentic self. He's a progressive Catholic. I'm a progressive. But, shit, why do I keep grokking around with Catholics for a subject? I'll never be a Catholic, and never was one. This profile's treatment of Colbert's mission as the acceptance of painful moments, this idea of his willingness to let suffering be sacred, appeals to me immensely.

Rock and roll shows are the only place that I feel church with any consistency. I don't know if that is why I still get up and go out to them. The first time I saw Bruce Springsteen live, I expected a lot and got more than I expected. My parents never listened to Springsteen; the first time I heard any of his lyrics, they came out of the mouth of Patti Smith on the radio in the car. I was born in 1981 and missed a lot of good stuff as a result.

There was this one teaching gig I took that had a hellish commute, like two and a half hours in the dark and the cold every morning. I was the wind's whipping post and it was beginning to take an emotional toll when I got seriously into Springsteen for the first time. A lot of uplifting stuff leaking out of my earbuds on the train every morning. Much of the time, I was the only white person waiting on those platforms at that hour. The hour of brown mechanics and black hotel housekeepers, and I was their children's public high school English teacher. Pretty working class romantic, and lovelier to dwell on than the icy wind and slushy puddles. The music saved my ass from a bad season.

[handwritten margin note, left:] as something as one children as a ground

[handwritten margin note, right:] Rock & Roll Church

But—haven't I always got a dependent clause for you? But I know a few other stories, ones with different details that nevertheless capture the same suffering I heard in those lyrics. Sometimes at concerts, my wife and I play a game where we try to count the number of people of color in the audience. Tell you what, not too many non-white faces at the Springsteen show. Maybe a fluke, or maybe a thing. I try to begin by being aware of it, and maybe it turns into a substantial criticism or maybe it ends up not being a big deal. Springsteen has to be loyal to his own experiences, as each of us must to our own.

We are meant to see ourselves in the music as a measure of our common ground, of which there is truly plenty. Stephen Colbert got his break as a correspondent on *The Daily Show with Jon Stewart*. Stewart's love of Springsteen is legendary. Springsteen and Colbert are both Catholics of some fresh kind. The Boss, as an icon and a writer, is fertile territory for manifold contemplations. Also, ground well covered and beloved. Why can't I leave hallowed ground alone?

★

Every musician's origin myth seems to take seed with either The Beatles or Elvis Presley. Both of these stories are more deeply about *The Ed Sullivan Show*, which is itself an epic tale of how America owes its popular culture to the Columbia Broadcast System. I've always liked its big eye logo, very all-knowing. Listening to musicians is one thing; looking at them is another overlapping, more expansive thing. Perhaps this is why musicians must tour to support their studio recordings and why we believe that musicians who deliver solid concerts are a cut above musicians who produce solid albums.

Springsteen sprung up on the Elvis side. He hopped the fence at Graceland and rang the bell, only to be gently escorted back to the curb by house security. My wife was raised in a house that revered Elvis. Even today, most rooms of our own house have a piece of Elvis-affiliated artwork hanging in them. We went to Graceland once. Despite the size of the place, the walkthrough produces a strange type of intimacy wherein one begins to believe one might unlock the psyche of the celebrity who lived there. I also began to imagine myself living there, walking the proverbial mile in his shoes.

There are still-unreleased Springsteen songs that directly rewrite the lyrics of Presley's songs. He taught himself the craft by emulating his hero in a way that prized fidelity to the original, except he would tell his own stories through those familiar melodies. But Springsteen will not transubstantiate into Presley; he builds something new out of the bones of his ancestors, something that is meaningful beyond its association to the art of the past, something capable of fresh revelations.

Perhaps there is a parallel universe where Pr[...]
and invites the twenty-seven year old Springste[...]
Springsteen himself admits to not knowing what he mig[...]
had opened that door, but the act of jumping the Gracela[...]
any way require a response from Presley in order to succeed. I[...]
do be better to trespass on hallowed ground than to be invited onto [...]
is to acknowledge the significance of a landscape, engaging oneself at [...]
in order to embed in an unknown territory that purports to be untoucha[...]

Presley's legacy and estate are too vast to incur damage from Springstee[...]
intrusions; the Boss therefore committed merely a very personally valuable
misdemeanor. The King's hip swiveling resulted in similar violations. Ed Sullivan
initially barred Elvis from performing on the show because CBS had a family
audience unfit to experience those rock 'n' roll gyrations and for Sullivan to
reverse his disapproving position in a naked bid for higher ratings than *The
Tonight Show* meant that Elvis was a relatively unwelcome guest. In fact, there
was a different host that night as Sullivan recovered from a car crash and thus
skirted appearing in what would later be widely considered a historic television
moment.

Sixty million people watched it, which at the time represented more than
eighty percent of all American television viewership. In his second set that
night, Elvis covered Little Richard's "Ready Teddy." During his third and last
appearance on the show, he covered the black gospel standard "Peace in the
Valley." Everybody does covers; they're a form of worship and also of generational
knowledge transmission.

★

"Mary Queen of Arkansas" / *Greetings from Asbury Park, N.J.* (1973)

Elvis King of Tennessee, I'm not too ugly for screamin'
My eyes were blown and earworm sewn
And my plastered love's got me creaming
Elvis, my king, you cost my skulk's surviving
Well, it might be fate to designate me as your servant rising
I'm more than just a domestic cat, don't inquire about my grades
I'm not a fine toy for your flaccid fat or a doormat profligate
Elvis, my king, suppose my freedom is hissing
I'm not man enough for you to rate or woman for dismissing
Teevee made me believer, you can break my purpose through to the batting order

hat jumps the border
w will be intervening
s are just bleeding
elievin'
t till you got me achievin'
lypso of Bruce
overwrite sends mourning doves to Zeus

'is
d start to resemble a queen
ı fervency machine

*

Dear Abby,

It's finally time to write this letter because I'm heading back to school without you at the end of this month, and I'm hoping to grieve it all out in advance so that I don't end up snot-crying and dry-heaving in my empty classroom for all our colleagues to see. The intensity of our friendship has always been a mystery to them, whereas for us it was just more of a surprise. When you got hired by the high school, I didn't have many friends and was still flying under the radar out there in my rusty trailer with a view of the bus lane. In some ways, I feel like you were sent to me. "Sent" implies a sender, so go on and insert your own Jesus joke in here.

Our friends have never understood how we fit together. They see you as a loud-mouthed, short-attentioned Christian from a Midwestern town, with a head full of casserole recipes where advanced literary analysis skills should be, boiling over with a pathos too bubbly for your own good. They say you're nice in a tone that bespeaks their lack of respect. They see me as a foul-mouthed, overly-political atheist from a Yankee city, with a head full of ambition where my grown-up cooperation skills should be, eye-knifing everybody with an ethos too sharp for my own good. They say I'm good at my job in a way that bespeaks their guardedness. I am an uptight punk and you are a wild church lady. They don't know us.

It's unbelievable that you were friends with my college roommate. She knows a young version of each of us that bears little resemblance to the people we are now. My side of the room was spotless and symmetrically organized, a shocking living space for a party animal of a debate team captain. She still can't believe I teach tenth grade English for a living, let alone that you and I are friends. You used to be a pretty solid member of your speech team and preserved your virginity until marriage.

In the beginning, I thought that at best I might have lucked into a reliable carpool situation. The first time we met for coffee, mainly I tried to reassure that my circumstances were similar to yours and I loved my job. We both came from blacker schools, attached to the idea that education is more about character than standardized testing, sent to the suburbs by an unfeeling county seniority system that might pick us up and drop us somewhere else next year or even next month. I remember that I stayed to talk with you for a half hour longer than I intended.

You saved me from a punishingly long and winding commute. I used to get up at 4:00 to scoot to the train at 5:15, then the end-of-the-line bus at 6:30, then meet my carpooler at a Starbucks at 7:15 to get to work by 7:45. With you, I woke up at 5:00, scooted to the train at 6:30, then got in the car with you at 6:45 to be at work by 7:45 with Dunkin' Donuts coffee in hand. Every Wednesday was coffee day. In a shitty week we would exercise our right to pastries, Boston Cream for me and anything with seasonal cheesecake or brownie batter filling for you. The cashiers at DD often asked if we were sisters. They appreciated us because we were the only regulars who didn't order the same beverage every time, though you always got large and I always got medium.

We were mostly on time. There were those two or three times we ran out of gas, in one car because the gauge was broken and in another car because we just forgot. Well, you forgot, but I learned to forgive and also to check your gas gauge every Tuesday and Thursday. There was that time we stopped for gas and found a twenty dollar bill tucked into the pump with a "pay it forward" note attached, and we both fervently hoped it was students of ours who had done this. There was that time an undocumented immigrant tapped the back bumper and after seeing no damage, you just told her not to worry about it and got back on the road. I thought she was going to hug you.

After four years, one hundred and eighty days of the year, five day a week, an hour every morning and as much as two or three hours every afternoon, I'll always have a fondness for a mid-'90s Toyota Camry, especially if it's got a blue-green exterior with paint on the seat covers and smells like Cheerios. This car braved Snowpocalypse, when all of Atlanta shut down and every other car had been left abandoned by the side of the road until the streets thawed out. We skirted the backs of strip malls where I occasionally had to get out to push us when two wheels couldn't get traction on the ice. We only took one break, to nap for three hours on top of boxes while using carpets as blankets at the

Home Depot, and eventually we made it back to my house fourteen hours after we'd set out from the school.

The Camry only had a tape deck, so I was bringing a new mix tape from my own teenage years every week for us to pop in when we didn't feel like talking. We went through both sides of that one cassette eleven times during Snowpocalypse. For the rest of my life, I will think of you whenever I hear Starship's "We Built This City." It somehow gave us the courage to press on, or at least it was there while we gave courage to each other. When we got to my house, I immediately made huge pasta. Then we drank a bottle of wine and napped. It was dark when we woke up, and you had your big cry while we watched a movie.

Mindy thought I was an insensitive prick for ignoring you while you cried, but I knew you were just having it out with yourself in consideration for what we'd just done and what was still left to do in finding a way home to your babies. Even my wife and your husband don't really get how we operate. They just trust that it works for us and tried to appreciate having to do a little less psychological labor because we processed so much of our daily baggage before we took it home to them. You helped me to allow my feelings and I helped you to get organized. We cried in the car a lot, and sometimes screamed, though never at each other.

We've gotten in remarkably few disagreements during the course of our two thousand plus hours together. I learned that Christians need not affiliate with conservatism. You learned that morally upright people need not affiliate with a church. Given any situation, whether actually in play in our classrooms or hypothetically proposed for the sake of amusing conversation, we agreed that we would take the same actions in about ninety percent of cases. Our justifications have different source material, but what does it matter?

Finally, you are going to divinity school. You will have a chapel of your own some day, ministering to youth the same way you always have in class, minus the stacks of papers to grade. Teaching and preaching are pretty similar endeavors. I'm proud of you for taking a leap this size and relieved there's an avenue for you to do what you're called to do. Meanwhile, I am going back to school, to fill the space in my classroom that is right next to your classroom, which will now belong to someone who doesn't know who the hell you are in the least. I will watch your freshmen sprout into sophomores, seeking shelter in my class and searching for the ghost of your voice coming through the wall we shared behind my whiteboard.

Your exit finally prompted me to get a car and a license to drive it, something that I have stalled for many reasons in the two decades during which I've been eligible to do it. But the thought of finding another ride to work was truly unbearable to me. Ours was the carpool to end all carpools. Thank you for the recycled license plate keychain with a giant V on it. You know how I love to put my name on stuff.

I will be so glad to have a little piece of you in the car with me every day, especially in the event that I run out of gas, tap someone's bumper or face a giant snowstorm.

We have been kinder to each other more than our biological sisters could ever fathom. We have learned more and grown more quickly than any other period in our lives so far, and we have loved each other well. We have been so lucky. We really became adults together, so that each of us now goes forth into the world capable of acts of feminism and acts of faith that would have previously been unthinkable. Happy graduation.

Love Always,
Megan

★

"4th of July, Asbury Park (Sandy*)*"/
The Wild, the Innocent, and the E Street Shuffle (1973)

Abby the fireworks are trailin' over graduation tonight
Endorsin' the light in all those freaked-out faces
Growing up this twenty-sixth of May
Simmered down the class's bull over jaded cheaters
So chaste so tiny such sparks
And the band geeks play with that drum line sway
In the bleachers after dark
And the noise from the lacrosse team advances
To rope in the flattened members of all those boards
Bracin' for cosmetology girls

Abby it's Pandora surprising aligned us
In headlights we carpool work wives forever
Study your rites for I will surely meet you again
It's Abby's world

How we teachers revamp worksheets
Or get tested on trying to read or give speeches or write
The poise of our psyched ideals ah Abby we're twins at first sight
I see you don't get wired from gradin' all them piles of papers
Handin' them scores through a screen
Unsatisfactory pearls inside oyster deadlocks

Where kids promise to follow routines
And you know that Snowpocalypse we had winter last
We drove all through the night and we never fought
Though that mix tape kept repeatin'
And probably zombies weren't far off

So Abby it's Pandora surprising aligned us
In headlights we carpool work wives alma mater
Runnin' out of reach at sight of the AP's slaughter
Well he ain't your boss for sure Abby

Abby, if angels are cranking it higher adjust
Spoke to 'em a thousand times
And they said you won't let yourself lose fire for work anymore
It's a bummer that the tether gets knots
We'll guide this ode from bereavement back to
Parley then scrum and then glow
'Cause I can see your blessed memoirs
No more of these weak signals from Mars hand of God
Beats the maybes piled on your status quo
You can start finally trusting youth ministry
And buildin' character outside the zoo
This classroom life for you is through
Although you won't skip out on me too

Abby Pandora surprising aligned us,
In headlights we carpool work wives forever
Go study your rites and don't doubt this friendship goes wherever

*

"Rosalita (Come Out Tonight)" came out in 1973 as part of the B-side of Bruce Springsteen's second album. The studio recording is more than seven minutes long and the song never charted. For the next ten years, the Boss closed pretty much every show with it. That's how a man begins to resent his audience, surely. For me, the story in this song isn't told in the voice of Bruce. I always imagined that it was an aging drag queen initiating a younger one, dropping the knowledge and providing some loving support in the face of worried, conservative parents.

Sloppy Sue and Big Bones Billy work at the night club. Jack the Rabbit and Weak Knees Willy are johns. Come out, indeed.

*

Springsteen cancelled a show in North Carolina to boycott the state's passage of a controversial bill that would arbitrarily and even dangerously dictate which restrooms transgendered people should use. An open letter on his website said he made the decision in order to support local freedom fighters against prejudice and bigotry. These so-called "religious freedom bills" were popping up in state legislatures across the South, including Georgia. If the Springsteen show in my city had been cancelled, I think I would have been pissed. I don't know how large a queer following Springsteen may have, but for myself, I'd have needed to go to a show more than ever if faced with such a legal landscape.

Stephen Colbert, a native of Charleston, challenged the Boss from the left. He said we should not withhold our talents from North Carolina, but instead use these very talents to troll the bigots. He wanted a bolder breed of activism, not a simple boycott. Toward this end, Colbert then proceeded to televise two men in Civil War garb making out on CBS. Cyndi Lauper, who has long been favored with predominately queer audiences, agreed with Colbert. She exercised a rider to her contract stipulating requirements for non-gendered restrooms and also donated all the concert's profits to Equality North Carolina.

By the time the state's legislature had closed for summer vacation, the law had been weakly tweaked to no effect, rather than repealed. However, most of the rest of the South was quick to point a finger at the barrage of negative publicity that followed in the wake of the bill's passage, and this public outcry had the impact of substantially dampening support for the bills in other states. The main focus of my own governor's remarks on the matter were echoed by leadership across the board: our state wants to stay inclusive for investors' sake.

The collective fiduciary consequences to the state of North Carolina due to boycotts like Springsteen's dramatically proves that rights for queers means more businesses willing to set up shop, more rockstars willing to do the show. I prefer the style of Colbert and Lauper, though their arguments were perhaps meant to address a different audience and their efforts were perhaps aligned with a different constellation of goals. It's still undeniably true that the people who have power to make decisions in a human rights case like this were ultimately most persuaded by Springsteen's type of argument. Wherever Rome is populated by ruthless pragmatists, it may be necessary to speak their language.

"Rosalita (Come Out Tonight)" / *The Wild, the Innocent, and the E Street Shuffle* (1973)

Shed doubt now Rosie, shock her from the noose of manly chains
You know prayin' for man enough is maybe too much shame
I'm gonna pick up an acolyte, you're gonna be a hot cross bun
And together we'll make the devout ignite and make our saint's day stun
You don't have to fall for more penance Rosie
And you don't have to be no son
The only mother you ever wanna heed
Should respect the way you've swung
Rosie's pure like none
Acolyte let yourself free, try on all the hats
Hot cross bun's cooled down confronting rebirth
Applying new attitude in all her spats
Cops cruisin' the corner waitin' for a bust
Drama she looks like a bimbo lookin' right past us
We'll recite the Lord's Prayer circle vessels made of squares
'Cause you know we won't succumb
We ain't got forgiveness
But who on earth could shun
When Rosie's pure like none

Rosalita hump a little higher
Senorita don't spit in my fire
I don't need another lover, not for hire
Rosalita you're my stoned esquire

Stack the abbot with calla lilies, 'cause it's time that we declare
Wandering Jews will all seem silly in our world of laissez-faire
We're gonna read bell hooks, smoke with crooks, get some looks
Grab the limelight, we're gonna be highlights
So Rosie come out forthright, baby come out outright
Windows are for dreamers, fire escapes for whores
Closets are for high heels, divas use the door
So use it Rosie, that's what I'm here for

Rosalita hump a little higher
Senorita don't spit in my fire
I don't need another lover, not for hire
Rosalita you're my stoned esquire

Now I know your mama she prays for me
'Cause I don't have mammary glands
And I know your daddy detests Rosie
'Cause he wants you to be a man
Papa entered your room, he beat you with a broom
I'm comin' to make a stand
I'm comin' to activate you, complicate you, I want to be your plan
Sometimes we're shook up, dismissed, but inside we'll be sunny
Olympiad, Dame Galahad
And your papa says he knows how you're making all your money
Tell him he can look askance or find his daughter in loving first glance
Because our subnormality, Rosie, just can't stave off our rain dance
My throat's not slashed and my face isn't smashed when johns have mercy
By the time we can sleep, I'm dead on my feet
From walking the streets of Jersey
Hold sunlight, it's a human right 'cause Rosie we damn sure belong
And in time we'll greet that justice fight as it's foretold by our harms
I know a city of some grace in Northern California down San Francisco Bay
It's a little cliché but we can be ourselves all the way
You can hear it in your heartbeat drumming
So keep faith Rosie 'cause this is your second coming

*

It's getting to the point in my life as a reader that I can discern very quickly whether I am going to like a book. Sometimes I can tell by the cover. More often, I know in about ten pages, no matter how many total pages there are. Peter Ames Carlin's *Bruce* is a little over five hundred pages and a *New York Times* bestseller. Oh man, do the critics love this book. I made it through the first fifty pages.

After the first chapter, things did not look good. So many superlative adjectives and so few facts. Somewhere around page thirty, he doesn't take the time to say what kind of motorcycle Bruce crashed—not even the make, let alone the model or the year. The prose was brightly emotive, full of figurative language and speculative pathos. It's exactly the kind of book a man might hope will be written about himself someday. Indeed, *Bruce* was touted as the only book authorized by Bruce in twenty-five years. His participation and blessing is its primary defense against superior biographies.

The book is far from lazy. On the contrary, it draws out every instance like the slow accumulation of sugared threads in a cotton candy machine. Replete with the highest and sweetest praise for any evidence of his goodness and erring for the glossiest shine on his minor misdeeds performed surely only in defense against unthinking or nefarious antagonists, *Bruce* is an easy project with which Bruce would of course want to cooperate. As I rounded the bend on chapter four, I thought in the final judgment of this portrait he might at best end up sometimes looking like a happy Don Quixote and at worst, like the hot hippie savior of progressive America.

But I had research to do and was doggedly determined to keep my mind partially open until at least the hundredth page. It was just as I reached this state of uneasy resolve that my friend Claire emerged from her guest room and came into the living room. She's a librarian and always wants to know what people in her life are reading, then she wants to know if it's any good. So I tell her my suspicions about getting sick on prose this shade of purple and yes, I may have done a dramatic reading of three randomly chosen sample paragraphs from different chunks of the book that easily and amply supported my impending conclusion.

Something in my grand performance jogged loose an odd little tidbit inside the palace of her memory, and she exclaimed: is that the one where they say, "he wore a condom over his heart"? That is a truly ridiculous sentence, but one which I had not encountered on my brief foray into the book. Claire then proceeded to smartly flip through to the chapters on Bruce's first wife and other places, skimming up on any part of the text that may have contained her golden turd. When she didn't find it, she hit the internet.

It turned out to be a line from Saul Bellow's novella *The Actual*. I'd put any of its ninety-six pages up against Peter Ames Carlin. Anyway, I quit the book. It's been sitting in the living room where I dropped it after Claire figured out the Bellow quote. Can I really just not read it? According to everyone, it's a major part of the canon on Springsteen. What would I miss out on if I just put it down? One can never know. That's the opportunity cost of a refusal to waste my time.

This happened again immediately after I admitted to myself that I wasn't going to read it. I thought it'd be smarter to maybe read more things that influenced Bruce and less things that were actually about him. So I bought a copy of *The Catechism of the Catholic Church.* That's eight-hundred and twenty-six pages I'll never ever read. I couldn't even make it through the table of contents in one piece. Ugh, the syntax.

I was having dinner with my favorite aunt, who was passing through town on her way to the family vacation in Orlando. Aunt Fran used to teach Sunday school. She was raised Catholic and knows all about this stuff. She even briefly considered becoming a nun, before getting an advanced degree in microbiology and becoming a mother of five. Fran sent me a book, *The Catholic Faith Handbook for Youth*, which she used to use with her middle schoolers on Sundays. I have to take good care of it, too, because she wants me to send it back when I'm finished.

Having Catholicism explained to me like I am thirteen years old is pretty much right on target to meet my needs at this point. I'm whipping through this little textbook, finding a surprising amount of things with which to agree and an unsurprising amount of things at which to laugh. Any time I have questions, I drop Abby a text message. Sample question: *If Jesus rose on the third day, where was he at for those three days and what passage in the Bible explains this?*

A nice thing about the Bible is that the passages are generally short. Abby sent me back the second half of Luke 16, which says something about "Abraham's bosom" in the story of Lazarus. She also said it's more like defunct Catholic lore that Jesus was hanging out in Hell for three days, and that it was more like only one day anyway. I love her for thinking I might care about the difference between one versus three days in Hell. She appreciates my attention to detail. She doesn't see me as an asshole wearing a condom over my heart.

I would like to pull ten random quotations from *Bruce* and ten from the Bible, and see if you can tell me which ones refer to Bruce and which ones refer to Jesus. Is this book potentially headed in the direction of arguing for the plausibility of historical, rhetorical, or political parallels between Springsteen and Christ? I guess I don't know enough about either man, or myself, to say. Biographies are so tricky, have so many uncontrollable agendas.

The quickest route to seeing such heroic, romantic things about yourself in print would be to write a memoir and just spell your ideal self-image out for everybody. When I put down the Peter Ames Carlin book, I thought that if that was how Bruce wanted it, he should just write the tall tale himself, like Bob Dylan did. I seriously cannot get through *Chronicles* either, so sue me. Sure enough though, Springsteen announced a few weeks ago that his memoir will be published in time for my next birthday. It's the same size as the biography, but hopefully of somewhat greater factual density.

"Thunder Road" / *Born to Run* (1975)

The window slams
Peter's shade plays
Like an incision between two worlds one scorched
One made of waves
Poseidon swinging for the holy
Offering me an adult testimony
We can go home again
I just can't race you when you roam again
Don't run and fly
Boy you know just what I'd leave for
You take to air because you're drinking
That fountain of our own youth evermore
I'll become a wraith while Tink stays at your side
I can grow old and hey it's all right
Oh so say goodnight to me

Or you can sail the undiscovered
Get muddy in rain
Cut the losses from your mother
Blow kisses to her pain
Braced for bummers, decay and pain
Misbehavior becomes obsolete
Well now I'm your hero
A captain good
All the preemption I can offer, boy
A crew against one like Hook's
Any chance you've understood somehow
Hey what else can I do now
Except hold fast the sails
And let these travails blow back my hair
While your flight path's tight-roping
The trade winds will take me everywhere
We've got a romance that you can make real
If you trade in your wings for the eels
Grab an oar, heaven's waiting on our marine corps

Don't forsake my hand
We're ditching out tonight on the base at Neverland
Oh wonder rowed, oh wonder rowed
Oh wonder rowed
Loving you here has been a pillar of sun
It's not over yet if we pick up water guns
Oh wonder rowed, wet sprite, behold
Wonder rowed

Well we've got this lodestar
And I know where there's a dry dock
And my ship's out back
If you're ready to leave this lame loch
From your tree fort to starboard seat
The boat's anchored but the sail ain't free
You're my one and only
Just try to let that soak in
Both tonight we'll be free
Or I can leave you heartbroken
There are ghosts in the cries
Of lost boys who grew up this way
They taunt this disgusting eroded
Vision of acclaim in your made-up pirates' bay

Drop dreams of fame tonight at your feet
My blues dressing gown gathers dust in your tree
And in the siren song offshore dawn
You'll see my sails unfurling strong
You best walk this plank before I'm gone on the wind
So Peter climb in
Pretend is for losers
I'm sailing out of here to begin.

★

I am using this book project as an excuse to learn how to play guitar. "Excuse" may be too strong—final impetus. Music has always been at the center of my self-medication. I made mix tapes off the radio during a nightly "Eighties at 8" program, listening intently to identify a song within the first few notes and immediately decide whether to push the record button. In sixth grade, I joined the school band as a percussionist. That was about the rhythm; I never considered being a rock star. There were a couple of months in an all-girl band in junior high that covered Joni Mitchell with four-part harmonies. That was about being in a community of girls; I never entertained the idea of being a professional musician.

Over time, I've noticed many parallels between motorcycles and guitars. They are both extensions of the body, instantly receptive to a profound miscellany of environmental factors that must be ridden like waves. There's a technical vocabulary, specialized equipment, long lines of tradition, objects of an iconic Americana. After a few rounds of experiment, I became aware of not feeling invested in a manual transmission. Shifting gears was a type of math that didn't interest me. Fretting notes down the neck is the guitarist's equivalent of driving a stick shift. It's also masochistic, and I'm too vain about my hands to grow the proper callouses for fretting.

The urge was always just to make my noise. I learned slide guitar instead, just as I learned to drive on two wheels instead of four. Friends who played guitar, none of whom could play slide, would ask me why I insist on learning everything the hard way. These are the same people who tried to reason me through the ways that bikes were more dangerous than cars. Sure, if you're a certain type of person, slide is harder and bikes are scarier. I must be some other type of person because I took to both instinctively.

Never played guitar standing up. For nearly a year, my cheap black-on-black lefty Strat knockoff sat untouched in the office. I named her Betty, and Betty and I eyed each other warily across the room for a long time before we sat down together. The first few weeks, I played the proper vertical way. Once I understood how to find the chords, Betty went flat on her back. A few weeks later, I plugged in the amp. Then I started buying slides made of different materials—chrome, brass, glass, porcelain—in different sizes. Nickel thumb picks, then finger picks. Then I realized, playing guitar with slide and pick is like driving a bike with half-finger gloves on. The covered parts of my hands are the ones really impacting the machine, not the fingertips greased up with street grime or the first knuckle joints torn up from sharp strings.

A full year went by and my playing was starting to demonstrate some skill. I ordered an electric lap steel that finally arrived last month. Her name is Ginger, partly in honor of Gingger Shankar, the world's only female double-violinist. We got to know each other right away, despite the fact that she came strung for a right-handed person. I'm not one to waste a perfectly good set of strings, so I've been playing upside down with the bass string furthest away from me. Gives me something new to think about, which is another characteristic I've always appreciated in bikes.

I understand how men displace their bodily desires into high-performance objects like bikes and guitars. If a woman buys a Porsche as a birthday present to herself, we don't deride it as compensation or midlife crisis, in part because we admire women's bodies directly. At the same time, there are very few prominent female rock guitarists or race car drivers. These objects more overtly convey masculinity to the American culture that valorizes them, and then we refer to the objects with feminine pronouns. I'm guilty of this with Betty and Ginger, though the root notes of those names are actually Tom Petty and George Harrison. My current bike is a genderqueer named Hooligan, who mostly prefers masculine pronouns.

Gender, as something we all constantly perform, is complicated by objects that are read in isolation as also gendered. I get "excuse me, sir" most often when I have left my helmet on to go into the grocery store for just a few minutes. That is not about not seeing my face. We have given intrinsically gendered qualities to guitars; we say "play like a girl" as if that is feminist reclamation. I don't know how often I do anything at all like a girl, given my preference in objects.

When I was in high school, I remember once coming across a snippet of mean Southern gothic literature that was filled with all kind of stereotypical epithets. My teacher wouldn't say the N-word, but didn't miss a beat on spitting "bulldagger." This was new slang to me, though I had heard of butch dykes—two words in which I have never tried to make a home. These three syllables washed over me like gasoline; I knew "bulldagger" was inflammatory but I still loved the smell of it. Even as a child, I knew I would ride a bull and carry a dagger.

*

"Born to Run" / *Born to Run* (1975)

In the morning we set out for high school like all typical American teens
At noon we read through newspaper stories looking for common themes
Flipping pages till hallway time
Revealed, disaffected
And colorin' outside the lines
Kids frown still gripping their phones in their hands
Macbeth or nap, put on your thinking cap
Better not let those pages burn
Teachers like us, I say we were sworn to learn
Students let me in, we got an hour to spend

Let's roll hard on big life decisions
Try to wrap your psychedelic limbs
Round stupid social divisions
Together we can shake your nap
We'll learn in workshops, I say however no hacks
Will you talk with vocab you've acquired
'Cause I know I'm a very long way from retired
So I gotta hope that this appeals
Before grades are due to be filed
Just show me that you're turning your wheels

Respond to office on lunch hour loan sign on a get well card
Then go home with unaware papers
And cowboys want to write like bards
The breakthrough score part prize is cold and dark
Students shuttled back and forth as the grist
I'm gonna cry on kiddos' answer sheets that's right
It's a never-ending test

The hallway's damned with token zeroes
Or a flash dance come alive
Beyond any doubt now about red lights
So all I can do is guide
Shoe leather, teachers, we can walk in this madness
Let's serve them with all the vastness that we know
Give it a whirl, someday friends,
Let's try to keep a straight face
While our salary is froze
We still rock and kids turn
Because teachers like us
I say we were sworn to learn

*

I looked around for gods and didn't find many, so I came down a notch to mortal
icons of progressive virtue and picked the Boss over Bono because I like talking
about America. Springsteen openly aspires to write the great American novel in
song, and though a familiarity with the history of the man's life might certainly
augment one's view of his work, I'm gravitating toward the music itself, framing

it in such a way that his biographical input isn't needed. A part of me has long shown deference to that notion of wanting to let a superstar's private life and the history of the band go publicly unexamined. But over time, I've come to see a discussion of his albums as a separate matter. The text is right there; he made that for us to read. To analyze Springsteen's literature doesn't require his participation.

It took about a week to read all of his lyrics. As I did so, I indexed each album taken in chronological order, track by track with a very specific target question: Does the speaker in this song at some point directly address a female listener? As a female and a listener, those were moments I was expected to slip into connection with a song. I began to notice that some of his lyrics were creeping me out, or making assumptions on my behalf, or fomenting otherwise bad vibes where before I had only good vibes toward his music. Reading through the songs, I became lost in a sea of girls, babies, darlings and belittling yet affectionate referents of that ilk.

I wrote down every way he referred to any woman in every single song. Patterns in the data emerged with ease. Springsteen began his career addressing women by name with some of his most successful singles through 1975. Then there is a long line of girls and babies, emphatically broken by "Bobby Jean" in 1983, followed by a decade of comparatively crap albums and an accompanying crutch of archival material headed into the next century. In 2002, the twin towers fall and the songs turn to address a less gendered "you" until the intimacy of that is stolen by a pile of darling. Then I winnowed down this collection of well over one hundred songs by starring my favorites, the top hits, and B-sides that I just felt had interesting language.

The result was a list of forty songs, which I then resolved to rewrite from the perspective of the female listener. These songs can talk back to their originals, homophonically applying precisely the same rhythm and beat structures to a different set of words—an English-to-English translation of my own experience. So this is not a letter to Bruce, but it does put us in an awkwardly palimpsestuous, parasocial relationship. It is not to better the man, but to better our hilariously queer feminist selves in his image. I love Springsteen's music for calling me to be an arsonist, the paradoxical gift of creating this thing that destroys—these things that light him up as they melt him down.

CHAPTER TWO

LET'S GET THE ELEPHANT OUT OF THE ROOM FIRST THING: I am voting for Hillary Clinton. Whether you want to debate the merits of that or dismiss me as an idiot, it remains universally true that her guest spot on *Broad City* is a subject of interest. When I first heard that this appearance would be forthcoming, I had many immediate questions: What did she hope to gain by the appearance? Would Clinton be able to vibe with the show's raunchiness, or would the show compromise to elevate its tone in order to include her effectively? Did this constitute a Clinton endorsement of the show, and then conversely also the show's endorsement of Clinton? Is she going to play herself? Is it a walk-on or a fully fleshed out character? And is Clinton even funny?

The buildup to this episode was killing me. The night before the first episode of the new season, Abbi Jacobson and Ilana Glazer appeared on Colbert, and I could not wait for them to talk about Clinton's appearance. Was it a pain to get the script approved? What was she like on set? Did she do any improvising? Are they voting for her? But it never came up. Colbert talked to comedy's two hottest rising television stars for eight minutes and nobody ever even breathed a word about their link to the presidency's longest rising hot-button candidate. Much of the point of having a guest on a show is to boost ratings and increase new viewership by piquing audience interest with the appearance of a favorite celebrity. Guest spots are widely publicized and talked about in advance on late night shows for this very reason. I was bummed not to get new info from the broads or Colbert, but also intrigued by the simple fact of their silence.

Is it just that *Broad City* is so straight-up amazing that Jacobson and Glazer don't need to tout their guest list? Perhaps, since it's true that none of this season's high profile add-ons were discussed during that interview. And yeah, I've been a serious fan of the show since the pilot episode. These two ladies have so many qualities that resonate with me. All dope-smoking aside, I just love them. Jacobson is awkward in the best possible way, down to earth but also down for adventure. Glazer is offensive in the best possible way, aggressively consuming physical space but intellectually committed to nothing.

Broad City is, for me, like the love child of Dick Van Dyke and Janeane Garofalo. It is the unlikely heir to classic 1960s sitcoms full of exaggerated physical comedy, wild misunderstandings that breed heroic adventures, and a leap of faith that everything always ends happily. On the other hand, it is also the most cutting-edge breed of feminism available for our modern, uncertain times, socking it to the worst elements of American culture with fully politicized lives and fully formed opinions couched in a stream of bitingly surreal witticisms that—coming out of a man's mouth instead of a woman's—would be hailed as pioneering, but are instead sometimes struggling to get out from under the label of vulgarity.

Because what is a "broad," really? Yes, their city is wide, but also, the title of the show implies that city belongs to these two broads. Broad: noun, North American slang for a woman, arguably meant to have derogatory connotation. Or consider this delightful clarification from Urban Dictionary, brought to you by Mos Def: "less respectable than lady but much more respectable than bitch." What makes Jacobson and Glazer, either as real life human beings or as the slightly exaggerated character versions of their own humanness, classifiable as "broads"? As I began watching this season, I was reminded of a lot of reasons to label these two as such.

For starters, they are broke. As Pierre Bourdieu pointed out way back in 1979 in his excellent toilet tank tome *Distinction: A Social Critique of the Judgment of Taste*, lower socioeconomic status is often tied directly to cultural opinion, meaning that women of little means are overwhelmingly rejected by more financially stable segments of society and this rejection takes the form of automatic discredit of their tastes. In the first episode of the season, Glazer accidentally drops the key to her bike lock down a sewer grate, which results in her having to walk around the entire day with a huge, unwieldy chain around her waist. Despite its obvious weirdness, nobody in the episode comments on it, even though she has to heft it repeatedly just to sit or walk around. Just one more crazy broad dismissed as having unusual fashion sense.

Add to this Jacobson and Glazer's status as unmarried, and the label of "broad" becomes even more applicable. In the second episode this season, Jacobson faces the wrath of the local co-op board for impersonating Glazer to fulfill Glazer's monthly volunteer hours in order to keep her membership. The only reason Jacobson is discovered is that she confesses in a desperate last attempt to connect with a sexy fellow volunteer who seems normal and interested in her, if only she can reveal herself as not actually Glazer. He is horrified that she would lie to the co-op and ends up rejecting her. Meanwhile, Glazer is fearfully approaching a doctor's appointment because she has to get a shot, so her occasional boyfriend has to soothe her in a variety of creative ways. Hannibal Buress always nails the perfectly measured reaction to Glazer's Tasmanian devil antics. For his above and beyond good behavior, he nets zero commitment from Glazer.

Glazer and Jacobson are serious besties for life, with more than a touch of homoerotic undertow in the longing side-eye and breathless mumbles emitted by Glazer. These sisters are doing it for themselves. They have no secrets from each other, they defend each other against any outsider even when one of them is being completely stupid, and they tell each other the truth in the most supportive way possible. They have legit Millennial problems, and despite the fact that they go dismissed or unseen by much of the city around them, they express joy and confidence in each other's constant company. The girls of *Broad City* are underdogs, but you'd never know it from their attitude.

This is part of a historical tradition of funny broads surpassing their alleged limitations. Just to get the ball rolling on a much longer line of broke, loud-mouthed women: Lucille Ball, Joan Rivers, Lily Tomlin, Roseanne Barr, Sandra Bernhard, and Amy Poehler. And Poehler is where the endorsement triangle begins. She is executive producer of *Broad City*, and perhaps best known for her terrific and terrifying impersonations of Hillary Clinton for *Saturday Night Live*. Clinton enthusiastically embraced Poehler's impersonation by appearing with her on the show. Poehler has been a vocal supporter of Clinton during her 2012 and 2016 bids for the presidency. Jacobson has also expressed support for Clinton.

In fact, many "broads" who have achieved some celebrity credibility endorse Clinton: Uzo Aduba of *Orange is the New Black*, Kat Dennings of *2 Broke Girls*, America Ferrera of *Ugly Betty*, Lena Dunham of *Girls*, and RuPaul, to name a few. Rebecca Traister's new book, *All the Single Ladies: Unmarried Women and the Rise of an Independent Nation*, excerpted beautifully in *New York Magazine*, makes the case for how the demographic category of "broads" is climbing at a rate that will make these voters the ultimate arbiters of Clinton's success. Amongst broads, Clinton has actually been trailing Bernie Sanders by double-digit margins. Her exit poll numbers in early primary states show a consistent lack of support from women under thirty-five.

Will Clinton's appearance on the beloved *Broad City* give her a bump with the broads? Though the show features two of them, broads are not necessarily the key demographic watching the show. In the YouTube era, Neilson ratings are a bit out of touch, but according to a recent article in the *New York Times Magazine*, the show's numbers for Season 2 claim a hefty 18.8 million online streams from various sources like YouTube, Facebook and Hulu, while also netting 1.2 million linear television viewings.

Though its host network, Comedy Central, generally skews male in viewership, last year's *YES! Magazine* article rounds up the reasons why the show is "the funniest coping mechanism" millennials have for examining their economically disadvantaged metropolitan lives. The age 18-34 demographic is definitely watching *Broad City*, and these progressive viewers, demonstrably skeptical of Clinton during early primary season, will take some convincing. Simply appearing on the show is likely not enough to get them to rally behind her in the voting booth. At show time, can she hack it?

In January of 1976, Betty Ford went on *The Mary Tyler Moore Show*, and Carter still did better with women in the election than Ford. She was the first First Lady to appear on a sitcom, but far from the last. Nancy Reagan was on *Diff'rent Strokes*. Michelle Obama was on *Parks and Recreation*. It's traditional for these female politicians to play themselves, and to promote some favorite cause. Clinton's IMDb record lists tons of news segments, late night and morning show appearances, plus the work on *Saturday Night Live*, always as herself. With a clear cause of winning the presidency and a viewing public conflicted over her political persona, the stakes for Clinton's appearance on *Broad City* are high (and I hope Jacobson and Glazer will be, too). Will she help broads everywhere to cast their doubts about her candidacy aside, or will she get in her own way?

When the long-awaited episode did finally air it was chock full of additional guest stars with larger roles and longer scenes than Clinton's. Any of these guests would have rated the headline on any other night. At the South by Southwest Festival in Austin last week, Jacobson went out of her way to clarify that Clinton's appearance did not necessarily constitute the show's endorsement of her candidacy. "We were not trying to make a statement, to be honest," Jacobson said. "We wrote season 3 a year ago, at this point. That's not our show really: Let's make a political stance here. It was really more that this is something Glazer's character would do. Hillary, even regardless of where we stand—and we love Hillary—is such an iconic figure. These girls being around her is not an everyday thing. That's how we felt being around her. It was like, 'Oh, this is a different world'."

Except every chunk of the episode actually reveals the importance of Clinton's agenda. The fact that the episode fit right in with the rest of the season is proof positive that lovers of *Broad City* should also be lovers of Hillary Clinton. In the opening segment, the two girls are on a park bench brainstorming possible inventions, including "boots that have magnets on the bottom so that when you're walking around you're just picking up change." Glazer declares it the most productive morning of her life. When they hit 63 dumb ideas, they go get bodega brunch. What else can you say, except that these ladies dream big? It might look a little silly to an outsider, but Jacobson and Glazer are plucky to the max, which is a pretty serious business.

The second segment begins Jacobson's plot line for the episode, in which she must go to the Department of Motor Vehicles to renew her driver's license. The place is portrayed as a post-apocalyptic wasteland where time stands still and everyone is a zombie or a creep. Most critics have said that Jacobson's DMV plot was much funnier than Glazer's plot about volunteering for the Clinton campaign. I think this is really due in large part to something nobody is talking about, which is the way in which the license problem is resolved. After a terrible haircut, a sublated disk in her neck and vomiting during the photo, Jacobson vows to try the DMV again another time. First she must hit up her chiropractor, played by Alan Alda.

Alda acts as if he were her grandfather, asking after her health, giving her many gentle words of praise and encouragement. Her visit even turns out to be free because he just sold one of the paintings Jacobson made that Alda displays in his office. They have a great visit and Jacobson feels much better, but she dreads returning to the DMV. At this point, Alda drops the knowledge. "Next time, when you make an appointment at the DMV, do it online. That way, when you get there, it just takes a minute." This is late-breaking news for Jacobson—seriously grown-up stuff. Alda may seem like just another helpful old dude, but he knows how to solve the problem. He's not going to sit around complaining about the DMV with Jacobson; he's going to point out a better DMV policy that she can implement. She makes the appointment online, and this time, enters into a magically utopian DMV somewhere between Oz and Wonka. The photo problem is now being resolved to such an extent that the professional photographer requests to snap additional pictures just because Jacobson looks so great. She even offers her a job as a model. It's all sunshine and lollipops, if you're an insider.

Meanwhile, Glazer is busy with another guest star, Rachel Dratch. Glazer was fired from her startup gig due to her responsibility for an inappropriate viral tweet. Dratch plays a one woman show of a temp agency, but fails to find any opportunities for Glazer. Instead, Dratch ends up crying over her own personal problems and Glazer is the one to comfort her. Basically, Glazer goes to ask for help and instead finds herself able to give it. She does succeed in becoming a bike messenger, revealing the surreal superpower of being able to identify people better by their rear ends than by their faces as she delivers their packages. After saving a broken Dratch and crushing it on her new job, she stumbled into Clinton's territory to deliver a package. Upon finding out where she is, cue the patriotic ballad, the industrial fan blowing back her hair, the slow motion salute, the bald eagle background. Glazer immediately respects the juju of the place, saying,

"Glazer Wexler and Hillary Clinton? Two powerful women working as one?" Then the front desk lady says Glazer will never meet Clinton, and Glazer reluctantly concedes this is probably true.

Cynthia Nixon plays manager to Glazer and the other volunteers. Nixon's character is not especially likable--because she is working and is seriously good at working. She keeps one ear on Glazer's outrageously casual phone conversations with prospective voters. She asks Glazer to turn down her constant peanut gallery "yaaaas" commentary during a staff meeting. She informs Glazer that this is a volunteer position immediately after inferring that Glazer's believes this is a paying gig. Nixon is on top of it all, briefing the phone bank volunteers on how to answer some of the more idiotic, chauvinistic questions they may encounter. "No, Hillary does not cry at the office. Yes, Hillary can read a map. No, Hillary will not enforce male birth control or male pregnancy, as that is not a thing. And no," she says, "Hillary is not a witch."

Glazer expressed disbelief that her fellow citizens could ask such dumb, annoying questions about Clinton, to which Nixon grinds her teeth and sighs, "daily." The *Broad City* girls also face this type of constant underestimation, and that is the root of their fondness for this candidate. They don't "feel the Bern" because they don't get mad about their daily suffering. They just get hyped and support each other until they can work around these problems, if not entirely solve them. Clinton is a mythical creature in that mode of survival, imbuing everything in her campaign office from the air to the floor with her awesomeness. Jacobson visits Glazer there and they assess the vibe as, "power...it smells decisive...smells like kawn-fuh-dawnce...smells like no bullshit." These are the qualities they admire--the essential qualities of broads.

In the final minute of the show, Clinton makes her walk-through. The girls appear to be having orgasms, again with the slow-motion as Clinton winks once from each eye and smiles broadly at them, waiting for them to calm down. She is graciously soaking up the adoration, but it's equally quite clear that she is used to this. For the fact is: Hillary Clinton is a celebrity. You genuinely could sub in Beyoncé for this guest spot, and the argument made by the show would be identical. Not only because she is political, but also due to this longtime celebrity, Hillary Clinton cannot really be funny. She can stand next to other funny women and appreciate what they're doing, but she can't make a lot of jokes. She has to keep it presidential, after all. And a president can't actually be human because humans are funny.

Fortunately, nobody at the water cooler at work the next day talks about how funny a show is anymore. Now, we just share the link on social media. Clinton just had to do something that would be worth a click, and she closes down the episode with a sufficiently weird moment to make the audience smile and give them something sharable. She brings in one of those stupid waving arm things you see on the roof of used car lots, because she says she wants to improve morale. Firstly, as Glazer and Jacobson have just amply demonstrated, morale could not be more improved. Secondly, why on earth would Clinton think one of those annoying things would boost morale? It's a hare-brained scheme, just like Jacobson's magnetized boot idea. Oh, right, this is Clinton making fun of herself for doing this guest spot.

Everyone is already going to say she is pandering to millennials by appearing on *Broad City*, so in order to do it right, Clinton is completely embracing both her status as an icon and her status as too old-school to be cool. Need we be reminded of her most famous meme, Texts From Hillary? Comedy Central teased the episode by offering up the best part of it in the preview, which is Jacobson and Glazer's orgasmic reaction to simply sharing airspace with Clinton. They think she's an icon. And when Clinton rolls out the stupid waving thing, they quickly get on board with genuine enthusiasm. Millennials love star power—an immeasurable, influential type of cultural charisma that both Clinton and Trump have been collecting since at least the early 1970s. That's why they're going to meet up in the general election—where Trump will be funny and Clinton will be female.

Glazer and Jacobson finish the episode by saying they thought the stupid waving thing was male, but Clinton assures them it's female. Just a simple, generic assertion of female space, just holding it down for the ladies. In the whole campaign setting, in fact, there is only one male. Everybody else is these scenes is a tough broad, projecting the kind of smarts and savvy to which Glazer and Jacobson aspire. Actually, it goes beyond real life skills to the realm of the supernatural. Glazer demonstrated her butt-recognition powers earlier in the episode. When Clinton meets Glazer, she greets her by name and Glazer is incredulous, as if Clinton looked straight into her soul to get that name, or had somehow heard of her as a fierce fellow queen. Clinton just points and deadpans that Glazer is wearing a name tag. It's not hocus-pocus; it's pragmatic reality. And forty years of stacking up pragmatic reality definitely congeals, despite all its seriousness, into star power. They rest their heads on Clinton's comforting, old-school shoulders, and roll the credits.

Notably, there are absolutely zero drug references in this episode, which may be a first in the show's short but remarkably consistent history. When they consider the virtues of Hillary Rodham Clinton, the ladies of *Broad City* are not stoned; they are stone cold sober.

"Badlands" / *Darkness on the Edge of Town* (1978)

White hot highlights
Double down on tart brand
Got a dead-on new vision
Cashin' out faux slut clans
I've brought in a satire
Of corporate contraband
Because those pages wear manure pearls
Here's an epigram
For most women's magazines
I think they're a scam
To slash our self-esteem
Money makes gaunt their art, avant control
Let's take a poll right now
Upsetting visions forecast they'll be
Hawking a new cream
Get it for a steal
Your make-up is so tight
that the face can't feel
Bend with strife dating
For a selfie that still looks dumb
You're on pace for prime hating

Newsstands, you gotta read 'em everyday
Let liposuction land
As a price too big to pay
Or keep smushin' till there's no girlhood
'Cause these newsstands are beating us good

Perkin' for the lens
Till you get your check earned
Jerkin' up your cleanse
Till you get your pounds burned
Maybe they've got their grounds
Laid too good right now,
The pressure pixelates, snarling,

Door man calls you a bitch
Pitch man hands you a ring
The right wing is fortified
As it schools us to sing
I wanna tear out eyesight,
I wanna strike out what is fraught

I'm perceived in the face that was made me
I achieve in the age that time gave me
I will reave all these tropes and I say
That some way it marries me
To ladies' newsstands

For a run of sale promotions
For potions that will hide
Don't tailspin because we don't need looks to thrive
I'm gonna make one place that ain't out to screw me
I'm gonna make air space
I'm gonna pack a suitcase of these newsstands

★

As a critic, my main job is to convey a clear sense of what is at stake with any particular art object by delivering a fully formed opinion about it to readers who have yet to encounter that object themselves. As a process, criticism gets more complicated when the object of this opinion is a book that itself treats another separate art object. This type of criticism can spawn a stream of tangents for one to follow ad infinitum. The tricky bit is knowing which rabbit holes are worth pursuing and then how deep to fall down into them before they bottom out.

When criticism bottoms out on a really profound sidebar, that often means it can't get back in touch with its art object and thusly can't conclude with an opinion that properly alerts readers as to what they should do next. Most critics consider this type of writing to be a failure. But not me. And not Alina Simone. So let me say right now: Alina Simone's *Madonnaland* is a totally excellent book, and if you don't bother to read it, you will be missing something significant in the development of modern cultural criticism. Simone did not set out to write criticism; she set out to write a biographical account of Madonna.

But she couldn't. She failed at that. Most writers do, because come on; it's Madonna: a living legend of popular culture whose daily media references are generated as such a rate that it is simply impossible either to say you have read all there is on the subject of her or to say you have something so fresh to add to the slush pile that it is worth publishing a book. There is no shortage of crap books about Madonna's life and work. It's to Simone's credit that she wanted to dive in to such an intimidating mess and even more to her credit that she chose to bail on it in favor of this project, which is essentially a catalogue of her failure to write the greatest Madonna book ever. As a result, she actually did succeed in writing the greatest Madonna book ever because the focal point of it is Alina Simone, not Madonna.

Simone herself had grand music ambitions once upon a time, and indeed did very well for herself at the high tide of college rock in the 90s. But her band didn't gather enough momentum to stay on top, so despite her skills and savvy, Simone now enjoys a somewhat more low key existence as a smart cultural commentator with a nice backstory to vouch for her ample musical street cred. She is plainly self-aware of her own jealousy of Madonna's success. She isn't a Madonna super fan, a nut job memorabilia hoarder, or sporting any full-back tattoos of the pop star's face. In the book, she does meet all those people.

She also meets a Madonna-specific fortune teller in an encounter I won't spoil for you by trying to describe it any further. There are a lot of weird people in the Madonna orbit, and Simone's taxonomy of all these characters is delightful through and through. The king of the heap is Gary Johnson, who also doesn't even adore Madonna that much. Johnson is like a real life version of the *Gilmore Girls* character of Taylor Doose, a fervent town hall meeting guy with a profound knack for the kind of researched bureaucracy that makes him a blustery thorn in the side of many local politicians. Johnson wants a sign outside the town of Bay City, Michigan, acknowledging it as the birthplace of Madonna.

Simone goes to Bay City to research Madonna's early years and is dumbstruck by the total lack of information available. Instead, there is Gary Johnson and his quest for signage. I say "quest," because apparently this has been something of a raging municipal battle for decades now. Then there's the ancillary problem of the town's official song, which may or may not be racist. Then there's this whole thing about multiple, giant, engraved keys to the city.

Then it turns out that Bay City is also the birthplace of Question Mark and the Mysterians! And then there is a chapter on Flying Wedge! Flying Wedge is a mythic, astoundingly excellent black classic rock band about whom nobody beyond the most serious vinyl hunter knows. They had one single and three fans; now they're gone and Death, an equally good band working in a similar vein, got its long-overdue documentary treatment first. These developments result in an interesting foray into the question of who first smuggled the word "masturbate" onto the Billboard Top 100. Also important, the word "mondegreen": noun, a misinterpreted word or phrase resulting from misheard song lyrics. Simone will give you an education, just not really about Madonna.

These are great tangents! They are so great they become central. Does the world need one more half-baked biographical update on Madonna? No, it does not. What the world does need is Alina Simone's productively clear-eyed assessment of her own musical and journalistic failures, told with deep affection for the detours unavoidably provoked by fame and fandom. *Madonnaland* is not the end-cap of Simone's existential musings; it is an intense jewel in the already sparkly crown of a consistently perceptive critic. I find myself jealous of her.

*

There are a bunch of things in Gillian G. Gaar's *Boss* about which is it worthwhile to complain. For starters, the photographs are improperly tracked; they don't coincide with the content of the text until almost a fourth of the way through the book. As far as visuals, it's like The Castiles never existed because the collection doesn't include much of anything before 1974. Hilariously, Gaar even discusses the early publicity shots of Springsteen's first band and then none of those shots are actually presented. The photos throughout the book are mostly one-note. There are a huge number of monochrome snaps of Springsteen tilting up the neck of his guitar with his mouth stretched open mid-phrase, or doing that thing where his knees bend inward toward each other and it seems like he might collapse, or him and Steven Van Zandt making eyes at each other while sharing a mic. For an illustrated history, the illustrations are very weak. However, odds are the publisher is to blame for this because it's mostly a matter of permissions or of layout, which are not within Gaar's control.

There are two types of inserts sprinkled throughout the book: Gaar's review of each album and some highlights of anecdotal behind-the-scenes stuff. The reviews are arguably comprehensive because there is definitely one sentence about every single song on each album. Gaar sacrifices depth in order to go broad. Moreover, she is primarily concerned to read the albums as literature, usually summarizing the plot of each song or analyzing its symbolism in place of dissecting the composition or giving analytic descriptions of Springsteen's voice. The second set of inserts is often interesting because Gaar chooses to focus on things like why The Bottom Line was such a respected place to perform, and other acts for whom Springsteen opened or with whom he guested. There's a little bit on the two wives, and a little bit on other members of the band.

For the main text, which is the real reason to buy this book, Gaar is often working at the margins slightly outside of traditional biographical territory. A lot of diehard Springsteen fans might complain about this because *Boss* basically does not reveal anything outside of what we all already know. The author sometimes leans on Dave Marsh's 1979 effort *Born to Run* and sometimes on Peter Ames Carlin's 2013 effort *Bruce*. The complete bibliography is highly respectable, but there is zero original research. Normally, that would relegate a book to the realm of the coffee table, but there is something bigger going on here. I think the truth is that Gaar respects Springsteen a great deal, but she is not possessed of the type of deep, lifelong obsession badge that most of his biographers are proud to display.

I cannot emphasize strongly enough: this is not only not a criticism of *Boss*, but in fact, a theory of its best asset. Gaar's bona fides come from the land of punk rock. She's written liner notes for Heart and Laurie Anderson. Her first book was *She's a Rebel: The History of Women in Rock and Roll*, which is still the definitive tome on the subject despite its 1992 publication date. She lives in Seattle and contributes a lot to the knowledge base on Nirvana. *Boss* is a solid book because the firm, understated power of Gaar's gutter feminist voice cuts through all that glitters around Springsteen.

The thing that regularly bothers me in reading up on the Boss is the near uncontrollable pathos with which critics lob their loftiest adjectives at him. Beyond the hyperbolic praise many of his albums garner in reviews, the biographical material available displays a narrative tone so romantic and overwrought that the facts are often glossed by thick layers of apologist psychoanalysis over any mistakes Springsteen might ever have made. The whole enterprise smacks of Don Quixote. Don't get me wrong, I think Springsteen is terrific musician and human being, but my stance is akin to Gaar's in that there is something in the mythologizing characteristics of so much prose written about him that just rubs me the wrong way. Lester Bangs once wrote for *Creem*, "if I seem to OD on superlatives, it's only because *Born to Run* demands them." Gaar's clean, cold statements are bracingly effective by comparison.

Let's examine some of her diction choices. The text is full of streamlined and slightly distanced uses of language more in line with proper journalism that most journalists usually keep to in analyzing Springsteen. When he gives up on his first pretty successful band, Gaar states, "He didn't want to rejigger Steel Mill; it was simpler to break it up and start over again." Other biographers have devoted very many pages to speculating on the agony of Springsteen's decision, apologizing for his ambitious abandonment of the other band members. This book simply outlines the two options and confirms that the decision made was easy. Or there's this little gem: "There was an awkward start to the first show, when Springsteen forgot the words to the opening song, 'Born to Run,' but the audience surprised him by singing the words themselves." There is no excuse made for why the Boss forgot the lyrics, no contextualizing information about how that show may have been a particular struggle in distracting ways, and there's a straightforward acknowledgement that this was awkward.

Gaar's syntax and use of punctuation are also something special. She hides her admiration in parentheticals, undermines or makes jokes in sidebars, and uses dependent clauses to great effect. "(In 2000, the compilation *Badlands: A Tribute to Bruce Springsteen's Nebraska* testified to how highly regarded the album came to be; the album was a straight recreation of Nebraska, with contributions from such artists as Chrissie Hynde, Los Lobos, Ani DiFranco, and Hank Williams III, among others)." Of all the things to praise *Nebraska* over, this is such an obscure, odd one to pick. It's a covers album filled with indy, outlaw musicians, showing plainly where Gaar's sympathies lie.

In the *Darkness on the Edge of Town* insert: "Side note: race car driver Ritchie Schultz later informed Springsteen of an error in his lyric: Fuelie heads wouldn't fit on a 1969 Chevy 396, as he sings in the opening line" of "Racing in the Street." What a terrifically irrelevant detail in a review; what a completely unanswerable jab in the ribs of a man who is selling the image of himself as a working class person intimately familiar with cars. "The Max's show also generated an item in *Rolling Stone*, but not because of the music; Hammond suffered a heart attack while at one of the shows, and his doctor charitably attributed it to 'Hammond's enthusiasm' for Springsteen's' onstage antics." First there's the valuable historical fact of the national news item, then there's the defiance of expectation about that item, then the actual news tidbit, and finally the real skinny shot through with opinion in the use of "charitably" and "antics." As an exercise in form, Gaar is succeeding at something totally different and often better than what many other biographers could accomplish in two or three times as many pages.

Beyond formal elements, the focus of her content is similarly shifting readers away from the usual aggregation of facts to something a little more progressive. She reminds readers more than once that Patti Smith rewrote many of the lyrics to "Because the Night" after Springsteen gave her the unfinished song; Gaar gives ownership of the song's success primarily to Smith. She also introduces Patty Scialfa into the text at several points before even so much as hinting at her future marriage to Springsteen, emphasizing instead that Scialfa is a talented musician herself, with perhaps more punk credibility than her husband: "There would also be a female vocalist in the lineup: Patti Scialfa. [...] 'We would only play on the streets,' she later said of Trickster. 'People would invite us to play clubs, but we thought playing clubs was selling out!'." Gaar doesn't spend any time on the drama of celebrities' personal lives. The entire opening paragraph on the Julianne Phillips insert reads, "Springsteen's relationship with Julianna Phillips started out as a white-hot romance. They married just over six months after they met. But by their third wedding anniversary the marriage had fallen apart."

The characterization of Springsteen himself proceeds with reverence not by overloading the pages with purple, but simply by cherry-picking the stories about him that the author herself most reveres in consideration of anyone's character. She focuses on anecdotes about Springsteen's rebellious nature, what his guest appearances say about his influences, and the steady escalation of his political involvement. This is my favorite paragraph in the entire book:

"At a few shows, Springsteen surprised the audience by returning to play a couple more songs once the house lights had come up and people were beginning to leave. As early as September he began playing 'Santa Clause is Comin' to Town'—just because he felt like it. But he was also happy to show he wore his fame lightly; while in L.A. over the Fourth of July holiday, he and some members of the band climbed up and defaced a billboard on the Sunset Strip promoting *Darkness*, spraying 'Prove It All Night' (one of the songs on *Darkness*) in block letters along the bottom."

These three stories are all fairly common knowledge, but they are often sprinkled in to show Springsteen's silly side. I've never seen them stacked together like this, where the total effect amounts to rebelliousness more than just prankishness. Gaar is working on an approach to Springsteen that the crusty dudes of rock criticism will not comprehend; she knows it and wants her readers to know it.

I laughed out loud when she played Captain Obvious against what is unquestionably the most famous quote about the Boss. On Jon Landau's crucially important May 22, 1974, declaration of love in *White Paper*, she writes, "the piece ultimately became best known for this pronouncement: 'I saw rock and roll future and its name is Bruce Springsteen. [...] (The somewhat awkward phrasing of the sentence meant it was also destined to be misquoted over the years, as 'I saw rock and roll's future' or 'I saw the future of rock and roll,' among other variations)."

Again, there's that clear cut acknowledgment of what is "awkward." You pay undying respect to Landau; you don't call him out for ugly syntax. Unless you're Gillian G. Gaar—and more power to her. The several best-selling books about Springsteen that have received universal acclaim would not dare engage in a moment like this, either in fact or in sentiment. With Springsteen finally launching his own memoir at the end of September, *Boss* is likely the most sober and most punk rendering of the man's life and work that we'll be seeing for a long while.

★

"Streets of Fire" / *Darkness on the Edge of Town* (1978)

When the fight's died but it doesn't end the war,
The guise unexpired you can't
Outrun what's in store
So you capsize you hit a plateau
And your demise from the bold balls you rat race
Defeats your strong strides when you have interfaced with
Cheats and liars

I'm wondering why losers clown my back
I'm spying, swirling from all the smack
And in the starkness I fear nobody wins this game
And we need real guys now no dicks in this line
And it's first prize for a sharp tongue that expires
All these cheats and liars

Combative vow, all these dangers
Peacocks all these dangers
Road blocks with anger that won't disgrace
Cheats and liars

★

I've been running up the credit card on a hot streak of amazing tickets because you can't put a price on true experience. In the span of three weeks I've got Dixie Chicks, Garbage, and Guns N' Roses, so it's a late nineties throwback of epic proportions in keeping with the politics of the summer where I am waiting to find out how seriously Trump has considered Newt Gingrich for his veep slot and generally trying to remember everything Hillary Clinton worked on during her tenure as First Lady.

The Dixie Chicks played a new arena in Vegas the day after Trump announced he was going not with Newt, but with Mike Pence, who is "a Christian, a conservative, and a Republican—in that order." I had no sense of what the concert audience might be like because Vegas is Vegas. Everyone there was overwhelmingly nice and there was a freakishly high count of bachelorette parties, tipsy ladies in white lace and cowboy hats with arms flung around their best gals, tipping those hats to my wife and I in their gleefully bubbly support for gay marriage. Indeed, the three musketeers on stage also including a giant rainbow heart on the backdrop behind them during the encore. I'd had high expectations, which were met and quickly exceeded. The Dixie Chicks have a perfectly calibrated, thematically relevant and visually stunning video production at their live shows to rival that of Rush.

We sat next to a charming NICU nurse who was amiable and chatty with us throughout. Within three minutes of finding our seats, she asked us, "how is the gay scene in Atlanta?" Every word spoken like a person in the desert who has just spotted the queer shimmer of a unicorn in the shape of my wife who was dressed as loudly as usual. She was there with her mother. We had the aisle seats, so we kept rotating around each other, ensuring everybody could dance in the aisle and grab some good photos. She found us on social media and sent us all the videos she took. We have plans to meet up intentionally next time we're in Vegas. Natalie Maines takes a few minutes to drop her guard now and most of the rants appear in visual rather than verbal form via the video behind her. I realized that so-called "outlaw country" audiences are actually just Southern and Western progressives and this is the label of their ostracism from Top 40 country radio that they wear quite proudly as a badge of honor.

They did a great cover of the late Prince's "Nothing Compares 2 U." I cried when they covered "Landslide," which is most likely more deeply a story about my intensely fraught love-hate relationship with Stevie Nicks, a story for another time. Emily Robison played some very good lap steel and I wish she had busted out the sitar. That may be my own next move. They closed with "I Believe in a Better Way." We flew home the next morning and woke up to the Republican National Convention's bleak and backdropless vision of America on the edge of apocalypse, where a prospective First Lady can plagiarize a chunk of her speech from the opposing party unpunished and there are no people of color besides those present to protest.

It was four long days of surrealism and then I went to see Garbage. Grunge did to Garbage what country did to the Dixie Chicks and the quality of fandom at the two shows is comparable. Funky cut and colored hair was everywhere and the dust was clearly brushed off some epically excellent goth swag. Everybody had fun while behaving kindly toward strangers and nobody left in the break before the encore. Shirley Manson cried when she paid tribute to a recently deceased local fan whose family was attending the show, she brought a birthday girl from the road crew up on stage so the crowd could sing to her, and then she gave a solid rant about how good things still happen every day and we should not be overwhelmed by what pours out of the television.

A half hour before the show, Hillary texted me to say that she picked Tim Kaine for her veep slot. The Democratic National Convention begins in two days, and on Wednesday I will be rocking out to Guns N' Roses while Clinton is accepting her nomination. On Thursday, I will begin putting summer and hangover aside to go back to the work of raising the next generation at new teacher orientation day. I thought it might be true that there is a wave of nineties nostalgia going on this year, but it may simply be that the women I fell in love with in high school are still counted among my strongest influences not because they were so great at the time—though of course they were—but because they are still kicking ass today in a here and now that is somehow the same but wildly different.

★

"Jackson Cage" / *The River* (1980)

Leaning in she has nothing complete
She's a charmer, survives to compete
With vertigo of spouse, kids there's no time to play
Just machinery of mother's day to day
Being a mouse with a mind disposed
To sleep and keep things cheap, she's on her tip toes
She goes online and clicks her balance sheet
The cruelty in sight breaks the hedge from the cheat

All for women's wage
Just for women's wage
You can cry about your rights
But they're too blind to feel the slight
Of numbers fudged by pairing knives
Down to women's wage

Overextend preconceived notions
Lost rewards and top billing poor
While kettle black gets to settle on not owing
The lard pledge that we're meddling for

Santa Claus is bust with more delays
And that's even though they always say
Here's some pearls you have frowned now belong
Then like hell they will say you must prove you're too strong to

Make women's wage
Just for women's wage
And don't be flattered by some small raise
You are smart enough to earn the pay they make
But will you spend your lifetime portrayed downplayed
Working for women's wage

Give me last rites or I'll scream as a debtor spurred
Till I fake up a stouthearted twirl
For men reeling both conspired and excused
For plunder of my worth trustees will skew
Just hating to be outrun
Never growing if that pay is never won
Stepping stones grandstand under our feet
We beat the drum of plans that yearn to be free of

Women's wage
All for women's wage
No helping hands with wedding bands
Surveys all say we earn less than
Run from the danger we face payday
Working for women's wage

★

Patti Smith's newer book, *M Train*, is better than *Just Kids*. There, I said it. When I read Smith's exceptional and touching chronology of her young life orbiting Robert Mapplethorpe's, I loved it as much as everybody else did and I was psyched when it won the National Book Award. After reading *M Train*, it will be clear to any reader that Smith's formidable twin powers of rhetoric and compassion were actually only operating at half-mast last time. *M Train* casts the kind of spell that one must return to over and over again.

Her first line proposes that "it's not so easy writing about nothing." Indeed, the surface of this book purports to be a meandering and even random collection of journal jottings that may have a few common threads but really no ultimate focal point or theme. Don't fall for it. In fact, each chapter treats an important loss in her life, from such heartbreaking historical moments as the death of her husband, Fred Sonic Smith, to such private griefs like the sudden misplacement of her favorite coat. Every chapter digs a fresh grave in the chambers of her memory.

She moves between these reflections on actual events through the use of dreamscapes. With the occasional aide of a guru cowboy present in her imagination, Smith crafts extremely fluid transitions between her event memory, her creative instincts to romantically transform the real event, and her meditations on how to cope with what she's learned from the event. Even carefully attentive readers will catch themselves in mid-flight, having to go back and skim the previous paragraph to be sure the trajectory of that arrow of their attention can strike true.

The train is her metaphor for this dreaminess. "I followed whatever train I wanted," she says. "I wrote about writing—of genies and hustlers and mythic travelers—my vagabondia." We glide into each station with her, holding on to whatever solid objects we can as Smith imbues each of them with a totemic holiness. She sees soul in the smallest pebbles. Literally, there is a great story in one of the first few chapters about embarking on a pilgrimage to French Guiana to see the prison at Devil's Island in order to pick up a pebble. Genet had always felt destined to be jailed there, but he ultimately was not. So Smith, displaying her characteristic deep empathy, travels across the world to go there on his behalf and collection three tiny rocks from the prison yard, intent on delivering them into Genet's hands via their mutual friend, William Burroughs. Nobody asked her to do it, but she felt called to perform this act of minuscule yet extreme service to a writer she loved.

Some of the stations are faraway sojourns like that. She goes to Greenland to give a talk on Wegener's Artic expeditions to the semi-secret society of the now-defunct Continental Drift Club, of which Smith somehow became member number twenty-three out of a total of twenty-seven. In one of the few moments where Smith recognizes her own celebrity, she is summoned in the middle of the night to have a long talk with chess master Bobby Fischer. But then, utterly humanly, they just sit around singing Buddy Holly songs together. She also visits Japan, brought there by her extreme fascination with Murakami's *The Wind-Up Bird Chronicles*, and ends up washing the tombstones of two fiction writers who each committed suicide. She has lost her CDC membership, Buddy Holly and Bobby Fischer, some Japanese short story writers, and then eventually her thoroughly annotated copy of the Murakami book in an airport bathroom somewhere.

Those are grand adventures, to be sure, but it's actually in her efforts to convey dailiness where *M Train* really shines out from the pack of brilliant writings Smith has produced to date. "Not all dreams need to be realized. That's what Fred used to say," she recalls. "We accomplished things that no one would ever know." To borrow a phrase from Michel de Certeau, it's Smith's practice of everyday living that should most intrigue readers of *M Train*. For starters, there are several kinds of lists a reader could make, if one is interested to take recommendations based on Smith's own preferences. On the food list: brown toast and olive oil for breakfast, dumplings in the middle of the night, green-tea soba noodles for celebration, spaghetti with green onions and anchovies for dinner at home, and coffee coffee coffee of all kinds at all times of day and night. She likes carbohydrates and caffeine. On the reading list just from the first fifty or so pages of this book: Dante, Verlaine, Mrabet, Genet, Bulgakov, Blake, Auden, Sebald, Wittgenstein, Sarrazin, Murakami, Nabokov, Aira, Daumal, Artaud, and Musil. Smith's tastes tend toward the romantic in poetry, mythology and philosophy.

Readers will also delight in the list of things that annoy her. There are several good jabs in there for airports, from security to check-in kiosks. Of course, she is also annoyed by war in all its various forms. The best is when she arrives at Café 'Ino for her precious morning ritual at her special corner table for one, only to find an obnoxious woman sitting in her favored seat. Smith won't sit in any other seat. Sometimes if her table is taken, she gets confrontational. Sometimes she just wigs out a little bit and hides in the bathroom until the other patron leaves.

Café 'Ino, run by a Mexican cook named Zak, is Smith's personal daily church. She eats and reads and writes there every day for many years, right across the street from her apartment, until one day Zak announces that he is leaving to open a new place on the boardwalk. The cover image on the book jacket was taken on the occasion of Smith's last mournful moments at Café 'Ino. The disruption to her everyday life is plain on her face. Zak gifts her the table and chair, carrying it over to her apartment for her after closing the shop.

She soon visited his new cafe in Rockaway Beach, stumbled across a dilapidated old house for sale, got obsessive about it, made a handshake deal with the inside of the house totally unseen, gigged all summer to save up money and then paid cash for it—and then Hurricane Sandy hit. Smith's profoundly strong ability to exercise patience is constantly on display during this and other such losses, despite her claim that she has "always hated loose ends. Dangling phrases, unopened packages, or a character that inexplicably disappears." She respects that life is nevertheless full of loose and lost ends.

In this same vein, Smith watches a lot of detective shows. She happily plops down in front of her little television to watch *CSI: Miami* and other such crime procedurals. There is an entire chapter near the end of the book devoted to a personality profile of Sarah Linden, from *The Killing*, and elsewhere a lengthy analysis of the difference between the American version and the original Danish version. Once, Smith stayed on an extra week in London just to watch a marathon of *Cracker*, a British crime drama that is apparently somewhat hard to find in the U.S. Smith refers to the job of a writer as "the visualization detective" and in struggling to complete a one-hundred line poem, remarks, "ninety-seven clues but nothing solved, another cold-case poem."

Through the book, she is preoccupied by time: the time elapsed since her husband's death, the time spent on airplanes and jet lag, the time slot for her television shows, the beauty of spending winter holidays in isolation, the occasional bouts of insomnia, the endless waiting that is such a part of every life and real time, and the writerly problem she faces in moving too seamlessly back and forth across memory in the not at all chronological recounting of these stories. Ultimately, she rests this dizzying thread of concern on an image of a clock with no hands.

The other place she rests the time problem is in the comfort of spaces. *M Train* is the first book to properly incorporate Smith's photography into her storytelling. All but a dozen of the images in *Just Kids* belonged to Mapplethorpe. All the images in *M Train* belong to Smith, and they serve both as a wonderfully tight anchor to the stories in the text as well as a sort of unusual history museum unto themselves. There are a few family photos, of course, but mainly Smith is invested in special objects: her father's desk, her husband's boat, Frieda Kahlo's crutches, Tolstoy's stuffed bear, Plath's gravesite, Hesse's typewriter, the pylons at Rockaway Beach. There are about fifty black and white photographs in the book, rendered into the most vivid colors by Smith's accompanying prose.

Like everyone on earth, Smith is a little unhappy sometimes. Time and loss provoke a restlessness in us all. She often plays a game with herself, developed to resolve her occasional insomnia: "One proceeds by uttering an uninterrupted stream of words beginning with a chosen letter, say, the letter M. *Madrigal minuet master monster maestro mayhem mercy mother marshmallow merengue mastiff mischief marigold mind*, on and on without stopping, advancing word by word, square by square." But none of these puts the M in *M Train*; it comes from chapter twelve: *Mu*, the Japanese word for nothingness and a bedrock concept of Buddhist koans meaning essentially to unask a question.

What are we asking of Patti Smith? If the premise of the question is so fundamentally flawed that it cannot be answered, one sinks into sadness. This happens to Smith herself: "Without noticing, I slip into a light yet lingering malaise. Not a depression, more like a fascination for melancholia, which I turn in my hand as if it were a small planet, streaked in shadow, impossibly blue." In the end, devotees of Smith's work should not be satisfied with the historical account of *Just Kids*, beautifully written though it definitely is.

The real delight of Smith's work is how simply and daily she strives to embrace those mundane realities with which we all struggle. In the constant grip of what has been lost and mourned and pulled toward the abyss, she just wants readers to be human with her, to be familiar as a throughput to the kind of compassion that ultimately bolsters an optimism needed for making life livable. "[Portals of the world] float through these pages often without explanation. Writers and their processes. Writers and their books. I cannot assume the reader will be familiar with them all, but in the end is the reader familiar with me? Does the reader wish to be so? I can only hope, as I offer my world on a platter filled with allusions."

*

"Fade Away" / *The River* (1980)

Somehow the weight and smother of this land
Are playthings for me made of sand
And the mad hatter that I am spills over the tao
Sunscreens me in the world
We cannot perceive what we pay
So we must not grieve as we gray
Crybabies

I don't wanna waste a day
No I don't wanna waste a day
Sail me to Xanadu but while I wait
Keep sparkin' I don't wanna waste a day

Meow I see that you are disinclined
To lean much in for peacetime minced
With falsehoods and fuss
And that software rack along your spine
Has frost your doves and tossed your dust
The fumes that burned full of fight are chilled now with numbing spite, hardenin'

Not saying it's breezy for me
Sometimes we all get lowly
While the world spins out moving as it's wont to do
Don't say that you'll kiss good-bye prospects for advancing
Birthdays are homicide cocked at you
Shelled pearls dismissed accrue
No fanfare for your coup
All pearls

So agree we don't hafta be under cover unless reverie lends us flashlights
We have to make the most out of heartbeats
And bloom nonstop now like feisty freaks
Hourglass in flight brandishing sweetness and light
Set to vanquish all appetites
Grow gravy

★

My religion is a hotly debated series of speculations. I eschew labels because most of them are an uncomfortable, imperfect fit. Into the void left behind in their wake is a bunch of anecdotal flotsam upon which spectators—my family, my students, my bartender—build a sense of what I might believe. My father's father was Catholic and my dad quit the church as soon as he was allowed. My mother was born a Jew, never bas mitzvahed, and skulked around as a Jew for Jesus until eventually being taken in by a megachurch. The only time I ever went to a weekly service of any kind was when I was in seventh grade on a summer trip to stay with my uncle in Philadelphia. I still feel gross for not telling him I'd rather not have gone. My wedding was a pretty pagan affair, though we did stomp on a glass blessed by a rabbi who was into supporting same-sex marriages. Most people who know me well would say I am a philosophical person with strong values. To judge by my actions, one could easily conclude I am some kind of secular humanist. I carpooled to work every day for years with Abby, a woman who is all about Jesus, and we are often surprised to find that we agree upon what should be done in any given dilemma about ninety-five percent of the time. The remaining five percent is about abortion. Even among the Southern states I have called home, my neighbors largely love me as an upright citizen, though they do not see me on Saturday or Sunday at their houses of worship.

In college, when I was anti-everything, I did a few turns at the wheel of atheism, but it was just so much work. Still, my own grandfather who lived happily as a Jew for much of his life recently declared at age eighty that he is an atheist. But he still talks to my grandmother, who died twenty years ago, as if she is right there and they will be reunited some way some day, though he is not at all senile. I recently saw an interview with Brian Wilson where he spoke to George Harrison in this same manner and it affected me surprisingly deeply.

Patti Smith gave a reading from *M Train* in my city a couple months ago and I had the opportunity to ask her a question. I told her that I was strangely moved by the consistency of her quest to care for the dead and to have ongoing relationships with them, then I asked her what she wants us to do for her when she is dead. She physically recoiled from my question, then gave a jokey, defensive answer about sending her stuff to charity instead of to a museum and proceeded onto a long tangent about how people are too attached to material objects. When she wrapped it up and the audience started clapping, she dropped her voice a notch into the lull of the audience applause, looked me dead in the eye and said, "but seriously: pray for me." I have few gods; Patti Smith may be one and I will do my best to honor her request.

All of this is a part of what religious people call "testimony." These are the stories I tell to convey a sense of my religion. It feels weird to say "my religion." I usually go with "spiritual" or "agnostic." My first year of college I attended a private Lutheran school where I was obligated to take so many required religion courses. In one of them, I learned that agnosticism doesn't mean that you believe in god but prefer not to practice any form of worship. Agnosticism actually means a radical openness to the unknowable, a willingness of appreciate paradox and forego the pressure of making answers where there are none.

Now we can talk about Lesley Hazleton's *Agnostic: A Spirited Manifesto*. Hazleton is to be trusted. She's a scholar of many kinds of religion and politics, hip to ancient texts and modern predicaments, willing to drop obscure quotations without making a reader feel stupid. She gives her own testimony and uses her own life experiences to illustrate how one might live happily within the sense of uncertainty that would devastate a lesser mortal in search of illusions of closure. She conveys an appreciation for the mystical without ever tipping over into congealed pronouncements of dogma. In the blind alley of life, Hazleton stands on her own two feet in an exemplary manner.

She digs in her heels against atheists and believers alike, devoting a part of every chapter to unpacking the assumptions of each. Hazleton begins by dismissing the need for dichotomous thinking, but not in a Hegelian way that simply picks a la carte from both bad options to create some ideological mash-up passing as synergy. In the second chapter, she goes to town on the personalization and personification of capital-G God and likens Pascal's famous wager to the pitch of a sleazy insurance salesman, ending up at a beautiful reflection on the Tomb of the Unknown Soldier. Hazleton's main objective is simply to hold open a space for contemplative thinking, never tricking the reader down a slippery slope from reasoning to following. She's not starting a cult or converting anybody.

She is a firm supporter of doubt and mystery, and argues that the eradication of these is at the root of any stripe of fundamentalism. She finishes by tackling death and the soul, the fear of those twin dragons that so often leads people into blinding comforts held out by religion. Hazleton grapples expertly with the modern dilemma of longer life and the possibility of eventually achieving immortality through science. She addresses the matter of soul in part through a linguistic consideration of the difference between "the soul" and "a soul" and in part through her viscerally negative reaction to watching the documentary *Jiro Dreams of Sushi*.

Agnostic is a profoundly personal work of memoir as testimony, an erudite exploration of the consequences of religious and atheistic tradition, a sound rhetorical analysis of faith-belief-religion-spirituality-values, and an excitingly fresh take on the long shadow cast by humanity's effort to make meaning out of itself. I found it very helpful in sharpening the vocabulary I use to describe my own spirituality, as well as for articulating and celebrating the unknowable with which we all must ultimately live. Agnostics get a bad rap as lazy or uncaring or uncommitted. I walked away from Hazleton's book actually feeling very proud of the space I occupy in the world conversation about belief. I expect to recommend this book to many people, beginning with my grandpa and my carpooler. Not to proselytize, but people of all religious orientations really should read *Agnostic*.

★

"The Price You Pay" / *The River* (1980)

We grow up designed to lose the stands we make
Implied by all your dismayed friends and their double takes
Can't undo the overload you smile in the doorway
Return to weep and fight in the space we save

And when badlands nearby impeach doubt from your endless mind
Cast out shibboleths and guilt in codes found under your breath
Conniving pews contrite, we're able to rake away
All the feckless leaves in the space we save

Oh, the space we save, oh, the space we save
How we will be okay in the space we save

How we've jumped the bar and awaited prolonged
All to mend this plot and its themes of bastards' swinging dongs
Beefy appetites hijack our rights through foul play
And we're gonna lock up tight in the space we save

Talk of the town always manned
Myth committee whittles crazy reprimands
But by November there's glory in these hinterlands
Now defrost our firebrands
Would-be defenders of our frozen hands
To give thanks for a sliver of faith
To grace the space we save

Forget reclaimed arts, we're gonna stun their brittle, vile farts
They're undone who call gunfights for holidays
This albatross of asinine, the angry jackass always first in line
Head counts women crawling their way to the space we save,
Our world of more transcendent ballet,
We're gonna hear unbound allegro some day

★

When my wife turned forty, she would say that the absolute best thing about
it is not having to justify her opinion anymore. She's forty and can do what she
wants because she's pretty much earned it. My mother has been saying since I
was twelve years old that I am forty on the inside. Most people characterize me
as someone who has an old soul. When I turned thirty-five, we celebrated it as
my own over the hill milestone. I kept cracking that, since I've been living most
days like they've got twenty-five hours in them, I've aged up into the forty
bracket sooner than linear real time would otherwise permit. Autumn's daylight
saving day is one of my favorite days of the year—also, Leap Day. Maximizing
my time on the planet is important to me, and artificially gaining an extra hour
or an extra day is, to me, like discovering a crisp twenty dollar bill between the
cushions on the living room couch.

Middle age is sturdy, and I always perceived that the common wisdom
surrounding my character is that I am more spry than sturdy. More flexible than

dependable, more loud-mouthed than hard-charging. More ambitious than professional. But in my heart, I know that I am sturdy. And on Election Day, as Hillary's chances faded to black, I began to see that everyone around me also knew what was in my heart. So many people, women especially, reached out to me for support. They were screaming, sobbing, vomiting. They were my editors, my in-laws, my colleagues—people older than I am that I had always looked up to as role models for my future self.

These strong, smart, sassy women all needed my faith, if only for a moment. They were losing sight of their human worth as Trump's electoral vote count marched steadily toward our country's ghastly final solution. I remixed a classic to help these women keep their heart: Today, courage. Tomorrow, serenity. In the stream of history, wisdom. For myself, courage lasted until nearly midnight on Tuesday, when the results looked bleak enough to know the fact to which we'd all be waking up. I had to try to get a couple hours of shut-eye before my day-long training on Wednesday. Because win or lose the White House, I still had to get up and go to work in the morning.

The training was a full day workshop on how best to raise our new teachers. I've reached the mentoring stage in my profession, where I'm responsible for pulling the next ones up. Somehow, I got ready and got myself to the training site. It was in the library of an elementary school on the south side of the county, its hallways filled with the laughter and footfalls of nine-year-old black boys and girls. It made me smile on the outside, but inside I was still quite numb, trying to process the fact of a Trump presidency. I kept reminding myself that Hillary had won the popular vote; the results were not so much a repudiation of my values as they were an underscoring of the logistical challenges of the Electoral College structure.

During the day, I was surrounded primarily by black women who teach in public schools in the Atlanta metro area, many of them much older than I am. A few other people there were as ashen and sunken as I was all morning. When it was time to break for lunch, an elderly black woman who has been in trainings with my before patted me on the shoulder. She did not need to ask me what was wrong.

"Buck up, girl."

"I know, I know! But it's so hard."

"What did you expect?"

"I expected that she'd win."

This very kind and wise woman hoisted up an easy belly laugh on that one. Then she touched my head very lightly and got up to go in search of the vending machines. She glanced over her shoulder at me and said, "that is why hope requires audacity." It was a good riff on Obama's book title. During the second half of the training, it gradually dawned on me that only the white people were sulking about the election. I felt gross about being one of them. I felt blinded by my privilege, confused into thinking that this election could simply be about one superhumanly qualified candidate versus one selfish asshole, and that the merits of the candidates would deliver Hillary the presidency with ease. After waiting so long to get out of my father's house, and having lived happily outside his influence for twenty years, the White House has become my father's house and the entire country cannot escape his influence.

But sitting in the training with these fierce ladies all day, I tried to embrace a blacker feminist approach to the results. These women still had laughter and they had so very, very much fight left in them that they took into their classrooms every day. With Hillary in the lead for many months, I let down my guard. I forgot all the work I have had to do on behalf of queers, on behalf of women, on behalf of my students. I thought that I'd racked up enough goodwill and resume bullet points on this earth to magically pole vault Hillary over the objections of angry white males and into the Oval Office. The women all around me reminded me that I should know better. We lost one very significant battle and I am hurting for Hillary as a person – but as she herself well knows, feminism is a war of attrition and none of us can ever give up.

These women around me were soldiering on, as always. Never had I felt so strongly called to teach high school English as I did sitting in that room with them. My current crop of sophomores in the purple state of Georgia will elect out next president. Last week, I'd laminated my giant Hillary poster, the official one with the sunrise background. Had hoped to put it up when she won, but losing the office hardly means she isn't a tremendous role model. So the poster is going up in my classroom wall as a reminder of many kinds of lessons. I've been the only openly queer teacher at my school for years; might as well be the safe space for feminists, too.

Someday, they'll find a reason to fire me. On a few occasions, they have come close. It has been scary and saddening, and I have sometimes trembled with uncertainty at what my own future may hold. What shape will my scarlet letter take? Will it be a Q, an F, an H? I'm getting Hillary's logo tattooed in red and blue on the inside of my right ankle on Inauguration Day, in part as a funeral for my misguided complacency centered on the idea that feminism has an endpoint.

Hillary Clinton went to the same high school that I did. In the main hallway, there was a picture of her posted behind glass as a sort of honorable mention of a famous alum. She was First Lady at the time. I walked by that picture of her probably fifteen times a day, five days a week, for four years. Many times, I blinked at it with a silent but deliberate salute. I've loved Hillary Clinton since I was fourteen years old. I've thought about her with extreme regularity for more than twenty years. I waited my whole adult life to vote for her. When she lost, I lost something, too. But I did not lose my faith in feminism. I'd just momentarily forgotten that women were already bloody but unbowed.

As Chrissie Hynde wrote in "Hymn to Her": "She will always carry on / something is lost, something is found / They will keep on speaking her name / some things change, some stay the same." I had the good fortune to finally cross the Pretenders off my concert bucketlist, just forty-eight hours before Election Day, and cried for so many reasons when she sang "I'll Stand by You." Before the show began, my wife was chatting up people sitting around us. I put my nose in my phone and kept to myself, too excited about sharing airspace with Chrissie Hynde to talk to anyone. My wife spoke to one lady who said she was a medium, that she told fortunes and read auras and other such hokum – and then she pointed a long, bejeweled finger at me apropos of nothing, and declared, "that one has many angels all around her."

This week in piano news: Leonard Cohen and Leon Russell are booked solid in heaven, and Kate McKinnon rises as national treasure on *Saturday Night Live* by blending Hillary with "Hallelujah." Whatever my political or religious beliefs have been, I've never lost faith in music.

CHAPTER THREE

I HAVE BEEN MIGHTILY TESTED THIS WEEK by a simple pair of concert tickets, because I hate Stevie Nicks. Since I don't actually know her, I suppose it's more fair to say I am annoyed by her and I don't know where I get it from.

When I was a kid, in the kitchen with my mom while she made dinner, she often had the tape deck going. She was a pretty good singer and would harmonize easily with Carole King and Fleetwood Mac. *Rumours* was always on the heaviest rotation. Surely it was my mother's way of making peace with her life, finding some interior space in which to chill out against the living room onslaughts of my perpetually angry and ungrateful father, against the verbal abuses he would lob at anyone passing by his Lay-Z-Boy. The kitchen was our safest space and Stevie was the aura in residence there.

To this day, I still know the words to very many Fleetwood Mac songs, often surprising myself with an ability to sing along, taking my mom's harmony lines now that there are—blessedly—a thousand miles between my home and the house in which I grew up. When they finally stopped being afraid of changes and got a divorce, my mom found a blue collar trucker to treat her nicely and they retired to a rundown farm somewhere just south of Chicago that I have never seen. Now she has control of all the rooms in the house and also her own life to a much greater extent, and good for her.

When I most lacked control over my own adult life, it was because my body and eventually even the part of my mind that contains language were ravaged by a GI disease. When I felt most victimized by it, I turned to music to save me, just like my mother taught me. My peaceful place was Tom Petty. We never had his tapes in the house. I don't know where I first picked up on him. He wasn't on the oldies station my dad always had on in the car. I guess I found him on MTV, maybe "Last Dance with Mary Jane" when I was in high school, and then working my way backward to the roots.

The second time I saw him live, we had lawn seats. He brought on Stevie Nicks as a surprise guest. Even then, I was humbuggy about it. When he called her an honorary Heartbreaker, I became furious. She doesn't even play any instruments, aside from tambourine, which a three year old can play. Even Mick Jagger plays more guitar than she does. I can agree that Tom and Stevie can do great harmonies, resonating from somewhere in their equally unmistakable nasal cavities.

I suppose I just don't like her persona. I don't like her because she let sexual tension and divahood fuck up her terrific band beyond repair. I don't like her because she probably introduced Petty's band to both coke and heroin, and they did not survive it as unscathed as she did. I don't like her because she purports to be so witchy, in a way that strikes me as so pretentious and self-serious that it is often laughable. Everything about her way of being a frontwoman just rubs me the wrong way—even when the songs are great and the show is great. There is simply some part of me that won't open to Stevie Nicks, even with Petty's ultimate endorsement.

I voluntarily bought tickets to see a regionally very successful Fleetwood Mac cover band. It was a really solid performance with one extra guitar player, and I focused my attentions there because the band itself was comprised entirely of assholes. The lady doing Stevie never broke character, even on her fifteen minute break in the middle of the set. They were using the turmoil and snootiness of the real band to give themselves emotional permission to be jerks to each other and their audience. It was an unflattering bare bones portrayal.

A few months ago I had the opportunity to see the Dixie Chicks, and I jumped at that. Those ladies are awful nice family and they can all play the shit out of multiple instruments. When they covered "Landslide" I noticed I was crying. I tried to concentrate on whether the tears were coming from the moment of experience or from Stevie's lyrics and honestly could not separate them at the time. I was mad at myself afterward, because it seemed lazy to be swept up at that bit when there are many Dixie Chicks songs that are much closer to my heart and to my personal journey than "Landslide" has ever been.

The Dixie Chicks are outlaw country, which allows them to maintain a punk rock attitude in a number of crucial ways that delight me. Stevie has never for a moment seemed punk rock to me until this week, when she announced that this tour's opening act would be the Pretenders. Chrissie Hynde is a bucket list performance for me and this is the first chance I've ever had to see her live. So there's the test.

Would I be willing to give a wad of cash to Stevie in order to see Chrissie? Would I be willing to actually sit through some or all of Stevie's show, so as to get my wad's worth after Chrissie's set is over? There are $40 nosebleed arena seats, and $60 tell yourself you don't need binoculars seats, and $89 now we're getting somewhere close to the giant screens seats, $150 floor seats, and of course $350 premium Stevie merch VIP experience seats. How close did I need to get?

My wife was psyched for Stevie Nicks, but in discussion about our ticketing budget bracket for this show, she reminded me of the time we had fourth row to see Lucinda Williams. Heroin has wrecked Lucinda, body and mind. She wears jeans that are too tight to let her breathe and she keeps all her lyrics in a giant binder next to the mic because she very often forgets them otherwise. Seeing her face right up close like that, in all its sad, dead weatheriness, was a total nightmare of melancholia.

But Chrissie Hynde has still got it, right? She's still the ultimate asskicker, full of innovative chord progressions, fucked up time signatures, sonorous punk howling and sparkling in the eye and sweating through the tee shirt. Right? Didn't I need to get close to that? Did I need to get $350 close to Chrissie for an hour and then come home with a pile of crap with Stevie's logo on it? We bought the $89 tickets, so I can leave before Stevie is over if I feel like it. The show is on a Sunday shortly before Thanksgiving, and we'll go back to work the morning after.

I suppose it's a fine line between tough and crazy, and I've been putting Stevie on the ugly side of that for a long time now. Sometimes I like to be wrong because it's a catalyst for personal growth, but I can't speculate as to whether that will be the case here. I'm trying to get open to Stevie as the current price of access to one of my heroes. If I instead walk away with a second hero, surely there's no harm in that. All signs seem to point at the need to pull my head out of my ass and succumb to the glorious power of Stevie Nicks. I'm just going to go there and see what speaks to me. Buy the ticket, take the ride, right? Worst case scenario is that it is illuminating.

★

"Atlantic City" / *Nebraska* (1982)

While I grew up in quickened sand
It's really alright now it's screwed up statehouse crew
Frown down the cross-talk
You're holdin' steady for the light apply direct sun
Target noises skewed
Backstairs knuckles blushin' skin asseverate
With the P.A. turned up to belief

Wanna start a crumbling doubt at the masquerade
Where these ramblin' admissions gangin' up on the sins underneath

Somehow every disguise diplomats refract
Gives way when worshipping those lines betrays their cracks
Like an Amazon split your talk real witty
That turnkey fits right in romantic fig leaf

Hell we're no heartthrobs ringside who're all honeyed decay
But our assets are out bogeyman clan sway
Foes I knew deadbeat dads and their diamond dust
Man I got noise from crickets for the resulting trust

How our love changed the tide and our luck still rolls bold
So I must endeavor to say
We're makin' out fair our stands earnin' stronghold
So good on our mock kings out of Oz our fight's netting gold
'Cause every disguise diplomats refract
Gives way when worshipping those lines betrays their cracks

I still grin cookin' for the mob these lips hardly mine
'Round here there's sinners and accusers and won't fret
When brought to bestride landmines
We're not hired for dumbing down on accusin' friends
Smart money dog bites your pets
When it wants to use committal flavor from them
So somehow every disguise diplomats refract
Gives way when worshipping those lines betrays their cracks
Roll this pair of dice and threaten gritty
That turnkey fits right in romantic fig leaf

*

Claire came back to town for the book festival and she brought her five year old,
whom we mainly referred to as Monkey. Monkey is actually only three, but she
is preternaturally witty and intellectually gifted for her age, and there is something
about assuming partial responsibility for a three year old for a weekend that
seems much more treacherous, so I prefer to think of Monkey as five.

   In my experience, nearly all parents like to claim that their children are well-behaved, not prone to get into unnecessary trouble, easy to manage in social situations involving childless adults. Most of them are lying to themselves, or lying to me. As a high school teacher, most small children don't interest me, and as far as I can gather, the kids feel the same way about me. But Monkey is a good friend of mine.

She's very discerning and made good recommendations for activities throughout the weekend. Our pajama party went well. Her Mexican restaurant of choice was delicious. She picked out a very nice necklace for her mom that Claire did ultimately purchase. She insisted the aquarium would not be too crowded, despite the holiday, and she was right. Her favorite movie is *Zootopia*, which turned out to be quite a deep plot structure maintained by a set of symbols so thoroughly progressive that as a piece of propaganda, I'm thinking of recommending the animated movie to my father. How can Trump supporters watch this cartoon and not see the error of their ways? Even the five year old understood better.

We also formed a band. I have been in three bands in my life. The first was in junior high, where I played drums and engaged in five-part harmonies with four other girls who loved Bananarama and Joni Mitchell. The second is ongoing and entirely in my mind, an all-girl punk rock Tom Petty cover band called Pretty Petty. I play rhythm guitar and sing. There are currently no other members, but I sometimes rehearse by myself. The third band is somewhere in the future.

Abby texted me last month and said that her younger daughter had something to ask me and she insisted on asking it herself, so I should call when I can. I assumed it was a queer-related query and that Abby was trying to teach the little one how to get answers for herself. Instead, the kid informed me that she would be starting a band someday and asked if I would agree to play lead guitar. Though I already see some of the most stereotypically ugly characteristics of frontwomen creeping up in her as she approaches her actual fifth birthday next month, I nevertheless agreed. She did not audition me whatsoever; it was purely based on my perceived coolness. Even her mom had to audition, so I felt honored.

Monkey also wanted to form a band and really went about it in an organized manner. She picked out one of Mindy's ukes from the line on the living room wall and plucked at it for a few minutes until it quickly dawned on her that acoustic instruments didn't feel right. Fortunately, Mindy has an electric uke, too. Monkey plugged in that bad boy and never looked back. She had a decent strumming pattern, could keep a beat for a couple of measures at a time, and was fond of fingerpicking with her fretboard hand like a cross between bluegrass and Tom Morello. She intuited that both hands ought to be playing the same string at the same time, and would look down at what her two hands were doing as least as often as she would look up at us to see how much we were enjoying the show.

She did have excellent living room stage presence, even dropping down to one knee during the bridge at the peak of her solo. Monkey did all this with an innate confidence that was unspoiled by schooling, marketing, or helicopter parenting. She had a powerful, intrinsic sense of self that probably all little girls possess before the world beats it out of them. She was wearing an oversized t-shirt that hung down to her knees with a koala bear on it that said, "Trust me, I'm koalafied." She explained to me that the shirt was a thought experiment wherein she imagined herself as a koala bear and presumed that as a koala bear she is trustworthy. I explained to her what "qualified" means, and then what a pun is.

Then she asked Mindy and me to join her band. She named us Time Receipt, clarifying that we would then always remember what a great time we were having together that weekend because a receipt would show the time. She went on to tell us what the first song was about, and give us a nod when we should come in on the chorus. Each of us had to invent some verses. They did not need to rhyme and we did not need to harmonize. In fact, we ultimately created a kind of delightfully atonal racket together.

Monkey was not fond of balladry. She did not ever want to do anything slowly all weekend, swooshing by us and always wanting to know what was next. So many children just ask "why," tone deaf to the nihilism implied by infinite regress, but this one wanted to know "and then what?" She mostly sped through eighth notes until I modeled some sixteenths for her, then we both shredded until she dropped to one knee again and I was forced to declare that my arms hurt from so much band rehearsal. Monkey agreed, and we called it a night.

We all assumed it would be fleeting, but after returning home from the aquarium the next day, Monkey immediately picked up her instrument and marched us all into the living room for another practice because, heads up, we had a show that night. About three minutes into the show, she informed us that it would be a long show. I ask her if it would be as long as Springsteen's record-breaking summer at Madison Square Garden. She made a face, indicating both that she did not care who the Boss was and that she did not appreciate being measured against any other bands.

Mindy had been calling her Boss throughout band practice, which Monkey did not mind at all. The show ultimately ran about a half hour with no encore because the venue was shutting down for bedtime. "You like circles and I like squares / but they're both shapes, so who really cares." The total effect was probably not unlike early practices in the garage with the Ramones. We have a lot of potential. I taught Monkey some basics of using her amp and when I tried to show her a more comfortable way of slinging her uke strap over her shoulder to better distribute the weight of the instrument across her tiny thirty-three pound frame, she once again scrunched up her face and declared she would do it the harder way because she was used to that.

★

"Cover Me" / *Born in the U.S.A.* (1984)

Confined enough somehow vetting rougher
But this broad is tough, there's no need to suffer
Under me, bygones if she's under me
It's swell working with another goodwill firing pin who's under me
Office suite maybe if you can align us
Fold it in your files, let that good work bind us
Under me, break glass floors from under me
It's swell working with another goodwill firing pin who's under me

Allied campaign, arriving slow
I don't fear the blowhards growing
Girl Scout bull fight matador
I am walking in the front door

This old broad will take care to pry open yours
I'm teenage tough commandant you can wean for sure
Under me, marathon under me
I'm working with another goodwill firing pin who's under me
Working with another goodwill firing pin who's under me

★

In the early nineties, there was one definitive handbook to being a progressive, politically aware queer kid. You had to get tickets to see Ani DiFranco. These were almost always general admission, so if you really wanted to prove your worth, you'd wait in line from sunrise to sunset to get in the front row. I did this several times, including once in sub-zero temperatures with Midwestern snow packed six inches high. But when you graduate from college, you also pretty much graduate from Ani. It's amazing to me that she's now approaching fifty years of age, and yet the average years on her crowd is still certainly hovering cumulatively just under the drinking age.

After Ani, you get a job and start dating people kind of seriously, and that brings you to Melissa Etheridge, who loves Bruce Springsteen. Whenever I tell the story of how I came to love "Bobby Jean," I begin by saying that the first time I ever heard it was on a duet with Melissa Etheridge. Having searched high and low for a copy of this performance, I can conclusively say that it does not exist. Etheridge has been a party to "Thunder Road," "Hungry Heart" and a handful of other performances over the years, but there is no evidence whatsoever that she's ever sung "Bobby Jean," with or without Springsteen in the mix.

So why did I project that song on to her? Well, it's a fucking gay song, isn't it? Gayer than even "Streets of Philadelphia," the lyrics for which actually contain no queer references of any kind. Springsteen grew up as a kind of sensitive misfit, a longhaired outsider in his own small town. Bobby Jean was one of the few true friends who understood him. The common wisdom about this song is that the title character is Steven Van Zandt, and that Springsteen is wishing him a fond farewell on the brink of taking his leave from the E Street Band for many years. I came around to that later. The first time I heard the song, I knew right away that I was Bobby Jean.

From the vantage point of my twenties, the lyrics reminisced about a teenage wasteland with the stand-out face of one real friend. The friend is suffering under the weight of being too big for her town, a town that doesn't respect or maybe even understand who she is trying to be. She was me, just getting out of there as quiet and fast as she could, to the point of ghosting out on her only pal. Bobby Jean is no kind of suicide case; she's just bailing on the boardwalk that was holding her down. But Springsteen and Bobby Jean still have a spiritual connection through the radio. Bobby Jean is out there somewhere, probably making her own music. I also think of her as something like Suzi Quatro—maybe the Boss ain't the only one coming through the radio.

Quatro is a Catholic from Detroit. She did things that females were not supposed to do, and she did them well. Still does. I gave up Etheridge when she got cancer and found Jesus. Then I paid cash for my first bike, named Star because it got a lot of attention, which I rode for about two years until it was stolen right in front of my house on the one night in its whole lifetime where I hadn't chained it up. The second bike was bigger, louder, faster, named Silver Bullet after Bob Seger. That one eventually got sold for parts to my beloved mechanic after several years, once it couldn't be trusted for a daily ride. My third and final bike never had a name—until I realized it was my final bike and immediately took to calling it Bobby Jean.

I got in a car accident a few weeks ago. My first one, nobody injured and blessedly it wasn't my fault. Some schmoo tapped my bumper in the pre-dawn rain on 400. Funnily enough, we were only doing about fifteen miles per hour because we were passing a serious collision on the side of the road. So the truck bumps me and we pull over where the police from the other crash are conveniently ready to help us. I dislike police, to say the least, so we handled it on our own. The guy was real nice about it, I suppose because he was thankful that I was real nice about it. Then I got back in the car and arrived at work full of the shakes.

Once I dropped the Bullet in a parking lot while sitting side saddle on it like an idiot, but there was barely a scratch and that's it. Statistically, it's quite rare to drive a bike for a decade and never crash it. I'm a lucky son of a bitch, I know. So now I've got this Prius because Abby's in divinity school and I'm not looking for another carpool situation. After a decade of the winds beating against my chest, the rain soaking my ass, the helmet smushing my hair, no radio, no phone, no GPS, no decent trunk space, no windshield wipers, no heat, that secondhand auto is starting to feel pretty good. Not only is my ass dry when I get to work every day, it's toasty from heated seats and I'm ready to spring in action thanks to lumbar support.

The final bike has been chained up for the entire semester and there's a fair chance now that it won't start up once the weather gets warm. It's going to sit on the yard for a couple more months, then I'll fix it up properly when summer comes, and then I'll hand it off to my beloved mechanic to put up for sale. I drove bikes for a decade and nothing bad happened. Seems like a solid high note to go out on. But damn, I'll miss it—the throttle, the counter-steering, the flat black, the heft of the chain over my shoulder, the sound of the wind in my ears, the grind of every tiny asphalt pebble under my two wheels, watching for the green and then doing sixty off the line next to sports cars that need four full seconds to catch up. People always told me to drive safe, which is the most patronizing fucking thing to say to a broad on a bike.

When people see me climbing into the Prius, nobody tells me to drive safe. It's a given. It's like I'm hiding out in there, just quietly snuck in undercover as a regular suburban asshole, filling up the trunk with shit I bought at CostCo and placing my latte gingerly in the center console cup holder. I didn't even decorate the bumper with any stickers, lest I give myself away as being interesting and intelligent. So I've got this hard outer shell of an automobile now that appears completely assimilated, and I've got to stop pussyfooting around the issue of whether to kiss my bike goodbye.

I'm gonna do it. Little Steven gave up E Street for fifteen years. I'm gonna sell the bike and make my peace with driving this Prius around like a normal adult until I retire—and then I'm going to buy any kind of souped-up, chopped-up, crazy-loud motorcycle I want and that's what I'm going to drive into my grave. We shall meet again, Bobby Jean.

★

"Bobby Jean" / *Born in the U.S.A.* (1984)

Tough guy drove by some mousey mother frayed, another dead I'm going gray
Ahead there's still something adulthood outruns
And it's something retirees betray
Sneak preview headstone blood brother every inch of gasoline
I hitched that iron horse home I ditched it unequalled blue
Trust highway banzai my machine

How it sung with me when I felt smothered spurned cliché burned up shadows
That bike my main cruiser that bike my badlands that bike my bulldoze
Feel bold godmother connoisseur of mileage, the mileage wings of teenage dream
Bow and kiss boyhood that sold it I miss that good I cocked and flew
Trust highway banzai my machine

We were a driving hurricane rocking out profane underworld tight lid
Prepare saint somebody somewhere
Somehow thrown together second hand squares away the bid
Carefree beastly nightmare postal code affair
Still a lust for lanes unravelled and wrong
This my farewell zoom melody tomorrow delaying
Disappear I shove along
One whiff voodoo plateau I'm honking at you enthrall to trials of Springsteen
I must be taking some fast ride hot and strange and blind
Rough justice prays I'm blessed you banshee, amok banzai, my machine

★

The wife and I are strolling along the boardwalk at Venice Beach. I am reasonably dressed in board shorts, a t-shirt, and a light hoodie that may later double as a towel. She is unreasonably dressed, as usual, in whatever loud and crazy fancy pants she felt like putting on that morning. Sometimes her childish sense of wonderment about getting dressed on an ordinary Tuesday reminds me of a six year old who insists on wearing a tutu and frog pajamas to pre-K. But she wears everything well, so rather than be embarrassed that my wife always stands out in a crowd, I just go with it. It works for her and that works for me. She even stood out on Venice Beach that day.

So did the missionaries, poised at the bottleneck of the main drag, awaiting their next victim. I drew a bead on them at twenty yards, but bless my wife, she did not notice them until the boldest one approached and complimented her shirt. It was a button down with a bunch of neon pink and blue fish all over it. Naturally, my wife paused to accept the compliment. Within two minutes, they were dropping J-bombs on us. Within ten minutes—yes, fully ten minutes, because my wife is not a rude asshole and the rude asshole she married was going to let her get herself out of it, however slowly—they laid hands on us and bowed their heads to pray on us. On us? Okay, they said "pray with us" but I'm quite sure they meant they want to pray "for us" and then it still felt to me like "on us."

They even took a photo with my wife, but I declined. Emphatically, for reasons I cannot really explain except that this tiny posse of Minnesotans had freaked me the fuck out and really harshed what was otherwise a good Venice Beach buzz. I don't know why I couldn't just laugh it off, but I couldn't. I went immediately into retail therapy mode. When we were finally extricated from the clutches of the weirdest thing on the boardwalk, I walked quickly to the nearest street artist and spent twenty-five bucks on half a broken skateboard that had a stencil of Kurt Cobain's face in black on a neon rainbow background. Thank you, Eddie de la Barca, for painting me a vision of Cobain on a busted board at precisely the moment when I most needed it.

The plank fit perfectly in my backpack, keeping my spine straight until the sun went down. Should we have run into the Minnesotans on our way back, I most likely would have whipped out the idol and held it in front of me like a shield, like a crucifix against an oncoming vampire. We did see them across the road, still easy striking distance, but they just smiled and waved. Having already hit us, they cast us aside in favor of fresher meat—some guy in khakis and dreadlocks.

★

"Dancing in the Dark" / *Born in the U.S.A.* (1984)

I clean up when I'm bleeding
And I'm facing cutting dismay

I free roam heed no warnings
No talking head reeling out clichés
One day gonna get fired
But I was hired for swords on my shelf
Send your babies, childhood adjusts with all my help

Our kids don't aspire
Cause teens can't aspire without benchmarks
My crumbs are wired
Make it look like we're walking through a park

Lesson looks in the mirror
Dominoes run and improve what's found in face
Paycheck we took getting nearer
They rearrange their pose, their airs, their ace
No complaints fretting my prayers
Must be giving in a clump of kids
This plumbing's dampening nightmares
Pacifies trust no brat resists

Their wits abound hitting bolder
Go for broke billionaires with all my seeds
I'll turn this herd to stakeholders
They're not lazy when staff turns key

Weighing the seats with grad gowns
Advisees starving for my advice
One day they're gonna stray set free
And maybe they're acting out charging despite
They're trying for some traction
Picnic for fit buccaneers vying to smite textbooks
I'm in awe of transaction
Sacred cow babies no one's overlooked

Our kids don't aspire spitting out dry holdovers of spoken arts
My crumbs are wired
Make it look like we're walking through a park
Our kids don't aspire hurrying
Without my whittled pearls state of the art

My crumbs are wired
Make it look like we're walking through a park
Young ladies

★

I've been "in a church," but never "to church." There have been weddings and funerals featuring a diversity of orthodoxies, some even in languages that I don't speak. The summer before eighth grade, my father's mother took me to visit an uncle in Philadelphia. His family was huge on church stuff, to the point of mission trips that lasted all summer and Christmas newsletters with prayer in the header. We stayed with these nut jobs for an entire week, and when Sunday rolled around I was not feeling mighty enough to say no.

I was thirteen and my uncle was much richer than my father, so I steeled myself and went along. All I remember is an intense feeling of not knowing their rules, the guarded terror of on the one hand definitively not belonging and on the other hand not necessarily knowing how to recognize their recruitment tactics. There seemed to be a lot of people, maybe two hundred or so. The only residual of the entire experience is that I have some regret over not being bold enough to tell my uncle to shove it, that he could find me at home with a good book whenever his family was finished with their silly talk about "the" good book.

This week was the first time I went to a church service voluntarily. Abby got invited to preach at her hipster Methodist place on the southeast side. I went because she asked me in a way that made clear it was important to her, and since I love Abby, I said I would show up for her. We have a mutual friend who also got invited. The friend is a real life Kimmy Schmidt type, raised in a cult and home-schooled within an inch of her life, until something broke inside of her in her early twenties and she found some critical distance. We have to do stuff like watch Grease and listen to Metallica, because she was isolated from all of that by censorious fascists when she was growing up. Church services trigger who knows what type of ugly shit storm in her mind, so we went together for safety in numbers.

I guess the Methodists have this universal calendar thing where certain bits of the Bible are the scheduled topic of each week, so you can walk into pretty much any Methodist church on Sunday and pick up where your other church left off. Abby got to preach on Acts 13: 42-52. I've never read it and her first fifteen minutes of fame was light on quotations. I know it's from the New Testament, and I know that Acts tries to explain why Jewish Jesus ended up

75

with a following of Gentiles instead. Sliding around under there somewhere is the idea that Jews were too dumb to appreciate Jesus, and I could pretty much feel my grandma heaping curses upon me from beyond the grave for tuning in to this knock at her people. So that was a bummer, but Lulu was as fiercely loyal to her friends as I am, so I figure she understood that I was not there to soak up the message inasmuch as I was just there to support the messenger.

Though I don't really know what it has to do with Acts, Abby's message was that people should privilege mercy over sacrifice. Sacrifice is a math of hardships we use to rack up the points on an eternal reward, whereas mercy is a daily detachment from our own narrow interests in favor of empathy, or a kindness and gentleness to others. She said that the crucifixion put a cap on the age of sacrifice and ushered in the age of mercy. She also quoted the line "shake the dust," which I personally felt was a wink at me from the pulpit, as she knows I have that sentence tattooed on my left ankle for wholly unrelated reasons.

Then there was a mildly terrible band going on and on about lead us not into temptation and protect us from whatever. So much of that rubs me the wrong way because the congregants are always on the wrong side of the action verb. The congregants are being delivered, being protected. My life experience has generally taught me to protect and deliver my own self, rather than rely upon something or someone else to do so. I have never counted on mercy, on the kindness of strangers. But Abby did a great job explaining it. She was operating in an area that was some cross between the form of a TED Talk and the content of many of our conversations carpooling together, threaded through with the surplus of verve afforded by her long training as a speech team kid.

We sat in the last seats in the back row, furthest from any action. Most of the congregants physically avoided entering our space, protecting it as we were with teenage witchery in the form of all the giggles and snide sidebars we could manufacture on the spot, but many of them fixed their peripherals on us as a fresh curiosity in an otherwise fairly predictable space. One old guy approached me with his hand out and I convinced him to fist bump me instead. He did so with glee, but then did not ask me for my name. He was wearing an official little name badge at which I did not even glance, and then it was communion time. I thought communion was just for Catholics, but I guess not.

Abby got to help give out the grape juice and I watched as the first few pews got to their feet to line up. The anxiety set in when the middle rows lined up. I know Abby would very much have liked to give me communion, but I couldn't do it. My friend and I had already invested maximum emotional labor in just showing up, and Abby knew that. She would be merciful about it. She got to give her own two little daughters their drink, as well as her husband. That would have to be enough. We went to brunch afterward and everybody had a bloody mary. The couple of church people that came with us kept exclaiming when I got introduced to them. I'm Abby's famous carpooler. She's been passing along my good words to them for half a decade.

She said it meant a lot to her that we were there, and it meant a lot to me as well because now I've been "to church." Really, I just went to see Abby's show. Context is everything though, isn't it? I didn't know how psychologically expensive an experience it might be due to the space and the crowd, but I wasn't going to miss her first official preach. Abby has said way more preachy stuff than this sermon to me before, in dive bars and in school auditoriums and in the car. But this time she said it in a church and though it was an uphill climb on a rocky road overgrown with the thorns of my youth, mercifully, I got there for her without ultimately feeling like I had sacrificed anything.

★

"Brilliant Disguise" / *Tunnel of Love* (1987)

I know we were all warned
That the man gets paid
Look at these turds slippered gayly
Fast as we burn doomsday
Jigsawed truth searchlight
Clout on alleged crackdown
It's guaranteed unkind
Ammo lust passing shots dismiss offspring to ground
Bombshell clearcut I mean
Send your rook for my prize
Quiz your doomed Hades
Robust resilience baptized

I stirred nobody stalled these games
Scrum bequeathed fandango
Chutzpah rushing fucked with blame
Bearing teeth for tableau
Justified vanguard safety
From the rust of creeds
That an old man might use
Undoing his deeds

Bombshell corkscrew I mean
Send your rook for my prize
Quiz your doomed Hades
Robust resilience baptized

They took us for lazy
Juggling all our worshipping fright
Till zen our stone wall jumpstarts
All aglow with rights
Stardust obeys this rhythm
Its clocks unfurled in stealth
Manifesto follows through a paintbrush
Pure program you've grown rusted wealth

How I prayed some policewoman
Keeps away the clergyman
Coloring books arose
Accrued the songs of this land
She could but did not falter
This dizzy lore of humor has bite
Calliope she showers
Our black tea family with tipsy guides
Kingpins your rook meets queen
You'll be hook scarred and shook nice
'Cause you're doomed Hades
Robust resilience baptized

This night our story's told
We fought off the tarnish from above
Controversy to the lambs
That tout their labor's love

★

Woke up yesterday morning to the worst mass shooting in U.S. history. It seems
the AR-15 has become the weapon of choice for aspiring mass murderers, so
congrats to Colt Industries on cornering a burgeoning market. I don't understand
why the Federal Assault Weapons Ban was allowed to expire a dozen years ago
and I don't understand how anyone could argue that civilians need access to a

military spec weapon that discharges thirty rounds in a dozen seconds. A magazine that size would tear up a deer so badly there'd be nothing left to eat.

If a man's wife leaves him because he beats her and she fears he is mentally unstable, if a man's own father worries about his vehement dislike for gay men publicly showing their affection, if a man's employer records his consistent display of anger management problems, if a man's internet usage is monitored not once but twice by the Federal Bureau of Investigation because of his suspected connection to actual terrorist groups, then this man can still legally purchase an assault rifle in the Sunshine State.

And if this man can still legally purchase an assault rifle without so much as a three-day waiting period, then bullets should cost a thousand dollars apiece. That first magazine would have cost the shooter thirty thousand dollars. I understand that a man like this man might want to do what he did, that violent extremism relies upon its converts' mental illness and social isolation, that this reliance is coupled with hilariously easy weapons acquisition in America. Imagine if these loons had to save up thirty large before they could kill anyone.

Not including the wounded and the additional bullets missing their mark because he was an amateur jackass, just covering the cost of his body count would have put this man in the hole by forty-nine thousand bucks. If a man survives committing a crime of this caliber, we give him the death penalty after his detention and trial cost the taxpayers certainly no less than forty-nine thousand bucks. That's what passes for deterrence in our country: an utterly obsolete consequence to the heart of a man who would be a martyr to any cause, a man that is unwilling and possibly unable to give calculated weight to what happens next.

We have a mental health crisis in this county that cannot be remedied by earnest moments of silence and a few million lit candles. I want to see legislation, and meanwhile for consolation, I wanted to turn to Springsteen's "American Skin (41 Shots)" because it's true in so many more ways beyond the police brutality that originally inspired the song: "You can get killed just for living in your American skin." But forty-nine are dead and fifty more are wounded, so forty-one shots no longer reaches the grotesque height of this increasingly common horror like it once could. He's playing Orlando in two months and I'll bet he gets into this song before the first hour is up. He can change the lyric to forty-nine shots without difficulty because it's the entire refrain of the chorus, so it need not rhyme with anything. It'll have been a dozen years since he debuted the song in my own city.

I found myself turning instead to Neil Young, working through "Rockin' in the Free World" and "Hey Hey, My My (Into the Black)" until one knuckle on my pick hand was bleeding and my slide hand couldn't hold tight anymore. Because I don't live in Orlando, but I live in the South. Because I don't go to night clubs anymore, but I am a queer. Because I "don't feel like Satan, but I am to them." Because I wasn't watching a movie in Aurora or teaching a class in Sandy Hook, but I know what people will whisper during my jazz funeral march through the Quarter if I am ever cut down by a madman's cheap bullets.

They'll say, "She worked her whole adult life in mental health service as an English teacher at a public high school, only for her life to be tragically shortened by one kid she didn't save." I try to relax any way I can about not being able to save every kid from everything. I'm working as goddamn hard as I can on both the saving and the relaxing about not saving, because extremism always reveals irony. It necessarily pulls us into the black, but I believe with my whole heart that Neil Young is on to something good when he professes his faith that rock and roll can never die. Therefore, we absolutely must keep on rocking in the free world.

CHAPTER FOUR

THERE IS NO ONE LEFT ON EARTH WHO DOESN'T KNOW Bruce Springsteen's memoir, *Born to Run*, debuts this week, as the publicity machine has been rolling out in full force all month long. Particularly in terms of television appearances, Springsteen has been stepping up in advance of the book in a way he hasn't had to do for albums. Even though the book includes an album of previously unreleased material, Springsteen has been sitting and talking more than he's been playing in order to promote the autobiography. This includes repeatedly highlighting the fact that Springsteen has depression, a mental illness that runs in his family. Clearly, the book is not meant to be construed as a tell-all bombshell, as this depression reveal has been the focus of the advance coverage and I doubt that anyone who's really listened to any of his lyrics will be surprised that the Boss sometimes gets pretty down.

Stephen Colbert's number finally came up on Friday, when Springsteen appeared on *The Late Show* for the entire hour after Colbert's monologue. They'd previously agreed on giving him three slots, which represents all the available interview time on the show. The fourth and final slot usually belongs to a musical act. At the end of the third segment, Colbert requested that Springsteen stay to continue their conversation into the final segment, which means one of four things: Springsteen was going to play and instead he agreed to talk more, Colbert bumped whatever unadvertised act was going to appear in the fourth slot, the show never slotted the fourth segment because they expected Springsteen to run over his talk time, or Springsteen had agreed to four segments all long and Colbert's request was simply a conceit to make the audience feel special. Those last two options are super cynical and substantially unlikely, but aren't any of the options a bit disappointing? Would we rather hear Springsteen talk, or play?

So, disregarding the two parts of their dialogue that replicate all of Springsteen's other appearances this month—his reflections on how writing a book is somewhat different from making a record and the fact of his depression—let's consider what Colbert was able to get out of Springsteen that was new. Springsteen is fond of casting mystery over everything he does by turning it into a metaphor. He is accustomed to constructing poetic comparisons so that his lyrics conjure up pathos. One reason these televised interviews are valuable is that they are an opportunity to force Springsteen to deal more directly in facts. His ability to convey those facts to Colbert is notable because it relied less on the emotional quality of his autobiography and more on his sense of place. Throughout the interview, Springsteen displayed repeated interest in the politics of space and how he inhabits it alongside his audience.

For his walk on music, Jon Batiste chose Bo Diddley's "You Can't Judge a Book." This is one of the tracks on the book's companion album that Springsteen recorded when he was just sixteen years old. Before he sat down, he briefly turned to wave at the band, momentarily looking a little uncomfortable to have to be somebody else's audience. But then when he sat down and Colbert asked him to name that tune, he couldn't do it. Springsteen turns sixty-seven this weekend, and indicated that his distance from the band multiplied by his decades of stage time prevented him from being able to hear what they were playing. He wasn't really open to being their audience.

Realizing the awkwardness of the answer, Colbert quickly turned to make a joke about judging the autobiography by its cover, and asked what the twenty-seven year old on the cover would say to the sixty-seven year old rock star today. "Where'd my car go? Who's the old man in the suit jacket? And what did he do with my hair?" The car has disappeared and a suit jacket has appeared in its place, two very different markers of what is cool. His hair has also disappeared. Springsteen never had good hair, if we're going to look at photographs of him honestly, but everybody knows the story about not being able to walk at his high school graduation because he refused to get a haircut, so the symbolism of this commentary is clear. The fact is, young Springsteen would disapprove of elder Springsteen. These questions from his younger self show a sense of bewilderment tinged with suspicion, and a very current preoccupation with the visual. He didn't have to focus on Colbert's question from the perspective of the photograph itself; that was one among many routes for an answer that he chose.

Colbert briefly returned to another part of Springsteen's origin story, and this is where the sense of space really takes hold. It was the vision of Elvis on *The Ed Sullivan Show* that brought Springsteen to music. Of course, Colbert's show is in the same theater, meaning that Springsteen was now in the space that a few times was briefly inhabited by his idol. Colbert asks him how it feels to be there, but Springsteen has higher standards. His eyes search the carpet and he gestures toward the expanse of floor. "I'm curious as to where he stood here." Being in the room where it happened is not enough. It's not in the air; he wants to put his feet right on the spot. He needs to get closer. Even the Boss can't touch his idols; even the Boss longs to physically overlap with a space he personally considers sacred.

When the conversation inevitably turns toward their mutual Catholic upbringing, Springsteen again focuses on how he might inhabit sacred space. Colbert quotes from the book that this upbringing is "where [he] found [his] song." They talk about how to a young boy, hell is a literal place and the fact that Springsteen's not wanting to be scared all the time turned him off of Catholicism early. He says he was "the worst altar boy on planet Earth," and aside from trouble with Latin, all the evidence offered is of a spatial nature. He remembers running down the street in a predawn hour, trying to get to the early service on time. He remembers telling another altar boy he needs major help because he didn't study his role well enough to perform it responsibly. When he has to simply light some candles, he can't do it. He finds himself face down on the altar, having been collared and put down by the angry priest, and remarks that he was "the only altar boy to be knocked down on stage."

Colbert returns to the subject of the memoir to ask, "What do you mean by 'the magic trick'?" Then he adds that he only really gets intimidated when interviewing musicians because they "have a magic I don't understand." Springsteen says, "You're there to manifest something. Before you go in there, it's an empty space. It's an empty building. So the audience is gonna come and you're gonna show up, and together you're gonna manifest something that is very, very real. It's very tangible, but you're gonna pull it out of thin air. It wasn't there before you showed up. It didn't exist." He describes this experience as one of catharsis and transcendence, and he views his purpose as assisting with the audience's deliverance.

It did not seem not lost on Colbert that this is pretty much a description of the functions of a good altar boy, and he makes a transubstantiation joke. He follows up by asking how Springsteen knows he's "turned the trick," and Springsteen replies that "it's in the air." This is in direct tension with his own desire to stand in the exact same spot as Elvis once did. In his elaboration he inadvertently harkens back to the previous topic by saying that an excellent concert experience can "alter you."

To begin wrapping the interview, Colbert turns to a softball question about how long the shows are, referencing the E Street Band's recent four-hour record-breaker. Springsteen says, "I'm here to take you out of time. I'm here to transport you someplace else. I'm here to alter time and space, and play with it myself, and help you move in and out." He also credits a "little man under the stage" who throws lyrics up on the teleprompter instantaneously when the Boss calls for a last-minute song that none of the band has rehearsed. Colbert then raises the specter of his own "man under the stage," and cuts to a live feed of the sound mixer who as a young man once helped Springsteen mix the version of "Henry Boy" that appears on the memoir's companion album. This is another thing connecting Springsteen to the place of the Ed Sullivan Theater.

Most of the reviews and clips of this episode of *The Late Show* focus on the final segment where Colbert asks the Boss to name his personal top five from his own catalog. He quickly lists "Born to Run," the title of the book he's ultimately there to hawk. Then he names "The Rising" and "Thunder Road," followed by "but 'Nebraska' was a good one." Then, at a loss, he turns to the audience and they immediately start shouting out a bunch of different songs. He veers toward "Jungleland" and then decides on "Racing in the Street" based on their suggestions.

I see very little merit whatsoever in this list itself, but as an activity it speaks volumes. At the end Colbert rightly declares that "these are everybody's top five, by the way." More to the point, Springsteen curated his list based on the audience that happened to be there with him and what they happened to shout when he momentarily ceded the floor to them. He makes a joke about people being planted in the audience. Taken in conjunction with his remarks about pulling the show's energy out of thin air together, it's clear that he would make a different list if you gave him a different space with a different crowd. The list is in no way meant to be definitive; it's a one-off moment between the idol and whichever of his fans were present.

The interview concludes with Colbert presenting Springsteen a birthday gift: a framed copy of the original schematic for the Ed Sullivan Theater. Colbert says the building historian informs them that Elvis would've played pretty much right where they've been sitting the whole time. Bruce goes "wooooo" and gives a thumbs up. He seems underwhelmed, and then all I kept thinking was: too bad the Boss didn't perform in that spot where Elvis performed; he could've gotten closer. But didn't he indeed perform? Springsteen quite clearly thinks of any stage he's standing on as his church. The Ed Sullivan Theater, under Colbert's progressive Catholic personal brand, is often described as his church.

On this episode of *The Late Show*, Springsteen's consistent attention to the space results in the same transubstantiated feat as his concerts. He was able to get it done in a new space, without a guitar. Can the book—an experience that happens everywhere and therefore nowhere—also get it done? I'm going to set the bar as high as possible for this memoir based on Springsteen's own preoccupation with the particularities of place: If *Born to Run* provides an equally transformative experience that is detached from the spatial politics of the concert stage and its attendant live audience, if it succeeds in a collaboration with readers despite their isolation from his sacred space and from his guitar, then the Word of Bruce will truly have achieved omnipotence.

*

"Roll of the Dice" / *Human Touch* (1992)

Hell I've read snoozers 'n' ramblers
Trust glowin' fake wise
Book saints dearly departed
Last page on the ground this mourner cries
An admission price
Without some other word of advice

Tall tale legends and devils all coverin' up
Tricky headlines
Convinced to shell for Bruce maybe
Grin thinkin' of exchangin' lines
We're creatin' lots of baptized
With some other word of advice

I'm humbled as the show we played overtakes
Yet that's right I wanna be swingin' till my own heart breaks

Hell it's clever to write so hang on Bruce
Your fables are baiting
Devotees and potluck acolytes
An end to their waiting
Thinkin' constraints devised
Without some other word of advice

Page-turners pray down your heads all amazed gems
Hell I hear the gods granted our waiver

Save me from dusk showdownin' hometowns
Cookin' up maladjusted
Give me grief's courthouse up above
With this rant unfunded
Hell I'll make Bruce the Christ
Without some other word of advice
Prove this pup
Manna heaven

Call me crazy
These lines are leavened

★

The night the book arrived, I sat down and made a list of five questions for myself before I started reading it. Then I woke up the next morning and dug in. Here are my answers.

How does Springsteen's writing style here compare and contrast with that of his song lyrics or stage monologues?

A set of song lyrics necessarily has a more compressed narrative than the one afforded by a six-hundred page work of prose. Because the themes of the book are essentially identical to the themes in his songs, Springsteen's attitude toward them in the book is indistinguishable from his mood in the songs. He strives equally for those quiet moments of reflection, nostalgia and melancholy alongside the robust, energetic, heartening moments of glory. The reader is left with the same overall mood as when listening to one of Springsteen's albums.

In the matter of pacing, these pages of prose stretch out at a much slower rate of unspooling than even Springsteen's longest songs, though the pages frequently bring to mind some of the stage monologues. On stage, Springsteen is prone to several types of slow-downs: he can get so deep into telling a story that he can't easily wrap it up, or he makes long lists of hyphenates as if a lengthening string of Shakespearean smash-word-style adjectives will get him closer to conveying the fullest possible meaning, and he often raises and lowers his vocal projection to mimic preachers in an effort to recapture the band's alertness before counting off the next song. All three of these rhetorical moves are present in the book, and it is sometimes jarring to see them rendered on the page.

For the story-telling deep-dive, well, that's why people want to buy the book—his audience is full of completists who want every little detail. Springsteen is by turns both funny and moving, but the entertainer in him often goes front and center when he gets anxious or shy about a good nugget of fresh information, so that some of the best stories kind of end up concealing more than they reveal. Over and over again, *Born to Run* adds more mysteries than it solves, in large part because Springsteen would rather talk about his feelings about whatever happened than actually stating what it was that happened. He describes his songwriting effort on *Greetings from Asbury Park* in a manner that transfers easily to this book: "Most of the songs were twisted autobiographies. [...] I wrote impressionistically and changes names to protect the guilty. I worked hard to find something that was identifiably mine." *Born to Run* is similarly twisted, for better and for worse.

The long strings of adjectives and the changes in volume do not translate easily from stage to page. They have the nice effect of feeling like a concert, but readers may find that Springsteen occasionally resembles a shouty old grandpa. He conveys high volume phrases by WRITING THEM IN ALL CAPS! And there are very, very many exclamation points! There are also many sentence fragments strung out with ellipses to convey some sense of pausing for reflection, of grasping at the straws of one's own inner life. Coming out of his mouth, all these devices seem quite natural. But to punctuate the pages in this way is rather clunky. I suppose the editors felt that Springsteen has earned his poetic license, but there is no real reason why they couldn't have cleaned up the copy with italicization and some less attention-hogging punctuation. It's well known that Springsteen was not a particularly good student; certainly he would appreciate that his ability to tell story can benefit from touching up some of the grammatical false moves.

There is something very interesting going on, syntactically speaking, that is in stark contrast to his declarative style of songwriting. In the book, Springsteen often puts the subject of a sentence at the end, as opposed to the beginning. He engages regularly in the use of passive voice that has the double effect of creating an ornate style of verbiage while distancing actions from their agents. This florid sentence structure often has echoes of the biblical, with some "delivered unto us a son" type language. It also relieves a variety of bandmates from owning their mistakes, with some "complaining was going on about this and that" where readers don't find out until the end of the sentence who was doing the complaining, and sometimes Springsteen omits the agents altogether by indulging in substantial tangents about his feelings that never circle back to the report of events.

The total effect of these style choices is that the voice in *Born to Run* absolutely resembles that of the Boss we've come to know and love. He knows how to sound like the many varieties of himself, either on page or stage. There is no way any part of this book was penned by a ghostwriter. It doesn't always look pretty or flow smoothly on the page, but it draws power from the same sources as Springsteen's songwriting and stagecraft always have, so it will no doubt please his fans. "Most of my writing is emotionally autobiographical," he reflects.

*

"Real World" / *Human Touch* (1992)

Sister double numb talkin' today
Hears con appeal spiked won song say
It's always jive bust that ceiling all night
Hell I gunned that cutthroat down in cheesecake ditty
Tilt my cockeyed arsenal reassert my dignity
Feeling headstrong somehow improving swan

Paint those perched birds singing
Saint their wings uncurled
In that tree of truth take hold of tears stinging
Home brew of feel words

I gilt the brine of my art because it fitted for free
Shut out the rule's cold reverie and years slide
Plow time sleddin' over the ice
I'm lurchin' toward a component of fountain youth
Gordian knot a brittle wraith
Watch while I proceed with dynamite
I'm hookin' it up in these lines

It's a fight I'm not checking out
It heals the holes spaced weep and shrinkin'
The abyss delivered from drought
Cosmic dust baptized and taught these songs diversified
And then rewarding drums dignify us amplified
A spotlight as my ride with its charms bona fide

Nevermind handsome dancers we're all on task for self-help
I'm fired and unimpaired
Maybe was once a sad sack
Remake my fears farewell expression soundtrack
Get rid of this roadless lowness depressed
Bygones walk on without distress and stars delight
Till we're crowin' with birds of paradise

★

Does this book contain any new information about him untapped by previous biographers?

My instinct is to say no, but this is in large part a matter of what a reader can appreciate as "new" or as "information" or as "untapped." As far as the main narrative thrusts and the facts of his circumstances, nothing much in this book is untapped material. Peter Ames Carlin's *Bruce* is barely five years old, so it's not as if there is much to update in the way of the life Springsteen has lived since the last "definitive" biography. I finally got to learn that the bike he crashed was a Yamaha, so there are some additional fine lines drawn on already widely circulated portraits of his life, but not a wealth of previously untold stories that round out or give fresh angles to a reader's sense of who Springsteen truly is.

The best elements tend to be those where he gives insight into his daily life as a musician or his everyman milestones. His first chord shape was an E-minor, on "Greensleeves." His first electric guitar was actually a Gibson bass sixer that he played with guitar strings. He played it for quite a while before some more experienced guitarist complimented Springsteen on a choice that he presumed had been deliberate. In matters of skill, he confesses he still doesn't know how to read music. Most amusingly, readers learn that all his early albums' fascination with car talk was not based in any substantive firsthand experience. Even at twenty-one, he didn't know how to drive a car. I've often wondered why Springsteen chose automobiles over motorcycles for his road symbolism, since he actually knew more about bikes than cars until he was about thirty, but I suppose he shoots for whatever will be most universal.

This is nothing like the tell-all memoirs of many rockers who've been around the block for forty years. Springsteen sticks to the straight and narrow, claiming to have avoided all drugs except alcohol. He writes that as the son of an alcoholic, he made sobriety into a kind of religion for himself and had confidence that his music was giving him as much of a high as he'd ever need. What he got from his father in this regard, he gave back in quite another with this funny little tidbit: "Through using the same facilities at the apartment, all I left behind for my pops was a case of crabs I picked up somewhere along the way" (164). Still, aside from some vague allusions to a more free-wheeling sexual past, this gentleman does not kiss and tell.

On the other hand, if Springsteen's feelings can be classified as information, then there is a tremendous amount of information in *Born to Run*. The press has seized upon one primary feeling-fact in this book: the Boss gets depressed.

Though this does qualify as "new" in the sense that Springsteen has not opened up about it until now, I would argue that it is both spoiled by the roll-out of the book's publicity and also in and of itself an unsurprising fact. Because the book is very extensively rooted in Springsteen's feelings, it does convey a more nuanced sense of his depression than his pre-publication interviews. Still, the depth of conversation around this element of the book ultimately undercuts the specificity with which he is able to treat it in the book itself. Readers will likely have a sense that this is ground already decently covered by the book's publicity; the business end of Springsteen's operation soft launched the topic too successfully in the press for the content of the text to be let to do its own work.

It's a bigger issue that the depression reveal is unsurprising. I've previously cracked that anybody who's listened to the *Nebraska* album will not be shocked to learn that the Boss sometimes feels a deep and chaotic sadness. Of course, depression is unquestionably a very serious, often paralyzing mental illness. Raising awareness about its existence, its impact and its treatment is a highly valuable cultural endeavor. It is undeniably good that someone with as much star power as Springsteen is willing to publicly own and share his experiences with depression so that we can all be more socially conscious people toward him and those that suffer similarly. But I still have questions.

Why does he situate his depression primarily as something occurring in his sixties, instead of tracing its life-long arc, especially given that he admits to going to therapy for it since at least his forties? Why doesn't he devote more than a paragraph to discussion of how he has treated it with medication, or give descriptions as to the nature of his therapy and how it has worked for him? Why does he allude to such dark depths and the rock bottom of it all, but then stop short of any discussion whatsoever of suicide, declining even to use the word? These are tremendous missed opportunities for education and empowerment; I'd venture to guess that the people who turn to his music as their medicine are likewise turning to this book for same, and that many of them could use the full weight of his knowledge on the issue.

Understandably, these are painful and personal topics. Well, that is true of ninety percent of causes the Boss has taken up in his work over the past forty years (the remaining ten percent is girls and cars). I'm not asking for the inclusion of grist for the gossip mill or divulgence of his specific, individual nightmares; I'm saying that if Springsteen finally felt ready to share this element of his experience, he should have held himself to the same standards for an emotional deep dive that he has with other serious societal ills that have been just as profoundly personal to him. It may be difficult to write about the black fog of depression when it is not upon him, but in the same vein, he's been fabulously wealthy for decades now and doesn't have much trouble writing about the plight of working class people with proper pathos. In his treatment of the subject of depression, Springsteen has far more power at his disposal than he chose to use.

★

"I Wish I Were Blind" / *Human Touch* (1992)

I play in key of brotherhood awesome
Grin a girly king
I'd write to read the blessing of doves
On these new words' wings
Amen carefree true rocking prelim
Crown lifelong headstand
I know I'll be fine
Cause I sit at your left hand

I keep a beat guitar whining
With a strong drummer's sight
Fingers hopscotch fretboard ride or die
A newcomer's fight
Our amps ablaze awake the band
Top notch now you rush in with your heart askance
And I know I'll be fine
Cause I sit at your left hand

Befuddled ears shut holler inhumane
Aristocrat rebuild me with a duty
Wow thrill me so sane
And the fight I remembered seared
Has vanished between
Endless harmless revolves maybe with expertise

I know your whirls are skilled
Commonplace and rooted in your band
And I know I'll be fine
Cause I sit at your left hand

★

Is he a self-aware individual? What are Springsteen's virtues and what are his sins?

Yes, Springsteen is self-aware. "It is my nature to 'dissemble' (a.k.a. fuck up), then bring roses, blow kisses and do backward somersaults in a manic frenzy trying to charm my way out of the hole I've dug. That's no good with kids (or a wife either)." He is aware of the perils of rock stardom at large—the gig requires you to be something of a misfit and an egomaniac. Springsteen has exercised as much caution against his own ambition as he can, given that his major weaknesses are also his primary strengths.

He'd been skating along this double-edged sword since he was born, wrestling with the "terrible freedom" of his younger years: "In this house, due to order of birth and circumstance, I was lord, king, and messiah all rolled into one. [...] Our ruin of a house and my own eccentricities and power shamed and embarrassed me."

Of course, one page later: "The grinding hypnotic power of this ruined place and these people would never leave me. [...] It ruined me and it made me." His first encounter with the dangers of charisma was his own grandfather, holding a crisp dollar bill in one hand and a death pinch for Springsteen's cheeks in the other. "He was exciting, scary, theatrical, self-mythologizing, bragging... like a rock star!" His family gave him the purpose and then Elvis gave him the motivation.

As Springsteen worked on his craft, every fear and shortcoming would be turned into fodder for his career, polishing his personal turds into recording gold. "At the first sound of thunder, I caterwauled until my parents would take me in the car until the storm subsided. I then proceeded to write about cars for the rest of my life." He says the best review he ever got was courtesy of his sister, who saw her own working class life—the same one Springsteen personally scrambled to flee—reflected in "The River."

One of the main reasons for running that threads through the songs has always been the hope of not turning out as careless and cruel as his father. The old man's playbook, as it was reflected in himself, included a significant part "that sought to reap damage and harvest shame, that wanted to wound and hurt and make sure those who loved me paid for it." But through most of *Born to Run*, there is quite a thorough effort to undercut all that, sitting somewhere between a soft-hearted walk-back and actually making peace. When they get together to try to patch up some of their long, awkward, fearsome history together, it doesn't stick.

And because he didn't make it stick, now it aches. His father did, once toward the end of his life, try explicitly to acknowledge his own fault in the matter. Springsteen attempts to pay that moment forward. "I can't lay it all at my pop's feet; plenty of it is my own weakness and inability at this late date to put it all away, my favorite harpies, the ones I count on to return to flit and nibble around the edges of my beautiful reward." That's as good as it gets. In talking about social healing after Vietnam, he reflects that "to move forward, we'd have to willingly bear the weight of our unreconciled past." So there's Springsteen with a devil on one shoulder and an angel on the other, both wearing the same face.

The sins of his father still rest upon him, and some of that weight indeed transfers to his own kids, despite Springsteen's best efforts to the contrary. He is keenly aware of his own shortcomings in the workaholic image he presented to his children, but has done his best to make good. To his credit, he gives all the credit to Patti Scialfa. She arrives on page 322, almost the precise center of the book and the fierce gravitational pull that brings the Boss down to real reality for the first and final time in his life. She gave him an ultimatum and he acquiesced—he stayed. His description of the arrival of their first born son sounds like baby Jesus. "CITIZENS OF LOS ANGELES: EVAN JAMES SPRINGSTEEN IS BORN. A SON OF NEW JERSEY, BORN IN EXILE, HERE IN BABYLON! [...] We are huddled together with seven pounds and eleven ounces of living proof." The holiness of his second marriage is balanced by the terror and sadness of his first marriage to Julianne and the trashy way he handled their separation, which is not a story told in much detail.

If his family growing up was the source of chaos, and the family he made for himself was a source of frightening responsibility, the refuge was always in his band. Springsteen exercised maximum control, for better and for worse, in what he thinks of as a benevolent dictatorship. For the E Street Band, he was "mayor, judge, jury and sheriff." "I needed disciples," he writes, but ultimately, "This would prove to be an Achilles' heel and in the future, after some costly enmeshments, I'd let it go."

Blessedly, Springsteen knows all about himself and shares in this book the basic human problem that our virtues are generally identical to our vices, and succeeds at laughing at himself a little bit. But after some sunny jabs at the fragility of human nature, after turning fault into fruit as often as he can manage, the sun still sets. Shit goes dark and nobody gets a do-over.

★

If I Should Fall Behind / *Lucky Town* (1992)

He bled he'd sing forever overcome doomsday
Become the spotlight would we choose his say
Whereas I'm talkin my band guarantees
I'll speak for Bruce
Sainthood why lose my mind
Speak for me

Legacies fragile but a mile wide
Keyed up discovering spirit guides
Impeached and perplexed all the stone ponies

The favorite son teams hand in glove recasting new
Impresario to follies of ruth
Undertakes cavalier hats another might flee

Vow I'm a dutiful scrivener of pep rally bloodshed
Bequeath sacred cows swooning thoroughbreds
Would we fuse or smother with the cargo of these meanings free

★

What is his mission, for the book and in his life? What kind of Catholic and what kind of political activist is he?

The use of a Unitarian minister in the wedding ceremony with Scialfa notwithstanding, it is commonly accepted as fact that Springsteen is Catholic. He sometimes slides in and out of verb tenses when referencing religion, so that the book is by turns dismissively vague and precisely ambivalent about whether he was one or is one. He is also fond of holding these contradictions in the same breath, for example, when looking back on one of his most treacherous surfing experiences. "I nearly drowned in a hurricane surf I should never have been out in. [...] I paddled like a windmill, immediately rediscovering my faith in Catholicism as I prayed like never before: 'Lord, please let me slip over the peak of this monster.' [...] I lay there for a long time, breathing in gulps, my heart pounding, thanking the God I did not believe in."

Springsteen is the doubting kind. On the one hand: "As funny as it sounds, I have a 'personal' relationship with Jesus. He remains one of my fathers, though

94

as with my own father, I no longer believe in his godly power. I believe deeply in his love, his ability to save...but not to damn...enough of that." And on the other hand, on the very same page: "I came to ruefully and bemusedly understand that once you're a Catholic, you're always a Catholic. So I stopped kidding myself. I don't often participate in my religion but I know somewhere...deep inside...I'm still on the team." This applies not only to his religious life, but to the politics of his work. "Along with (when necessary) supreme confidence, doubt and all of its many manifestations is in my wheelhouse. You work that right and it's a blessing. You work it wrong and you're paralyzed. Doubt can be the starting point for deeper critical thought. It can keep you from selling yourself and your audience short and it can bring you hard down to Earth if needed."

While his faith in religious practice may be lapsed or shot through with doubt, his commitment to the rhetorical mode of belief-based mission itself never waivers. He talks like a preacher. Even when he undercuts or downplays his personal faith, his diction stays firmly rooted in the Biblical. The opening chapter of *Born to Run* explicitly connects his writing to the notion of church, ending with, "Let the service begin." Early on, he found miracles in the pastoral care of Elvis. "A 'man' did this. A 'man' searching for something new. He willed it into existence. Elvis's great act of love rocked the country and was an early echo of the coming civil rights movement."

The Boss had a self-concept of epic proportions, complete with quest, test and the mysterious joys of survival. "I determined that there on the streets of my hometown was the beginning of my purpose, my reason, my passion. Along with Catholicism, in my family's neighborhood experience, I found my other 'genesis' piece, the beginning of my song: home, roots, blood, community, responsibility, stay hard, stay hungry, stay alive. Sweetened by cars, girls and fortune, these are the things that guided my musical journey." The albums are meant to convey these bedrock themes as a better means of approaching one's own life. "Each record was a statement of purpose. I wanted playfulness, good times, but also an underlying philosophical seriousness, a code of living, fusing it all together and making it more than just a collection of my ten latest songs." After Clarence Clemons passed away, the Boss sought to heal his band's gaping wound with the understanding that "it was less of a 'job' than a position of faith that had some distinctly shamanistic requirements."

He is humbled by the activism of other bands, like U2. "I never had the frontline courage of many of my more committed musical brethren. If anything, over the years, too much has been made of whatever service we've provided. But I did look to develop a consistent approach." Springsteen views his band as having a mission, and that mission is transcendence. He states this humbly and directly: "A lot of what the E Street Band does is hand-me-down shtick transformed by will, power and an intense communication with our audience into something transcendent." "[The E Street Band is] more than an idea, an aesthetic. We are a philosophy, a collective, with a professional code of honor. It is based on principle that we bring our best, everything we have, on this night, to remind you of everything you have, your best."

So he ends up treating a concert hall as if it is a church. "It's a life-giving, joyful, sweat-drenched, muscle-aching, voice-blowing, mind-clearing, exhausting, soul-invigorating, cathartic pleasure and privilege every night. You can sing about your misery, the world's misery, your most devastating experiences, but there is something in the gathering of souls that blows the blues away. Something that lets some sun in, that keeps you breathing, that lifts you in a way that can't be explained, only experienced." The achievement of this mission on a nightly basis, the temporary experience of this transcendence, is a form of communion. "Something that before the faithful were gathered here today was just a song-filled rumor. I am here to provide proof of life to that ever elusive, never completely believable 'us.' That is my magic trick."

Springsteen insists on the authenticity of this magic trick. "The shows were real, always…my friends were real, always…the audience was real, always. I was not alone. I was carrying a lot of weight, but I was not alone. The men I'd chosen to travel with were at my side. Their comfort, their partnership, was invaluable. No matter how weird it got out there, on the bandstand, when I turned around, I saw home." In his home space of the stage, he preaches primarily on the gap between our daily life and our ideal selves. "By the end of the *River* tour, I thought perhaps mapping that territory, the distance between the American dream and American reality, might be my service, one I could provide that would accompany my entertainment and the good times I brought my fans. I hoped it might give roots and mission to our band."

From time to time, he has doubts about whether he is out of touch with daily life. "As my success increased, there was something about that 'rich man in a poor man's shirt' that left an uneasy taste in my mouth surrounding this type of writing [on social issues]." He has doubts about whether rock music in America is itself out of touch as a means of real dialogue, but his fundamental faith in the power of his own words keeps him steady. "When people wanted a dialogue, a conversation about events, internal and external, we developed a language that suited those moments. We were there. It was a language I hoped would entertain, inspire, comfort and reveal. The professionalism, the showmanship, the hours of hard work are all very important, but I always believed that it was the dialogue, this language, that was at the heart of our resiliency with our audience."

He believes this is the purpose of rock music at large, this communion. "Rock 'n' roll music, in the end is a source of religious and mystical power." The power of rock shows is not that they inform or educate, but that they are evocative of something beyond our individual selves. "One plus one equals two. It keeps the world spinning. But artists, musicians, con men, poets, mystics and such are paid to turn that math on its head, to rub two sticks together and bring forth fire. […] People don't come to rock show to learn something. They come to be reminded of something they already know and feel deep down in their gut."

The mission of the book is human, to reveal Springsteen's inner thoughts and the motives in his gut. He has worked hard with his psychologist to arrive at the right moment to do this. With more questions than answers, more feelings than facts, more philosophy than reportage, Springsteen adds layers upon layers. If the Bible is meant to narrate the life of Jesus in order to acknowledge the mysteries of God, *Born to Run* narrates the life of Springsteen in order to acknowledge the mysteries of rock. And here, the Boss is a god. "There is something to be said for living. Personally, I like my gods old, grizzled and here."

★

"Living Proof" / *Lucky Town* (1992)

Hellbound on the drummer's right for a funky tune
When the riddle ceases the chords still dynamite
Prying open the hollow of diary's rune
Buried in those charms resolves a duty undertake
Reminiscing herds thoroughfare ally chats clever made
For some girls vanguard of yearning in souls so misused
Carnivorous mother wit feminism
I'm crowned bulletproof

State of the art black hole barefoot and smiling to myself
Annexed by the wraiths that bathe in our frost overwhelmed
I want frowns accrued as dirt that's pretty
This train so far woodshedding kin
Sprawling sweeping toward my mind's catharsis
Pushing to slow the deathly pace of venial sin
And when my comrade sings maybe
Amen truth applied to Bruce

I'll welcome scared and hateful kings
I'm queen bulletproof
Say goodbye to anchor and cage
Ammo for this mission stardust in middle age
On a fresh breeze through yards
Past some whitened clan who were predisposed to war

Still on my grand tour of the bully's yard
Bowie knife in trust from Hildegarde
Jazz agile to disband shibboleths
That destroy anything we've said
So fight and die for our beliefs
One-woman band of campy griefs
And at curtain call threaten encores
Reveal bogeymen by the measure of their swords
Just grin with headstrong doubt weighty
Passenger train baring down in my spoof
Carnivorous mother wit feminism
I'm crowned bulletproof

★

How does this book compare and contrast with the autobiographies of Bob Dylan and Patti Smith?

Chronicles and *Just Kids* are the two greatest music memoirs of the twenty-first century, correct? Confessions before we proceed: I have never made it past page fifty or so in *Chronicles* despite having tried to read it three times in ten years, and I'm already on record saying that *M Train* is a way better book than *Just Kids*. Go ahead and get started on your hate mail.

Springsteen himself would not agree with me. "Songwriters with their own voice, their own story to tell, who could draw you into a world they created and sustain your interest in the things that obsessed them. Not many, but a handful at best. Dylan was preeminent amongst these types of writers. Bob Dylan is the father of my country." I want to say that this "father of my country" bit is about as much over the top mythologizing as Jon Landau gave to the Boss in that "future of rock" prophecy he called a review. And now that Dylan has won a Nobel Prize for Literature, I suppose I'll try to take a fourth pass at the autobiography that has even fewer facts in it than Springsteen's.

They've earned it though, right? "You have to make thoughtful compromises that don't sell out your soul, that let you reach just a little bit higher until your moment comes and then you set the rules." Their license has pros and cons. "What makes something great may also be one of its weaknesses, just like in people." "Rock 'n' roll is a music of stakes. The higher they're pushed, the deeper and more thrilling the moment becomes." As men like Dylan and Springsteen age up into their legendary obscurity, of course they'll want to write a book that dumps out all the gris-gris rattling around in their heads. "All I know is that as we age the weight of our unsorted baggage becomes heavier…much heavier. With each passing year, the price of our refusal to do that sorting rises higher and higher."

Springsteen is still in search of salvation. "It's a common malady, a profile of sorts, that floods my profession. We're travelers, 'runners,' not 'stayers'." He can run all he wants, but he's stuck with himself. "There is but one life. Nobody likes that…but there's just one. And we're lucky to have it. God bless us and have mercy on us that we may have the understanding and the abilities to live it…and know that the 'possibility of everything'…is just 'nothing' dressed up in a monkey suit…and I'd had the best monkey suit in town."

This monkey suit does often put his realness at risk, which he well knows. Despite his hall of mirrors and these Dylanesque feats of mystery, Springsteen's book is humble enough and properly pained to fall more in line with Patti Smith's two memoirs. Unfortunately, the Boss doesn't devote more than a sentence or two to Smith's work (why on Earth doesn't *Born to Run* have an index? That is cruel!), even though it would be amazing to hear his take on everything surrounding "Because the Night."

The only woman besides Scialfa he gives professional thanks to is Bonnie Raitt, because she let him open for her so often in the early days. She comments on his need for a nightly exorcism. "My pal Bonnie Raitt, upon visiting me backstage, used to smilingly shake her head at me and say, 'The boy has it in him, and it's got to come out.' So there, with you, I'm near free and it's party 'till the lights go out. I don't know why, but I've never gotten anywhere near as far or as high as when I count the band in and feel what seems like all life itself and a small flash of eternity pulsing through me."

At every turn, readers are reminded of the high stakes of transcendence. "The theory of relativity holds. Onstage your exhilaration is in direct proportion to the void you're dancing over." So, too, are readers reminded of the paradox of this entire endeavor that is Springsteen's life's work. "Your blessings and your curses often come in the same package." In some ways, he's known all along about the futility of trying to explicitly tell in this book the things he has been trying to creatively demonstrate on stage all these many years. "I know how it works. I've done it. Play and shut up. My business is SHOW business and that is the business of SHOWING...not TELLING. You don't TELL people anything, you SHOW them, and let them decide. That's how I got here, by SHOWING people."

This book is not a very clean exercise in telling, but what it does show is more shades of that predictably driven, mystical Boss we already know. Why does reading Springsteen's memoir feel like a test? You may like to know that, as I write this, I am thinking about having just turned thirty-five two weeks ago. The problem then is not that life is too short, but rather, that it is long. Springsteen just turned sixty-seven. We're both Libras. It's all about balance. *Born to Run* refers to two innate tendencies that are arguably a paradox but unarguably human: to flee from a thing and also to work really hard on it. What he says of his father is surely true of the son. "The Sphinx spoke! My dad showed himself, or some part of himself, though under tenuous conditions. So, rather than revelation, his pronouncements brought only more mystery and a longing to understand what was ultimately unfathomable."

So, that's my final verdict: *Born to Run* is unfathomable. It is unfathomable because Bruce Springsteen is a soul man. "Soul man, soul man, soul man...that's the term. As an R&B singer, I will never be more than 'pretty close,' but 'soul man' is a much broader term. It encompasses your life, your work and the way you approach both. Joe Strummer, Neil Young, Bob Dylan, Mick and Keith, Joey Ramone, John and Paul—all white boys who could rest comfortably with that sobriquet. It's an all-inclusive, and I'd be perfectly happy with just those two words on my gravestone."

If you can get it down to just two words, that's excellent.

CHAPTER FIVE

MY WIFE WAS ONCE A PROFESSIONAL COMEDIAN. Everybody with whom she worked is now famous, but she didn't have the stomach for it. Literally— she felt gross living out of a suitcase and the amount of drugs that it takes to fuel a permanent road show are obviously way beyond what is healthy to ingest, if you can ever get them all down on top of your own self-loathing. But as her anecdotes about life on the road trickle out to me over our years together, she has consistently expressed admiration for Paula Poundstone. They would do two sets a night and Poundstone's shows rarely had very much overlapping material. According to my wife, Poundstone was gifted with such a fearless capacity for improvisation that she could invent three fresh hours of material each night.

Poundstone, clearly a venerated veteran at this point, has been delivering apt social critique from the stage since the eighties. This near to unattainable level of longevity surely counts for a lot in the comedy business. Doing it longest is one thing, doing it best is another thing, and doing it first is yet another. When comedians talk about the greats in their profession, they often go back to George Carlin, who began working in the sixties. Carlin's career spanned several decades, he got in a good deal of legal trouble for his work, and his legacy of social satire is unparalleled—or, nearly unparalleled. After reading Lenny Bruce's autobiography, *How to Talk Dirty and Influence People*, I realized that everything I have ever loved about Poundstone or Carlin and their genre of hilarity actually began in the late forties with Bruce.

When asked about his own influences, Bruce is dismissive. "What an absurd question. I am influenced by every second of my waking hour." His work was based on experience and completely of the moment. He could rework a bit hundreds of times, but it was never done quite the same way twice, either in form or in content. Many of his most famous bits caused him to be labelled a "sick comic" from the whitewashed suburban viewpoint of the fifties, about which he shrugs, "It is impossible to label me. I develop, on the average, four minutes of new material a night, constantly growing and changing my point of view; I am heinously guilty of the paradoxes I assail in our society."

Chief among Bruce's peeves is hypocrisy of any stripe, and chief among his virtues is his constant willingness to cop to his own sordid contradictions. "Every man reading this has at one time pissed in the sink. I have, and I am part of every guy in the world. We're all included. I know you've pissed in the sink. You may have pretended to be washing your hands, but you were definitely pissing in the sink." This profound dislike for pretense would shape up into anecdotal evidence and storytelling of all kinds during his set, and Bruce could run the gamut of diverse social issues from marijuana legalization to the treatment of women to his view of institutionalized religion. His "Religion, Inc." bit was a major catalyst for his success.

"Of course I disagree with [church-goers] and of course they have the right to believe whatever they do; all I want is for them to come out and admit it and stop issuing sanctimonious bulls saying one thing while they pursue the opposite." He also believed that this widespread insincerity was setting society up for failure. "The what-should-be never did exist, but people keep trying to live up to it. There is only what is." When it did not come at too high a cost, he tried to live up to his own standards of charitable behavior, albeit often in an unusual fashion. The autobiography spins a great yarn about getting busted for impersonating a priest in Miami to garner financial donations—half to the legitimate charity, half to Bruce's rent payment.

The first part of the book is concerned with Bruce's formative years, and his memories serve more as evidence of moral development than development of his comedic craft. He begins with childhood and then moves to his time in the Navy. As he grows older, he shifts from learning about communication between men and women toward cross-cultural communication between citizens of the world. As a result of these reminisces, he arrives at a deep, firsthand understanding of the scant virtues of capitalism and war. Despite his heavy-hearted cynicism, he is surprised to find himself making room for love.

The antics of his courtship and marriage to stripper Honey Harlow are surprisingly heart-warming both to Bruce and his readers. When she was nearly killed in a car crash, he found himself frantically bargaining with God—when she survived, he followed through on his promises despite not necessarily believing in their efficacy in her recovery. Of course, they later divorced, whereupon he reflects, "How can I ever get married again? I'd have to say the same things to another woman that I said to Honey. And I couldn't say the same things to another woman because somehow that would be corrupt to me."

He wasn't generally interested in elaborating on the "somehow" that lands people in the middle of corruption. He focuses on the symptoms of it and then asks why we don't treat the disease. This rhetorical question is perhaps his greatest asset as a comedian, because audiences laugh uncomfortably in the empty space where they should be able to provide an answer. But the fact of human nature's attraction to contradiction cannot be answered for, and Bruce knew this. He opted for the only rational response—faith in the essential productivity of generating confusion over our own hypocrisies. "As a child I loved confusion: a freezing blizzard that would stop all traffic and mail; toilets that would get stopped up and overflow and run down the halls; electrical failures—anything that would stop the flow and make it back up and find a new direction. Confusion was entertainment to me."

What was entertainment to Bruce was often construed as unlawful by others. He was famously arrested several times in the early sixties, sometimes for drugs and sometimes for the obscenity of his comedic work on stage. "Believe it or not," he says, "I have a dread of being a martyr." Nevertheless, his obscenity trial was a major sensation. He was hauled in for using the word "cocksucker." It wasn't even the punchline to the joke, just a casual part of the dialogue that he used in order to properly characterize two people and set the tone in a scene he was narrating. The second half of the book primarily concerns his legal troubles. Bruce provides excerpts from the court transcripts, his own recollections, letters and petitions on his behalf, and so on.

This stunning farce of decency forced Bruce to play the straight man against very many unintentional laugh lines given by witness and experts in court. In the book, he provides thorough context and is really quite fair to his critics. Given his willingness to admit his faults, the court documents showing his persecution are especially disturbing. Though his show is far from arousing, he's even willing to concede the point. "Well, I want to know what's wrong with appealing to prurient interest. I really want the Supreme Court to stand up and tell me that fucking is dirty and no good." Subsequent arrests were greased by the sensationalism of the first obscenity trial and compounded by rumors of his drug use. "It is because of newspapers—their disregard for the truth when it comes to reporting—that my reputation has been hurt."

The autobiography was written as his case was awaiting appeal, and timed no doubt in part to drum up funding and support for his legal woes. That's not a criticism. "Of course, there are some people who sell themselves for money. That 'some' constitutes ninety percent of the people I've known in my life, including myself. We all sell out some part of us." Bruce recalls that the best letter he got during this time period was from the Reverend Sidney Lanier, vicar of Saint Clement's Church in New York, who wrote to him that "it is never popular to be so scathingly honest, whether it is from a night-club stage or from a pulpit, and I was not surprised to hear you were having some 'trouble."

Bruce got many comparisons to other satirists in the vein of Jonathan Swift and even Aristophanes, but he himself seems to return over and over again to religious leaders rather than other comedians. Indeed, he felt that his performance was a type of calling from deep within his heart. "I felt—and still do feel—that all so-called 'men of God' are self-ordained. The 'calling' they hear is just their own echo." Much of his childhood reflection centers on having been brought up culturally Jewish. Much of his stage act is framed by the fundamentalist hypocrisy he saw in religious institutions. Much of his legal battle was predicated upon a churchgoer's sense of indecency. His own best scam was to imitate a priest.

Unconcerned by matters of personal faith but deeply invested in the double-standards of its public application, Bruce's worldview consists of both authentic empathy and social responsibility. This perspective caused him to be both revered and vilified for most of his short life. "Constant, abrasive irritation produces the pearl: it is a disease of the oyster," reflects Kenneth Tynan in the introduction. There are three introductions, in fact—two that are new to the 2016 fiftieth anniversary edition, and the original from Tynan in 1965. Tynan locates Bruce as "a tightrope walker between morality and nihilism." In some ways, he's above us.

Lewis Black also likes the idea of the God's eye view. In acknowledging his debt to Bruce, he says he's made "a career out of expressing [his] dissatisfaction with the world." But Tynan and Black disagree about the extent to which a comedian can be viewed as a preacher. Black maintains that, "I don't think about changing minds; I think about getting laughs. Changing a mind is collateral damage, if you will." Tynan says that Bruce was "seldom funny without an ulterior motive. You squirm as you smile. With Bruce a smile is not an end in itself, it is invariably a means." One page later, he declares, "Bruce has the heart of an unfrocked evangelist."

The other new introduction is from Howard Reich, jazz critic. He seems at first to agree with Black. "Bruce was no preacher, telling others how to live. He was simply saying what he believed: not to win converts but only to make his case to those who bothered to encounter it." "Perhaps thinking about Bruce as a preacher is not quite the right word, perhaps conversion is not quite the best frame for the relationship between comedian and audience. To most effectively value his work and to take his self-concept into our own hearts, we must simply remember that "like all genuine sages, Bruce directs as much criticism toward himself as anyone else, which lends credibility to his skepticism of others." Lenny Bruce was a sage—possessed of unique experience, performing with excellent judgment, and perpetuating a profound wisdom.

★

The night before I hauled off my motorcycle to be sold, I went to see The Flaming Lips. I had to get my mind right, in part by getting messed up. The next morning,

I got up at 8 AM and made a giant pot of macaroni and cheese for breakfast. Then I washed my bike and had it towed, following along with the truck to the sound of "Freebird" on the radio, and I didn't cry about it. Unscrewed my license plate, signed the paperwork and didn't look back. Drove home in a tornado warning, thinking about my bike sitting outside the shop, battered by gray sheets of rain while I was safe and dry inside my auto.

Before the second encore, standing alone in the glare of the bright white spot, his speech halted no doubt by the power of hallucinations that only he could translate, Wayne Coyne delivered this monologue: "It may seem like a sombre moment. We do not want you guys to become sombre and sad, okay? The best thing that can happen is that you could—and hopefully you will—just continue to laugh, and scream, and have the fucking best night of your whole life. There is plenty of sadness waiting for you once you leave this building. Remember, sad songs are not really meant to make you sad; they're just so we remember. Even though we know life—it's not fair, it can be brutal, and the little things in the world take—sometimes they get the worst of people. But, we can still say life is fucking fucking fucking amazing. Ha!"

Then he launched into "Waitin' for a Superman." I wasn't waiting; I left the building and could hear the keening prayer of "Do You Realize?" pouring out through the roof of the Tabernacle as I strode toward the train station.

★

"Youngstown" / *The Ghost of Tom Joad* (1995)

Queer in northwest Chicago
Kicking in the nineties
All my uncles beating
Round the chore of tellin' me not to speak
Their guilt made them nervous
Feared so strong my score
So they rolled the bowling balls
That kept me ruined on the floor

Pulling rungs down
Pulling rungs down
Uncle Kenny, I'm climbin' round
Queer pulling your rungs down

While my uncles parked in furniture
Kitchen daughter I dwelt
I stayed calm like bombs corked the weight of warfare
In shoes so full of pebbles from hell
Tuesday night, bowl and beer zone
High score hidden and barred from play
Their setbacks preachin' all the norms for broads
About my duty to guys barefoot and splayed

I went batty from all of those fireworks
And the outcome was cut them loose
But their jaws still flap and fumble
They say, "We're annoyed at what bitter women spew"
My chills are gilt with lamps and moms
That stun these gendered scores
Dissent begun new ideas and opened qualms
While I'm climbing the rungs up to their front door

And the more girls that I can rally
To climb the ladders of this rage
With their cold minds to best combat it
Our quarry will face a change
Heaven's jungle tongues these petals of page
Transfer from hell Ken's dreams exchanged
Published paid and hitched he's chuffed
Proud and puffed to stake his claim

As I rise I'm undaunted by concessions
I can spot his intention's smell
I weigh the level sums and stakes we
Demand in the airy sureness of our swell

*

We'd have been fine if Pennsylvania and Michigan had ponied up, if white
working-class Yankee women had not voted for Trump. Personally, I blame Bruce
for not doing more gigs because the votes we lost pretty much comprise
Springsteen's entire audience. When *Rolling Stone* asked him why he had not
done any campaign events for Hillary with less than a month before Election

Day, he said he liked Hillary a lot and wasn't aware that they'd been asked to do anything. You've got to be kidding me. You think this campaign that's been in the works for over a decade simply neglected to put in a call asking the Boss for help? No, my man. Whatever happened, and I don't pretend to know, that is not why Springsteen didn't stump for Hillary. Hell, a phone works both ways. You're telling me Hillary wouldn't have picked up the phone for Bruce? Completely unlikely.

So I hope that of all the people who woke up on November 10th to regret not having done more for Democrats in this cycle, Bruce was chief among them. Meanwhile, in a cruel twist, the B-Street cover band was nearly forced to perform at New Jersey's Inaugural Gala for Trump because they signed a contract to do so after performing there the second time Obama got elected. It's really just a big Jersey party, no matter who's been elected, but of course the headlines don't tell it that way. So these poor guys in their sixties who've been riding the coattails of the world's best bar band for more than twenty years are facing all kinds of flack for performing for Trump. Living in mortal fear of offending Springsteen, they're going to back out of the contract and refuse to play, even though neither they nor the event are at all political.

Gary Tallent said the whole debacle must be a joke. Steven Van Zandt said he wasn't going to judge B-Street, but then also that there's no separation between art and politics. Bruce has stayed mum. Personally, I think E Street should pay whatever fine B-Street is going to incur from failing to uphold the contract. Most professional cover bands saddle themselves with the band's image as well as the music. The B-Street Band has faithfully carried the burdens of the Boss for more than two hundred gigs a year since 1980, and not only do they deserve to be cut a break in this instance, they deserve an active legal and financial assist from their personal god of rock.

★

Anne Lamott has written a book about mercy, which I am now going to mercilessly review. Consider yourself warned.

Lamott is classified by some as writing in the genre of literary particularism. The idea is that the details inside each book should matter more than whatever connections can be made to other books, that each situation can be taken independently and in isolation as, um, situational. It's not a very well-defined genre, but the gist is that it has allowed Lamott to write another single motherhood or alcoholism or religion or whatever other big idea through the insights uniquely afforded by her own experience and its particulars. To appreciate the author's particulars requires some degree of empathy on the part of the reader, who may not be parenting alone or going to AA meetings or showing up at church. The minute that reader cross-applies some understandings from another work of art or channels Lamott's words into their own life's parallels, the particularism fuzzes and fades away, perhaps of necessity. A universally appreciated book is a bestselling book, after all.

Moral philosophy has a much more emphatic and clear cut notion of particularism. Ethical concepts such as "love" or "mercy" are thick with particularity. In short, there is no universal way to determine how to act upon these concepts. Particularity is different from relativism to the extent that it is more moderate; it suggests that by examining the details of a given situation we can accommodate a variety of values for a generic principle like mercy. We could even go so far as to begin grouping these situations into appropriate categories of response. Lamott's *Hallelujah Anyway* contends that mercy ought to be applied in one hundred percent of the cases where it is possible to do so. Situationally, she is happy to admit that it may not always be possible to apply mercy as an ethical principle (because each and every one of us is simply an awful, morally ugly person sometimes).

This willingness to concede the essential impossibility of perfect mercy is one of Lamott's best assets for two reasons. Most obviously, it enacts the very virtue she prescribes by letting us all off the hook a little bit for our inability to follow through with her suggestion of continually being merciful. It performatively makes her case because we are glad that her suggested diet of ethical principles is not too strict. Secondarily, it harbors an ideological permissiveness that is a trademark of her tone. Lamott lives in the San Francisco Bay area (and I hope you will unpack all the ugliness sliding around under my reportage of that fact and the place where I chose to insert it in this review). Or, let me be clear: Lamott writes in that relatively privileged mode of white women trying to better themselves, trying to work past the valid struggles they have encountered in their often invalidly smallish bubble.

She is a poet whose flow of language is operating under the aegis of narrative nonfiction, with the result that her work's primary effect is to suck readers into her sense of pathos. She appeals to our finest feelings. Particularism is a style that ultimately succeeds in putting sentimentality within easy reach. One cannot argue with emotional truths; when Lamott describes how she felt joy at someone else's misery, a reader has no choice but to accept her feelings at face value. The beauty of arguments based on pathos is that there is really no counter-factual available to refute them. But the author's reliance on the particularities of her pathos—though charming and reassuring and noble and fun—also hobble her anecdotal considerations and prevent them from rising to the level of a coherent moral position.

Let's first define "mercy" as the essential term of art in this debate. The author is correct to begin here. She cites the Old Testament prophet Micah, who said, "What doth God require of thee but to do justice and to love mercy, and to walk humbly with thy God," in order to set forth the basis for a purposeful life. From a rhetorical perspective, we can say that these three virtues correspond to the three forms of appeal—mercy is pathos (argument by feeling), humility is ethos (argument by character), and justice is logos (argument by reasoning). Although we access mercy as a kind of pathos, Lamott's definition further breaks mercy into three categories, "kindness, compassion, forgiveness." Kindness is a generosity of service toward others; often it is born on the wings of compassion, a feeling of sympathy or empathy toward the plight of another. Still, kindness travels the road of ethos perhaps more readily than the road of pathos. Because kindness is an act rather than a feeling, it feeds other people's perceptions of us and results in a sense of our character. Forgiveness may also be born of compassion, but I would argue that forgiveness falls conceptually under logos because it is neither an act nor a feeling. To forgive is to judge—or even if it is a letting go of judgment, that is still a matter for logos.

Most people would agree that justice is a situational enterprise. In passing judgment, we always consider the circumstances. This would seem to be in line with Lamott's affinity for literary particularism, but her reliance on poetic sentiment too frequently glosses the empirical dimension of moral particularism. After an initial foray into the definition of mercy, she waives away the distinctions between kindness, compassion and forgiveness in order to continually err on the more vague side of her own encounters with mercy. Her tendency to smooth experiences into parables and allegories, the mythic treatment of her self-improvements and predictable lapses, the strings of shiny adjectives that point to picturesque nouns, all serve to hide sets of situations that her merciful intention is not prepared to adequately address.

Many of her anecdotes are strawperson fallacies, presenting one-off situations that do not translate into the practical everyday merciful living that the book asks us to cultivate. There's the story of the Senegalese women stuck in a desert without water, who had visions of a massive underground lake that eventually was revealed by aid workers to actually exist. Mercy here belongs to the men who finally stopping dismissing the women's visions, and perhaps to the aid workers who dug the lake. There's the congregation who forgave the shooter in their Charleston church or survivors of war crimes testifying before tribunals in front of their oppressors. I think human beings can easily find their way to mercy in the face of massive tragedy. We call these triumphs of the human spirit; they strike us singularly at our core.

But these moments of profundity do not translate into the banality of daily evils we inflict upon each other. "Polite inclusion is the gateway drug to mercy,"

Lamott offers. I suppose I'll just be grateful to my conservative family for finally agreeing to allow my wife to show up at holiday dinners so that we can suffer severe awkwardness for a few hours together. Or we can go bigger, more impersonal on the merits of incrementalism: the now-defunct Don't Ask Don't Tell, Jim Crow's separate but equal policies. Were these polite inclusions on the right road to salvation? How long ought we to wait to arrive at genuine mercy? She argues that instead of failing and then trying harder, we should simply resist less. Sorry, but that's too close to the complicity of the good German for my comfort.

Here's another daily question hanging over the globe lately, and particularly over our collective American consciousness: ought we to forgive Donald Trump? Ought we to treat him mercifully as impeachment increasingly becomes actionable? Can we show him compassion and still seek justice? Or, if you're one of those, go ahead and make the question more hypothetically about Hillary Clinton. Let's leave that question to hang—pun intended. As Lamott concedes, "God doesn't give us answers. God gives us grace and mercy. [...] Left to my own devices, I would prefer answers." To fill the gap she offers up the wisdom of Krishnamurti, the famed Indian spiritual teacher who said his secret was that, "I don't care what happens." Lamott retorts, "I desperately want to stop minding so much about other people, life, and myself," but it is so very hard.

I have no positive feelings attached to the prospect of "resist less" or "stop minding." I'm an opinion writer, after all. It is my calling to care deeply about things that I suppose are technically none of my business. Again, Lamott concedes, "I hate this, but in judgment's defense, it's also an indication that I have a brain." I'm paid to pass judgment not only as a journalist, but also as a teacher. There are an uncountable number of anecdotes I can give—at least one for each kid that has passed through my classroom during more than a decade of teaching high school English—regarding the variety of ways I've considered to what extent it is appropriate to be merciful.

Here's a relatively easy one: do I round up that 69.4% to a passing grade at the end of the semester, or not? More complex: do I round it up for both the wealthy lacrosse team captain who will be an alumni legacy admit at an Ivy League school, as well as the student who speaks a foreign language at home while his mother works two jobs to pay for the summer school classes he already needs to keep from falling behind? Still more complex: the rich kid's parents just told him two weeks ago that they are getting a divorce, and the immigrant kid makes a good living dealing drugs during study hall.

The profession of teaching has taught me that Lamott's view of merciful action is impractical and improper. She thinks that "over and over, in spite of our awfulness and having squandered our funds, the ticket-taker at the venue waves us on through."

I tend to err on the side of believing there is no such thing as a free lunch. What is merciful is not always just. What is just is not always compassionate. Justice can be very unkind. Lamott glosses logical contradictions by seeming to embrace the inevitability of hypocrisy. She is even charmed by it. It's so cute how humanity struggles to do the right thing so often. And yet, we must "hallelujah anyway." We must keeping working on being better people—more just, more merciful, more humble—anyway. I agree completely with the action suggested by her conclusion, but I disagree with these modes and means by which she argues it.

Considering these particulars, would the most merciful thing simply have been to write a glowing review tightly focused on the point on which we agree? Or is it more merciful to push Lamott to do better in her forms of argument, seeing as how there's a strong probability that *Hallelujah Anyway* is unlikely to garner any widely read negative reviews? Or it is more merciful to just not have written a review at all? Not that I expect her to read this, but if she does, perhaps I'm just giving Lamott an opportunity to work on her own instincts toward mercy. How she processes her feelings about this criticism may offer a chance for personal growth. In describing a personal rivalry she quietly built up inside herself with regard to another unnamed writer, she says she understood well how "a blend of damage, obsessiveness, envy, and empathy was an occupational requirement for writers. Live by the sword, die by the sword." Of my sword I shall make mercy? Ugh.

Probably I'm not cut out to give opinions on contemporary spiritual teachers like Lamott. Good for her for feeling the feels and trying to get them on paper. I lack the pathos for it, or at least pathos lacks the credibility for it with me. Pathos may be a reason to act, but it never builds a strong argument because at a minimum it defies intellectual rigor and sometimes even basic fairness. It rarely transfers easily from situation to situation. Mercy must be more than what your heart tells you to do. Though I am happy to agree that the perfect is the enemy of the good, pathos is not necessarily its most natural ally. But I can hallelujah anyway.

★

"Mary Lou" / *Tracks* (1998)

More yearbooks drilled with strictures awful your bleeding then
So maybe don't make a fixture of squares condemned
Won't take it belittled worlds deemed trash cans forever blue
You better quit stewing on me, I'm not screwing with you

Uncle Drew, stop acting like you're some big prize
Uncle Drew, you should kill that petty dread sparkling in your eyes
Uncle Drew, you seem too clever, severed, beggared, peer reviewed
Uncle Drew, you ought to reassert the classified version of you

You seem all too frantic and moody, you scream and fake to the bone
But your real ace of spades must be out on loan
It hits a nerve don't reminisce, get rid of all that cargo
Quit the quaint slaying head fakes, like some dumb cut rate sideshow

No, Uncle Drew, don't hitchhike on a smothered girl
Uncle Drew, you should pray to wake up with your soul unfurled

Any fight you tough out cooking up your thin-skinned distraction
Keeps you ablaze and upset flinging unjust fights breeding factions
Try to set more apropos goals pull back on layers of pretending
You gotta get stoked and started booking some fat sappy mending

Uncle Drew, I've cleaned up the meanies blue
Uncle Drew, you can still convert from such scheming purviews
No Uncle Drew, don't wanna send up my grandmother's phony prick by scold
Uncle Drew, try and atone don't repeat it as a jealous troll

*

This review singing the praises of Bonnie McFarlane's new memoir, *You're Better Than Me*, will be delightfully easy to write, because she's very helpfully provided "Appendix C: How to Properly Give a Compliment to a Working Comedian." Assuming these compliments cross-apply from comedy shows to comedy books, here are my options, to paraphrase from McFarlane: I can state my enjoyment and reflect that I had a good time, I can describe the show as fun and the comedian as funny, and I can say thank you. Indeed, I'll gladly employ all three of those compliments for *You're Better Than Me*.

This book was a good time to read, and I enjoyed it. One of the main reasons that it felt nice to read was that I often do not have "the appropriate emotional response to things," which McFarlane considers to be the generative bedrock of all comedy as well as the source of an audience's responsiveness to comedy. The book's first chapter drills down into Wikipedia's entry on seven signs of serial killers, analyzing via unusual childhood reminisces how close she came to being a criminal but ended up a comedian instead. Maybe this is a good time to mention that McFarlane is Canadian.

She is also an enjoyable read on a more serious level, which is due to her astute rendering of the many horrific particularities of being a female comedian. For those who loved her 2014 "cockumentary," *Women Aren't Funny,* this text is a gloriously personal trek into the anecdotal evidence supporting how thoroughly sexist the comedy playing field is. Where the film leans on a cornucopia of funny ladies to give their opinions, this book unloads McFarlane's own laundry list of largely factual occurrences. And yet, she does many of the worst offenders the courtesy of anonymity when she could have instead written a true tell-all that calls out funny dude culture.

True to her form on stage, McFarlane stays fierce without tipping over into scathing. When discussing other human beings, she's simply never mean about it. She reserves the truly harsh barbs for herself, focuses punchlines on more broadly appealing types of vulgarity, and only uses names of other comedians if she is acknowledging them in a positive manner. The exceptions to this would be her personality profiles of Rich Vos, her current husband who agreed to be ridiculed when he put a ring on it, and Marc Maron, her long-ago long-time boyfriend who shouldn't dish it if he can't take it. She keeps it fun throughout.

And she keeps it funny, despite shifting in and out of a few different non-fiction modes. The beginning of the text is most directly in line with classic memoir, and as readers turn more pages, they will feel the author's compulsion to turn back toward something fragmentary and more in the vein of her stage show. By the end, she's engaging in outright reflection on her own progress as well as dispensing advice to aspiring comics. The beginning of the book uproariously mocks this tendency of veteran comics to want to drop their infinite wisdom on the newbies. The things McFarlane is most annoyed by in others are frequently revealed to be things she dislikes about herself—she's always in on the hypocrisy and the hilarity of that.

I'm trying to do justice to the book's content, but I'm also trying not to spoil it for you by relaying any of the most funny material in it. Just go pick up a copy of *You're Better Than Me* and revel in all the tiny ways you are actually neither better nor worse than its author. You'll thank me. And I've got to thank McFarlane as well. For the book, yes, but moreover, for a great anecdote that accurately reflects much about the book's content and vibe but is not itself in the book and therefore contains no spoilers. You see, once upon a time in a kingdom far away, my wife used to be a professional comedian.

She and McFarlane sometimes had occasion to work together. I have never personally shared airspace with McFarlane, but she'll easily convey to you repeatedly throughout the book the fact that her airspace used to be saturated with a fine fog of marijuana. The first time my wife got high, it was with thanks due to McFarlane. Their little baggie of sad, brown flakes came with one rolling paper stuffed into it. Back at the hotel ready to roll up, they discovered that one paper was torn in such a way as to prevent the production of a structurally sound joint. While my inexperienced wife bemoaned their bad luck, McFarlane spun her head with slow and steady resolve toward the nightstand—where, as we all know, one can generally find a copy of the exceedingly thin-papered Gideon Bible.

*

Kurt Cobain died when I was in 8th grade. For those of us straddling Gen X and Gen Y, it is an understatement to say his suicide was formative. Even amongst us fourteen year old kids, blame got pretty evenly divided between heroin and Courtney Love. For most of us, Love provoked the same intense polarization as Yoko Ono did for the generation before us. We blamed her for monkeywrenching Nirvana, for enabling Cobain's drug abuse, but none of us ever doubted how much he loved her. Looking at the two of them together was like looking at the sun, so bright was their connection, even when enfeebled by opiates.

Some of the best footage of the two of them together can be found in the documentary *Hit So Hard*, directed by P. David Ebersole and filmed mostly by Patty Schemel, the drummer for Hole. As a teen, I never got into Hole the way I got into Nirvana. I wasn't ready to understand the beauty of a feminist vulgarity or the power of confrontational performance art, and like I said, the high drama of Kurt and Courtney blotted out a lot of the rest of the subculture. And Cobain's death blotted out a lot of others, including the fatal overdose of Hole bassist Kristen Pfaff and the quite constant near-deaths of Patty Schemel. The film purports to be about Schemel's life, about the long list of follies stemming from her addiction to heroin and crack. But Kurt and Courtney often steal the show.

A half-decade later, Schemel's memoir of same title is now available. The content entirely overlaps that of the documentary, and I admit that I went into it looking for more of the first family of grunge, but quickly found myself able to focus on the intense delight of Schemel's own story. Cobain is dead by page seventy-five. *Hit So Hard* is one of the most honest—but moreover, one of the most useful—addiction memoirs in recent history. Most books like this operate as tell-alls, where the reader gets to indulge in juicy gossip and ridiculous rockstar antics for two hundred pages, followed by three pages of some kind of hazy but harrowing rock bottom moment, followed by fewer than fifty pages about getting cleaned up and the assurance that the author has definitely put those days behind him. And I'm using "him" deliberately, because there simply aren't that many books like this where the rockstar is female and they're usually focused on alcoholism—they don't hit so hard.

Hole's drummer is descended from alcoholics, but *Hit So Hard* spends most of its time on heroin and then adds crack about halfway through the story. Schemel is not only an apt explainer of drug culture, she's also a gifted humorist in that fine tradition of blackness that can really only emerge from the depths of such despairing pursuit of death by overdose. Her description of the nature of the highs is much clearer than any of Lou Reed's compositions. Her explication of how to buy hard drugs from strangers in strange cities and get them on the airplane is reported with a level of detail that does more to examine junky psychology than any straightforward testimonial could. Her analysis of the comparative merits of various rehab and detox procedures is deeply wise to the nuances of how best to kick, and why these programs are not one size fits all.

Hit So Hard pulls no punches. It's an unvarnished and unsensational account of how Patty Schemel survived—how she outlasted her addiction, but also how she coped with coming out, with the sudden fame and chaotic demands of Hole, with the prolonged agony of Cobain's legacy, and so on. She admits that relapse is always a possibility, that the baggage of addiction never fully leaves no matter how long one has been clean. She admits she literally and metaphorically sold off everything that Hole had given her. She admits that she glossed so much of her chemical dependency by harnessing the power of dysfunctional romantic relationships.

Regret and shame are useless feelings in the context of Schemel's noble effort to carry on. Far more valuable are her ability to look the facts in the face and her knack for landing bleak punchlines. This type of humor is often found amongst successful twelve-steppers and may be the best weapon Schemel has in the ongoing daily management of her sobriety. She's not joking around to minimize the real consequences of her failings, or to strut her ballsy rock star stuff. Jonesing for crack and going on the hunt for it is an extremely serious business; a heroin junky finds it impossible to laugh because the pain and emergency are just too overwhelmingly depressing to be funny. Forget about picking up the pieces of the life she once had; Schemel's memoir is proof of something much more foundational: that through a committed combination of clarity and wit, even the most enabled and damaged rock star might get a second chance at both love and music. Courtney Love should probably read it.

★

"Cynthia" / *Tracks* (1998)

Mindy Dawn, in your home late at night you're an attiring wife
Mindy Dawn, when you style I get high cause lady you're my life
I never want to scold you or waste your gifts
We're still dykes growing, Mindy Dawn, every kiss, just two girls persist

Mindy Dawn, with your sass it means that the knockdown stops
Mindy Dawn, you say that it's for me, maybe, but please school schmucks
As they launch their gawks
Doesn't matter what season all stardust in your smile
Done up, grand, dapper, resolute textiles
Clash Mindy Dawn

Somehow the saint of highest bling when you are clad
Lynchpin of show the heart your sleeve first lady and my comrade
So bright Mindy Dawn

So let's paint cavemen this keyhole now let's play blow their minds
We queer the streets walking, leading lady heal the blind
The outbreak of sappy, sunny, your spree launch pad
To get us understood in a swirl of plaid
Saville Mindy Dawn, go clash

Mindy Dawn, while I doze you slumber, dreams of clothes like a sieve
Mindy Dawn, the thunder in your open hand long range ring forgives
You got us all beat by a mile, the history of argyle
You are my jewel my rock unfurled like a child
A banshee of goodwill, Mindy Dawn
Hell I just wear my heart on my sleeve when I preach your truth
You know I don't ever wanna leave my front row view
Every night, I will gather seams to mend for you, Mindy Dawn
When we're eighty, still warpaint no big yawns
No frocks donned, Mindy Dawn, socks drawn

★

The name of the game is "normal or abnormal." Here's how you play: When some
exceedingly shocking political news pops up on your radar, turn to the person

next to you, read them the headline and ask, "Is this normal or abnormal?" If you want to up the stakes, drink a shot every time the answer is abnormal. If that's too many shots, alter the rules so that you drink only when things are normal—which is basically never now. Hilarious, right?

There are at least two problems with the above proposal. First, it's not that funny the way progressives often use alcohol as a shorthand marker of our need to cope with life under Trump. There are just as many liberal asses in chairs at Alcoholics Anonymous meetings as there are conservative asses. A tip of the iceberg footnote to that is the stereotypical image of white ladies drinking wine. Second, if your sense of irony has only gotten as far as the idea that "abnormal" is "the new normal," you're way behind.

You're most likely behind because you have not noticed or have not given meaningful weight to the fact that many kinds of people have long been oppressed, abused, marginalized or have otherwise been suffering way before Trump's election. Though the extent to which white women voted against their own interests in the 2016 election is indeed shocking, lots of other kinds of women are perhaps most shocked by the fact that white women have finally gotten around to wringing their hands about it. For a protest organized mostly by women of color, the Women's March sure filled the streets full of white ladies, didn't it?

It would be easier to think about how all our drinking jokes ostracize women who're trying to keep away from fire water. Yes, our empathy can certainly extend to women who struggle with drinking. It can sometimes even extend to women who live in poverty. To lesbians, but not really to transgender or gender non-confirming women. Maybe to black women, but not really to brown ones or immigrants or refugees. Or our empathy does extend to all these kinds of women—but our actions don't. We feel for these women without really seeing them. Or we see them but think we can't help, or can't help right now because their issues are made lesser simply because they're not our issues.

Oh, but they are our issues. All women are covered in skin, use money, know illness, have traveled—need rights, face trouble, hope for better. Don't we know this already? Yes, we do. And yet. (The use of "we" in the above paragraph refers to white women and it is paining me to count myself among the blind, but it is also the only intellectually honest approach to pronouns available to me because I'm white and a woman. Also a queer. Also sort of a Jew. Also left-handed. Also a public servant. Et cetera, but no excuses.)

Samhita Mukhopadhyay and Kate Harding have collected a bunch of women in a really solid book of essays, *Nasty Women: Feminism, Resistance, and Revolution in Trump's America*. All of the writers treat differing intersections of women's stuff and this infinite variety of other stuff. Even for readers well-versed in the theory of intersectionality, there is a quantity of lived experience and specific testimony here that will surely be eye-opening. Hey, it takes a village to raise a feminist, right? Many of the essays attempt to litigate why we ended up with Trump in the Oval Office; these explanations vary and sometimes clash between essayists. But the deeper work of the collection is focused on the how more than the why.

What emerges above all from *Nasty Women* is a conversation focused on the particulars of how women suffer, not why we suffer. Injustice has no reason; there is no why in matters of unfairness. We defeat unfairness by policing how it operates, by limiting its resources and its means of getting traction. But instead, feminists often end up policing each other—at least, this is the position held by many women who feel attacked when anybody points out that they are white, or wealthy, or privileged in some other kind of way. *Nasty Women* is filled with call-outs that are well-deserved—from union organizers, from Native Americans, from alcoholics, and so on. The strength of the anthology is that it provides space for disagreement without devolving into unproductive in-fighting.

Because another thing we have in common as people who have been fighting the good fight much longer than Trump has been or will be in office is this: a sense of humor. Many of the essays in *Nasty Women* are laugh out loud funny. Yeah, I'm pretty concerned that there's a maniac in the White House. But if you're focused on the admittedly big problem of Trump himself, again: you're behind. Women are not fighting against one man; we are fighting against the myriad moving pieces of a system that has always been rigged against us. ("Us": all women, not just newly semi-woke white ones.) A fight as many centuries old as this one is undoubtedly the definition of a war of attrition. Wars of attrition are a matter of stamina, of who has the most tools with which to keep fighting—and our sense of humor is easily our most renewable resource.

★

"Janey, Don't You Lose Heart" / *Tracks* (1998)

You've sought a look with sway beyond your years
Make that money with your barber's shears
High stakes and borrowed time are your tattoos
Some color code in your hairdo
Kissing carefree

Frankie get a head start
Frankie get a head start
Frankie get a head start
Frankie get a head start

Every day you taught the trans team to brush
You heal dykes in danger of a royal flush
You cannot wait to unbind your breast
You fly ahead knowing you are blessed
Still kissing carefree

You are delivered we see a good guy
Refilled a son stunning born butterfly
On the frontier of heartfelt glee
Live on rumblin' round win true the key
Kissing carefree

★

As a gigantic fan of Stephen Colbert, my confession is this: I thought his *Midnight Confessions* book pretty much sucked. I'm a *Late Show* diehard and have never missed an episode; I've been to a live taping; I track ongoing themes in his recurring bits and very much enjoy the "Midnight Confessions" segments on the show. So, what gives? Am I not the intended audience for this little toilet tank tome, which collects some of the beloved segment's jokes in a beautifully fonted, nicely illustrated keepsake package? Why does this book fail me?

First there's the matter of truthiness. "Truthiness" is an idea first proposed by Colbert on his old Comedy Central show, and it means that although something is factually untrue, it may still ring emotionally true and therefore sticks with us as real. Obviously, nobody expects the bulk of Colbert's confessions to be factually true. But if they don't resonate with that certain kind of pathos, which is what allows our identification with whatever frail part of our humanity the confession is predicated upon to produce the laughs that are our cathartic purge of this frailty, then the confessions are just jokes. They're just two-liners with punchlines, and though the punchlines may never miss a beat, the selections in this book are on balance much less warm than the selections that appear on the show. Reading the book cover to cover is a little like watching Peter Pan's shadow run around the room. It's amusing to look at the shadow's hijinks, but much less satisfying than watching Peter try to attach the shadow back onto his own foot. *Midnight Confessions* is heavy on punchlines but comparatively weak on accessible human frailties.

Certainly, jokes that are performed will engage a different set of comedy tools than jokes that are on the page. On the stage, you have props. On the page, you have illustrations. This book's illustrations are done by award-winning political cartoonist Sean Kelly, perhaps best known for his contributions to the *New York Times* Op-Ed page and the "Metropolitan Diary" column. His *Midnight Confessions* drawings properly enrich the punchlines provided by the text, but they simply cannot reinforce the content in a way that captures the emotion of the performances. If Colbert says he feels guilty about eating an entire canister of cake frosting, it's one thing to look at an image of the demolished canister and it's another thing to watch as Colbert shovels in several big mouthfuls while groaning with pleasure. The performance of eating the frosting unquestionably ups the emotional ante, prolongs our ability to appreciate the punchline by making the audience covetous of the frosting in ways the static image can't accomplish. The performance of the confessions is often funnier than the text of the punchline or even the text plus accompanying imagery in the book.

Colbert is well-known for having a love of food and beverage. In the show's first season, there were food options on the ultimately discarded "wheel of news" bit as well as interviews with people involved in the food industry or food-based non-profits, and Colbert's remarks about his life at home were usually connected to food. By season two, a lot of that had fallen away and been replaced by the long-running "Hungry for Power Games" satirical primary campaign coverage where his Flickerman character had a champagne flute ever in hand, or simply by drinking a cocktail with an actor who was known to enjoy them. As a sense of his enslavement to the Columbia Broadcasting System sunk in, laden with types of censorship that he was certainly unaccustomed to during his long run on Comedy Central, my own theory is that alcohol remains one of the most fertile territories for more adultish content available to Colbert now that his jokes must truly suffer scrutiny from the lawyers. As a result, you can see him genuinely savor that short glass of bourbon whenever it appears on screen.

Knowing how much he enjoys that bourbon aids in the viewers' emotional investment. We have a lot of empathy for Colbert whenever he takes a sip. In the *Midnight Confessions* book, obviously, he can't take that sip. So the book simply doesn't include many of the food and beverage confessions even though these jokes are very close to Colbert's true passions, one of the best ways of pushing back against the tone set by CBS, and some of the most recurring content of the confession bit. To not include these jokes means that the *Midnight Confessions* book actually isn't a very good representative sample of the show's bit. We should probably want the book to be a representative sample of the show's bit, but it can't be.

Instead, the book places a lot more emphasis on murderous feelings. Based on the confessions collected in the book, readers could generate a pretty long list of types of people that Colbert would like to die—people walking slowly in front of us on the sidewalk, people who sing "Don't Stop Believin'" at karaoke, and so on. Readers could also generate an even longer secondary list of ways that Colbert enjoys intentionally putting people on tilt—inserting a few Skittles in the M&Ms bowl, aiming sneezes at people who didn't say "bless you" the first time, and so on. We all recognize these people, but because we are not sociopaths, we generally do very little about them. These jokes hit so hard precisely because of our unwillingness to act; the jokes become our only defense and a way of acknowledging these people have broken some of the fine print of the social contract.

I've always felt that the excellence of this category of considerations would be better suited for a different bit on the show, and I think actually that Colbert's writers know it. The "what to do about annoying people" ideas generally end up funneled into other major *Late Show* bit, "Big Furry Hat." Colbert puts on a big furry hat, which he claims is something all dictators and divas have in common, then he goes up to the balcony of the set and pronounces the consequences these annoying people ought to receive. The confession bit and the hat bit are equally declarative in structure and they play with precisely the same type of content.

Their major contrast is that the hat bit is more empowering because it takes ownership of solutions, whereas the confession bit only takes ownership of guilty feelings while leaving solutions in the hands of God. Many of the jokes in the *Midnight Confessions* book may have had a stronger shelf life if they'd been funneled into a "Big Furry Hat" book instead. Therefore, far from making me feel hopeless about CBS shamefully cashing in on the success of *The Late Show* by flinging this somewhat watered down *Midnight Confessions* book our way just in time for no holiday season whatsoever, it actually clarified in my mind the prospect of a really excellent "Big Furry Hat" book. The ranting nature of that bit, its more proactive and energetic vibe, and the fact that it never relies on any props other than the easily illustratable hat itself, means that Colbert's "Big Furry Hat" book could succeed pretty mightily where *Midnight Confessions* has not. And lest we forget, the hat bit indulges Colbert's Catholicism just as much as the confession bit; it simply shifts focus from the quiet contemplation of the booth to the political noise of the pulpit.

There's been no whispering among publicists whatsoever that such a book will one day exist. But look, a lot of people are going to buy *Midnight Confessions* for the Colbert-lover in their lives. They should. It's kind of silly and makes a good coffee table badge for devotees of *The Late Show*. Serious freaks like me who know the performed version of the bit inside and out already will not be pleased with it much at all by the time they turn the last page, but CBS will have made a pretty penny nonetheless and I think we ought to all be looking forward to the "Big Furry Hat" book to resolve some of the flaws in *Midnight Confessions*.

Meanwhile, to Stephen and the good people writing for *The Late Show*: I feel overwhelmingly guilty about this negative review because I very highly prize the work that you do. I'm even grateful to CBS for the extent to which they are allowing you to get away with it and of course giving you a bigger stage on which to stand. You deserve maybe seven percent of the blame for this book; the rest of it belongs to your corporate overlords. I hope this isn't making sell-outs out of all of us. I hope you can forgive me enough to call and collect this bottle of bourbon I've got with all your names on it. Cheers, truly.

★

"The Wish" / *Tracks* (1998)

Surly deadbeat all dressed up for a painful show
Real McCoy and her pa bickering cockeyed at sundown was the status quo
Some fights are all about third degree burns and fists full of char
While crying right beneath the issue is a cracked bell jar

I'm dismembered in my mourning, pa, leering at penny stock swings
I'd just play dead and christen your pew holdin' steady for jerks
The rounds of your made up grace on the blink
And when Hades has a coffin, you can't pick, a tomb and hustlin' hurts
But how loud and sappy you could praise rooked talking homes at work

If my cries were minnows swimming into the river of you
You would eavesdrop on what's cooking yet my wept pleas got barbecued
So if I'm a running bold squirrel, papa, there your brittle toy militia's through
Hell I plot screws in my sockets an electric mistrust of you

No quaint house call for doomsday, hours for a father's day scarred
No saint to douse out your will with my hardened and list price whittled heart
You hoist your petard round this time sheet, I smolder

And forego your fresh advance
You might as well go look for a crowbar cause daddy you don't stand a chance

Sailing new seas in my Chelsea boots,
you slink with burglars and dinosaur stance
Pushin' me into a crouch with balling fists for your jungle of rants
Hell I drowned that girl from your home prow, pa,
I stopped her heartbeat and rode its wave
With hook baited by a blow torch smile too rebelling for your cookout stare
I slay all your draws it's anchors aweigh

That's right all your platitudes chafing at the stings that your corps taught us
Cause I prayed and ached sinking snout deep in the drought you wrought us
So you might try makin' confess and start new missions
Too late for you, pa, knock your scum lights out repay shit
It's nothing new, but daddy, if you're crooking up a birdsong,
I'm just gonna fillet it

★

I have often thought about writing a biography of Chrissie Hynde. In my opinion, she is the George Harrison of punk rock: an utterly original guitarist possessed of a unique sense of both self and influence, with a strong spiritual guidance system and a public attitude that is equal parts mysterious and misunderstood. As a result of a bizarre cocktail of humility and fame, of working class Midwestern pragmatism and right-place-right-time English expatriatism, the Pretenders' bandleader is one of the most ornery stars in the history of rock music. She is an extremely tough broad whose life and work are certainly worth a detailed fifty-thousand word treatment, and yet, the only commentary on her unique place in the rock pantheon comes courtesy of her own memoir, *Reckless*. *Reckless* is Hynde's impression of her own life, up to a point. Published in 2015, its account stops at the early eighties with the deaths of two of her bandmates. Though Hynde has been married three times, twice to other rock stars, her memoir only devotes about two or three pages to these relationships in total. Her early relationship with a bandmate begins and concludes in a single sentence acknowledgment, and her two daughters are likewise quite hidden. Many of the good stories in the book are a few tales that were already classifiable as oft-repeated from her interviews, and large chunks of the book are about the dumb things she did while on drugs. Her discussion of one of those things, wandering addled into a situation where she was raped by some heavy bikers, ultimately tanked the publicity for *Reckless* in a firestorm of feminist condemnation when Hynde attempted to take responsibility for her own poor judgment. Lambasted as the writing of a rape apologist, *Reckless* never got the more positive attention it deserved as the lone account of Hynde's legacy.

Enter Adam Sobsey, with *Chrissie Hynde: A Musical Biography*. Oh, I was so skeptical! Sobsey's other book is about baseball, which at first thought might not appear to offer much in the way of credibility to any take on the Pretenders. But baseball is a dispassionate fandom, and Sobsey documents Hynde's music with that same statistically-minded, historical approach. This book is thick with detail and seldom strays into editorializing that is unsupported by the facts. His ability to root out the facts in this case is itself quite admirable. Hynde is a very guarded person, to put it mildly. Even direct quotations from her interviews or from *Reckless* are not straightforwardly reliable, in Dylanesque fashion, so Sobsey is not working with a huge pile of research to begin with and then additionally, he has to thoroughly parse what little background there is for hints of corroborated truth.

Despite the analytic difficulties inherently present in Hynde as a subject, Sobsey truly does deliver the goods. He has enough musicianship to accurately analyze chord progressions and time signatures, embedding these in considerations of genre, bands in the Pretenders' orbit and other appropriate contexts. He has enough literary comprehension to trace themes and motifs across the lyrical compositions of multiple albums, including most obviously Hynde's lifelong ecological concern for children and animals as well as her ongoing fascination with biker culture and the state of Ohio, where she grew up.

The subtitle points toward a preferential focus on Hynde's work over Hynde's life, but Sobsey does succeed in quite a thorough account of her life to the extent that it provides fairly direct parallels or accompaniments to her work in the band. Hynde's life has been sensational, but Sobsey does not sensationalize it. He often draws attention to places in her story where proper details have not been forthcoming, and whenever he is compelled to lightly speculate, he makes clear that these are nothing more than open rhetorical questions sitting atop some plausibly fact-based or timeline-adjacent connections.

This is as gloriously comprehensive as it gets on the subject of Chrissie Hynde. Sobsey's effort to weave a consistent, continuous understanding out of an extremely cool person who defies most modern classifications is a noble effort. It's such a noble effort and so much a satisfying read that I am happy to admit something I almost never do, which is that I couldn't have written it better myself—and I have really given serious thought to writing it myself! *Chrissie Hynde: A Musical Biography* will please both diehard fans starving for any trickle of concrete detail and those with a passing interest who might like to know a bit more about the leader of one of the world's most enigmatic bands. Sobsey's portrait casts away all doubt that the Great Pretender is in fact one of the most underrated, authentic people to have survived the music industry mostly intact. We are lucky to finally have this book, and even though the band has recently released its first album of new material since 2008's excellent *Break Up the Concrete*, I doubt there will be a need for another Hynde biography for some time as a result of the quality of this one.

The only useful entry since then has been the hour-long documentary that aired on the BBC Four's *show Arena* in February of 2017. This prestigious prospect no doubt got fans salivating. Surely somewhere for a split second in there glimmers a different side of the icon who begrudgingly lets us love her. If you're looking for new factoids about Hynde, look elsewhere. If you're looking for talking heads on her legacy, in Hynde's own words, just fuck off. She thinks biopics are gross, so this is not that and it nevertheless fascinates. Basically, she allowed some cameras to follow her around for a little while in 2016 during the making of the *Alone* album, the band's first new recording since 2008's *Break Up the Concrete*.

The documentary crew seems to have done a lot of watching and waiting; there is very little effort to question Hynde or direct her attention in a particular way. The crew traveled to her flats in Paris and London, her recording studio in Nashville, some promo gigs in New York, and her hometown in Akron. Dan Auerbach of the Black Keys makes a brief appearance in the studio. Sandra Bernhard makes a longer appearance, interviewing Hynde for her radio show and then having lunch with her afterward. Most of the footage is just Hynde by herself, often in the middle of a crowd—which is the very thing worth contemplating.

She tries on a bunch of men's jackets and vests. She shows off two dozen paintings that she's done, in various impressionistic and abstract modes. She sits in very cool-looking chairs in otherwise basically empty rooms. She stares out many windows. She moseys through hotel lobbies and down staircases. She meanders through graveyards, parks, forests, and parking lots. She milks a cow, even though it's been decades since she drank milk herself. She talks about being a vegan, about not being a feminist, about how bands and tours work—and mainly she is saying something about loneliness. Hynde is alone, but for the most part not lonely. She construes being alone as a tremendous luxury and privilege.

This is why people think Hynde is so gorgeous; she exudes a genuine asceticism that can seem opaque and offensive, or at the very least ornery, to people who wrongly assume that rock necessitates shlock. She is a grown up punk, that late seventies species of which not many true examples remain. All this time, she's said exactly what's on her mind. People get frustrated because what's on her mind has only ever been about seven things. That's why there are so few documents about Hynde and why those documents tend to disappoint. Hynde has more lines in her face now, but she always wore clothes like that, made faces and moved like that, played guitar and sang like that, smirked and lobbed her opinions like that. The seamlessness of this footage fitting in alongside other video available is warmly reassuring of Hynde's constancy.

There is no new information because Hynde gave us all of it already. She's been unblinking about saying her thoughts aloud and also about sitting comfortably in silence, so it can be hard for people and even for cameras to look her in the eye without feeling as though they are confronting something hostile, something preternaturally intelligent. She intimidates, and though this has not been a reaction she's cultivated overmuch on purpose, she is totally aware that to most people she's a wolf best left alone. It suits her and she is content. She continues prowling through the world solo, absorbed by her surroundings but searching them for nothing. Hynde doesn't need answers, so it's difficult to ask her questions. Is there anything more confusing to modern culture than a woman who is alone and at peace?

★

Ah, Glenn O'Brien, requiescat in pace. Any eulogy for a man such as he was will inevitably go astray if it begins, "perhaps best known for"—what? O'Brien went to Catholic school, then Georgetown, then film school at Columbia. He was the first editor at *Andy Warhol's Interview*. There was a screenplay here and a television show there, a decade of columns for *ArtForum*. He wrote for *High Times* and *Rolling Stone*; he did the *Style Guy* column for *GQ* for years and was Creative Director at Barney's New York. He kept busy and had many irons in many fires. O'Brien could be counted upon to have a point of view. Regardless of any medium, if it was part of popular culture, he was qualified to give his opinion.

Whenever paid professors of cultural criticism forget that pop culture journalism can be just as rigorous and pointed and vital as the work of the tenured caste, O'Brien is one of the guys holding the line for us. I think the primary difference between the inside and outside of the ivory tower is that the meek shall inherit the academy. The fearful have no sense of humor. O'Brien once tried his hand at stand-up comedy. We'll be scrambling to retrieve every scrap of him, now that he's gone. There's a posthumous publication, *Like Art: Glenn O'Brien on Advertising*, which was the last thing he did before he died. I'm sure it's a good one, but the scope of it is too narrow to think of it as the man's last word. I mean, he also published a book on cognac this year, and it's not going to be the capstone either. That honor should belong to *Cool School: Writings from America's Hip Underground*, published by the Library of America in 2013.

This is a five-hundred page anthology that he edited. He wrote a fifteen-part forward to it, collected himself alongside sixty-six other cool kids, arranged the selections and wrote an introductory paragraph for every single one of them. In short, these are his foundational influences, the keys to that kingdom of cool for which O'Brien has served as arbiter for half a century. Coolness, as a specific type of charisma, is very difficult to fake because it involves a natural tension of opposites. On the one hand, to be cool is to be fascinating—witty, astute, colorful, vivacious, communicative, instinctive, fraught, conscious. On the other hand, to be cool is to be an asshole—aloof, icy, bold, capricious, flippant, cutting, vulgar, selfish. As a way of being in the world, to be cool is to be a fascinating asshole.

Cool is a vibe that we can study as somebody else performs it. What cool subjects do cool people talk about? What diction and syntax do they use to talk cool? Does cool have a structure, even an improvised one? This is what O'Brien's *Cool School* is getting on to, though he readily admits any anthology of the matter cannot be exhaustive. He could choose sixty-seven other hepcats and form a totally different product with precisely the same desired result. It's funny because it's true. O'Brien was always self-aware, as his "Beatnik Executives" poem once made plain.

So the question of who got in is not an important one to the editor. Personally, I felt there definitely could've been more effort to include the ladies. There's Diane Di Prima, Bobbie Louise Hawkins, Iris Owens, Cookie Mueller and Emily XYZ each doing a really marvelous job of cutting down the men around them, just baldly slicing right through the machismo implicit in the brand of coolness supplied by Kerouac, Sinatra, fictive boyfriends and real rapists. But I mean, where's Patti Smith on Mapplethorpe, Eileen Myles on Kennedy? Nikki Giovanni, Ellen Willis, Diane Wakoski, Ntozake Shange? But okay, not all my cool influences are the same as O'Brien's.

More at issue than who's who in the table of contents is the question of what the cool kids are talking about. Interestingly, most of them are talking about other cool kids, their own set of influences. In this beautiful way, *Cool School* becomes a hall of mirrors. Miles Davis is talking about Charlie Bird

Parker. There's Cassady on Kerouac, Joyce Johnson on Kerouac, and of course Kerouac on himself. Delmore Schwartz on Hamlet, cloudy with a chance of Lou Reed. Gary Indiana making fun of Roy Cohn. Arthur Miller and Chandler Brossard making fun of different kinds of parties. Corso and Kaufman and many others in Ginsberg's orbit, but not Ginsberg. Burroughs and Brautigan, Tosches and Thompson. The absolute best, most fascinating assholes America has to offer, speculating on the past and future of cool.

Cool seems to be a phenomenon located mainly between the end of Hitler's war and the beginning of Kurt Cobain's band. As such, it carries the linguistic baggage of its era, transmitted equally through poems and essays, through fiction and memoir. It uses black and white working class slangs as well as hippie parlance, verbs like flip and nouns like head, interjections like dig and, well, like. The favored curse word is motherfucker (cf. Lenny Bruce, George Carlin, both in this book). Talking is riffing, and either you pick up on it or you don't. Del Close's hilariously on point "Dictionary of Hip Words and Phrases" should've been placed closer to the front of the anthology simply for actual use to aid in the comprehension of many of the jazzier pieces.

This begs the question of how cool is structured, if at all. Obviously, there is a great deal of emphasis on the magic of improvisation. Sometimes it seems like O'Brien put all these pieces in a pile and flung them down at random in choosing what goes where. Sure, there are threads. Maybe two comedians back to back, or maybe four or five mentions in a row about the trumpet. Seems like a lot of the beatnik stuff is in one place and the younger folks who're still alive appear mostly toward the end. But O'Brien is operating neither chronologically nor alphabetically, neither thematically nor by genre. He goes by feeling. The contents of this anthology are freely associated, but somehow building bridges across the stylish conjectures of the editor's own experience. Only he really knows why Mort Sahl goes with Bob Dylan, why Chandler Broussard goes with Terry Southern.

Cool School is an unusually fine and eclectic aggregation of the voices that shaped Glenn O'Brien and his generation. If it's got enough macho dudes for a genuine sausage fest, or if Norman Mailer's "The White Negro" feels like a psycho bunch of essentialist claptrap, or if its romantic portrayals of heroin seem idiotic, that's the beauty of our hindsight. Cool is a vibe that you soak in, even though some of the wavelength can seem pretty screwed up. The next generation's responsibility is to evolve the performance of cool. Take what you want and leave the rest. That's how this anthology ought to be studied and that's how Glenn O'Brien ought to be remembered.

CHAPTER SIX

IT'S NICE TO FEEL VALIDATED BY POPULAR TRENDS in the death industry. The National Funeral Directors Association predicts that cremation rates will be more than seventy percent by the time I am seventy years old. I always wanted to be cremated because I'm afraid of zombies. The primary distinguishing feature of zombies is that they have no intellect. That, to me, is the worst possible afterlife. So, poof! No body to rob of its best asset.

But I've never quite been sure about what I want done with my ashes. I could have them buried alongside my wife, who tentatively wants to rest beside the eventual gravesite of her parents in Florida. I have no great love of Florida itself, but would like for what remains of me and my wife to stay close together. We've lived in Atlanta so long, it might be nice to stay affiliated with it after death. Then again, my biography does heavily lean on being born and raised in Chicago.

The idea of burying ashes in the first place wasn't something that interested me. I figured on being scattered somewhere. But then one of my dearest friends and mentors said to me that the passage of time will reveal my greatness and I should not deprive the earth of a chance to visit my gravesite by putting my ashes out on the wind. She raised the stakes and may have been only half-joking when she said I should commission a statue for my ashes to reside in, but she at least said Atlanta was likely the right place.

I'm pretty sure I want my ashes scattered in New Orleans, with a rock and roll funeral through the Quarter, down Decatur Street and into the Mississippi Delta. I only lived in Baton Rouge for three years and a lot of the time it was terrible. But it was there that I learned the overwhelming power of water. How it walks through the air, the depths of its filth, where it finds its own level, the ways we need it and can't avoid it. Water transcends, so scatter me in that. Forget about looking up at some bronze bust; anyone that wants to visit me can open up any tap. I'm hoping to be in more than one place at a time.

Haunting does not much interest me, but I am open to it. The future after death is really very wide open or else shut in a way that doesn't matter. In my experience, Louisiana is a uniquely chthonic place. I've seen more unusual shit there than any other place on earth. They got their mojo working down there on the river, if it turns out I'm in need of any expert assistance after dying. Also, they got the best music playing outdoors. I could soak in that for the millennia. That's the extent of my supernatural wagers. I'm a practical person who plans ahead, who uses the best information she has at the time.

★

I survived Hurricane Katrina. This was the beginning of my second year in graduate school in Baton Rouge. My supply of batteries ran out long before the electricity came back on. The guy next door knocked one afternoon and we stood around on the catwalk in front of our blessedly second-story apartments picking at a plate of sliced nectarines that he'd brought over because they were about to go bad and he'd gotten sick of eating them alone. This was close enough to hear the announcer coming from Tiger Stadium on Sundays, yet I was the only white person in my apartment complex—save the building manager, naturally.

There are many ways to think about New Orleans "after Katrina." For a long time, I would have to turn off the television if any kind of commemorative stuff was showing for the anniversary of one of the world's deadliest and most destructive storms. Actually, I still have a fair amount of trouble looking at footage of any natural disaster involving bodies of water, be it a tsunami in Japan or flooded banks of the Mississippi. But at the end of a couple of weeks, nearly everybody's lights came back on and we all went back to school—that's a satisfying conclusion to a white person's version of the events of August 2005.

Richard Brent Turner's impeccably updated new edition of *Jazz Religion, the Second Line, and Black New Orleans after Hurricane Katrina* tells far more important stories than mine. I began to think immediately about the gap between black and white experience in NOLA in the most productive and actionable terms, which can be illustrated with two memories I have about bones. Before or after the storm, trash in the gutter is common in the French Quarter. Tourists are drunk and have little respect. I've stepped into a pile of discarded hot wings or similar detritus a dozen times crossing Bourbon Street and never bothered to give the bones a second look. But I once heard that dull, familiar snap under my heel while crossing the stones in Congo Square and froze immediately in terror for my accidental offense. The bone was laid neatly across a preternaturally bright blue feather. I dropped to one knee, touched two fingers to my lips, then to the broken bone, then held them toward the sky.

A white person's Quarter trash is sometimes a black person's ancestral Vodou. Turner's archival research and participatory observation of religious practices rooted in West or Central Africa and Haiti provides essential context for the second line activities in the Crescent City. "Second line" most directly refers to the group of celebrants in a procession that follow behind the "main line" of the band members and other people immediately relevant to the proceedings, such as the members of a club. Second line activities have a connection to music and dancing, such as at a jazz funeral or during Mardi Gras parades. These activities have a very long heritage, which Turner details as both a matter of street festivals and healing arts, in Louisiana and abroad.

An entry point into this sound for those not intimate with it already might be Jon Batiste and Stay Human, the band on *The Late Show with Stephen Colbert*. His family has a storied musical lineage in New Orleans and Stay Human's mission of spontaneous "love riot" street performances are undoubtedly shot through with the influences of Caribbean and African spiritual practices. Turner capably demystifies the racist stereotype of Vodou as malevolent sorcery stuck hopelessly in the past, but one of the best things about *Jazz Religion* is the way that it looks at what's to come just as much as it looks at bygones.

I have seen and felt for myself how gloriously uplifting it is to bend and swing, slide and stomp, galloping down the street to follow the sounds of a Dirty Dozen or Rebirth outfit right to the water line. The culture of the second line has restorative power in the extreme. It is healing the Lower Ninth and the Seventh. It is an activist type of performance art, pushing up against the oversimplified pigeonhole of black masculinity. Before Katrina, the city was majority black. Before Katrina, the majority of black people were employed. I live in Atlanta now, one of many cities hosting Katrina's black diaspora. Louisiana remains the prison capital of the world.

Richard Brent Turner looks all of this in the eye. He is unflinching, necessarily personal, properly professional, historically and culturally aware, artfully academic. He worked at Xavier University for just four years, but the proof of his constancy to the Crescent City is evident in the thoroughness and polish of his prose, the diligence with which he fleshes out this strategy for future embodiments of hope and heritage. *Jazz Religion* quickened my heart so many times. It certainly brought me back, but it also helped me to see a way forward from my own paralyzing slice of experience with Katrina. People who were there should read this book. People who were not there must read it.

★

"Into the Fire" / *The Rising* (2002)

Yell while tides were squalling and peaked with mud
I feared your stalling deeds, when you got in gear boats all untrussed
Sailor's airs, rescuers mired
Yeah sailor's airs, rescuers mired
All bleeds dismissed, sort of a movie stalled youth's straight-faced fighters
Armchair sailor's airs, rescuers mired

Pray your tenth lives as tenth
Pray your eighth lives as eighth
Pray your rope lives as rope
Pray your gloves live as gloves

We saved our doves from seas, air fields of dead land all around
We saved our doves the fee of boats moored flung oddly drowned
Sailor's airs, rescuers mired
Yeah sailor's airs, rescuers mired
All bleeds with fear, sort of a movie stalled youth's straight-faced fighters
Armchair sailor's airs, rescuers mired

All was stark, the sharks were freed, they smelled of dim search lights and knaves
Who played your band country, docked in all that arctic cold of dopey brave
Sailor's airs, rescuers mired
Yeah sailor's airs, rescuers mired
All bleeds dismissed, sort of a movie stalled youth's straight-faced fighters
Armchair sailor's airs, rescuers mired

*

In my experience, which I have been given every reason to believe is archetypical, graduate school is more about stomach than mind. You don't really go deeper into the netherworld of the ivory tower in order to grow as an intelligent human; you go to test the limits of alcohol abuse and hack your own ability to be critical until it becomes functionally delimited. Grad school is an extremely suspicious endeavor. On television, it's easy to find depictions of cutthroat competition amongst medical students or young lawyers. I would love to see a show track the stunningly ugly and paranoid orbits of a couple twenty-somethings in an MFA program.

When I arrived to pursue a PhD in critical theory and contemporary American literature, the ultimate plan was to write a book about the work of Bret Easton Ellis. Immediately following my orientation in the English Department, where I announced this lofty and frankly useless intention, some second or third year student jerked a finger over his shoulder at me and popped his neighbor with a one-liner than she'd better look out—I was a slightly younger and possibly intellectually hotter model of the personal brand and specialization this other student had been cultivating for the past couple of years. She was all about Jay McInerney, not Ellis, but that is a semantic distinction that did not give either of us cause for relief.

So now we each had our target, and acting a frenemies, would work very hard to bloodlessly destroy each other by passive aggression for the next two semesters. I eventually bailed on the PhD for an MFA, in part because the poets were nicer people than the doctoral students, but in large part because the poets didn't know anything about how to read or discuss Derrida and I would be able to dominate them with comparative ease. This is bragging, but it is still true: I am equally conversant in French, German and American philosophy and gifted enough to synthesize connections between them in improvised conversations, even after the hurdle of three whiskeys. This is known as "strong theory"—densely transitioning, keyword heavy, supersaturated with footnotes, largely lacking in pragmatic or real world value of any kind, insular and selfish, destined to cement a tenure-track professorship quickly.

What an asshole I was! This is Machiavellian, but it is still true: in practice, there is little value distinction between being formidable and being respectable in the academy. When I took a job as a high school English teacher instead of moving to New York to begin my life as one of America's cultural elite, everybody was relieved and disappointed in me. See, I did it for love. I found my person and began to settle down, lead a comparatively normal life with her instead of going in search of tenure and awards. My peers were uncomprehending; why would I choose to try to be a caring person in a mutually supportive long-term relationship when I could keep winning at the game of academics?

I was a very successful commodity. Rehabilitating my interpersonal skills and reviving my ability to empathize was a long and difficult—in fact, still ongoing—process in which I am continually beholden to my wife for her patience and commitment to helping me lead a full and satisfying life that considers and even sometimes prioritizes the welfare of others above my own needs. We take it day by day and I have had to apologize often; I don't think I ever issued a genuine apology to anyone about anything until after graduate school.

One of the more impactful academic events in my life actually happened a year after I finished my MFA: I went to a reading by the poet Jennifer Bartlett. This was part of a series I regularly attended at a local university, so I didn't bother reading about her at all before I went. When she opened her mouth, my world kind of fell apart in ten seconds. Bartlett has cerebral palsy. Her reading was full long pauses, the occasional stutter and slurring, guttural throat-clearing, salivary noises of various kinds, and so on. She was perfectly comprehensible always, but she could take a fair amount of extra time to get through reading a single page. As a fast talker and faster thinker, the first five minutes of this reading were agonizing to me. I had an alarming amount of extra thinking space during her reading, which left me unsettled. Having done a decent amount of disability studies work in grad school, I fell back on what I knew in order to give the appearance of accommodation and support, which in retrospect led me to kind of baby her and shy away from any deep conversation or critical engagement with her work. In truth, I could barely get to the content because I was so preoccupied by her form of delivery.

We began an email correspondence in which I sought her assistance on a matter that was challenging my will to live: I'd been in severe chronic pain for a while and had just achieved a diagnosis of ulcerative colitis. Treatment was not yet successful and I was selfishly so glad that I'd chosen a wife and a high school gig over the ivory tower. I was too weak now, physically and consequently emotionally, for professoring. I was disabled by disease, but the disease itself was invisible to others. Bartlett was wonderfully helpful, challenging me on my instinctive desire to pass as normal, or as strong. I learned a lot from talking to her about her own life's challenges as a professor with cerebral palsy.

Six months later, I attended another reading given by Simon Pettet. Pettet read each of his poems two times, and the first time for each poem he went quite slowly. There was no physical reason why he needed to do this; he simply wanted each piece to linger in the audience's thinking space. I found it delightful, primarily because of the interval of time that I was obsessed with the many issues presented by engagement with Bartlett. The rest of the audience, primarily comprised of people still enmeshed in the competitive trappings of grad school, did a bunch of grumbling about how stupid it was for Pettet to repeat everything twice. I stayed mum; it's so hard to map how one has begun to lean toward an ethic of care over competition. I knew I was standing on a terrain where they wouldn't hear me calling back to them about it, as the terrain was still rocky even to me.

There were a few times during my three years of grad school where my personal life or biological needs became overwhelming and I sought care from my professors. One of them always responded to this in a supportive manner.

My clearest memories of those three years are the times I sat in her office, crying or yelling or generally raging against the dying of my own light. We remain the very best of friends—actually, chosen family. I was less than ten pages into the hundred pages of William Cheng's *Just Vibrations* when I texted that professor to say she needs to read this book immediately.

Cheng's work poses the only essential question left unanswered by the academy and the secret of its truly massive failure: an absence of any instinct to repair. Cheng is a musicologist utterly capable of strong theory—a capability he has abandoned for weak and low theory, for personal narrative and disjointed anecdotal investigations into why his profession must turn toward what high school teachers used to call "whole child education." Brains live in bodies; bodies have needs and feelings have failures. Cheng tells his own story about these considerations, which include being Taiwanese and gay, as well as suffering years of chronically disabling pain due to a nerve disorder in the wall of his abdomen. He has not played the piano in a very long time and he teaches at Dartmouth College.

Building on foundations laid by Eve Kosofsky Sedgwick and Jack/Judith Halberstam, he crafts four achingly lovely chapters that meditate on the necessity of hope in an institutional system that has paradigmatically relied upon suspicion, cynicism and competition to the detriment of everyone invested in that system. It is not a "scathing" book. It is a gentle inquiry supported through the firm positing that a better academy is possible. It is not prescriptive as to how a graduate program might accomplish this, except that he makes clear that the powerful professors—those who already have tenure and awards—should make this leap first.

It's all too easy for me to say that my experience jives with Cheng's assessment and that I could have been a better person all along if I had not been so rewarded for my ugliness—I'm not a tenured professor. But I'm reminded of my wealthy brother-in-law who votes for Democrats even though it is surely somewhat to his own fiscal detriment. I'm also reminded of the general consensus that successful professional comedians are all substantially self-loathing individuals. My experience is that tenured professors must also be comedians. Those in the academy who are capable of strong theory are currently most able to turn their resources to Cheng's less self-serving ethic of care. The world could easily get better.

Except not nearly enough people will read Cheng's book. It's for academics and those of us who made it out alive. Many people will write it off because he's a musicologist, even though theory is theory and his varied examples are highly accessible throughout. Some people will write it off because there is sizable consideration of sound as a weapon—personally, I found his evaluation of the militarization of music and the under-researched impacts of Long Range Acoustic Devices against protesters by police to be highly interesting. Is it so hard to see that if one sounds good, one should use that power to effect good in the wider world? So very many people should read Cheng's book, teach it in grad schools and continue to pass it along. I suppose pretension and coercion do have their place, but must they pervade the academy to the point of totally excluding collaboration and reparative dialogue?

How can I convey the urgency with which I recommend this book to everyone? I'm sure more people who need to read it would order a copy if I went back and dotted every I-statement with some Foucault. I'm strong enough to opt to showcase my humanity instead. Isn't it messy and so much less persuasive? That's a problem.

*

"Empty Sky" / *The Rising* (2002)

This close-up of mourning, levees rarely sieged
Must forget the old lessons in our threadbare diffused dignity
That haunts abyss drip by drip, to taunt the high and the dry
This close-up of mourning for a rising tide

Rising tide, rising tide, this close-up of mourning for a rising tide

Moldy receipts, our bold slowly drowned
We fear our hold growing cold corpses float around

In the rains we bargain for what's somehow understood
In a flood's upheaval, in the blood we stood
That haunts abyss drip by drip, to taunt the high and the dry
This close-up of mourning for a rising tide

*

Me talking about Chris Kraus talking about Kathy Acker talking about Bernadette Mayer is like Camille Paglia talking about Susan Sontag talking about Simone Weil talking about Jesus Christ—it's not a comparison that I find particularly favorable to me. Yet here we are. Chris Kraus and I have never met and never spoken and yet—we both care deeply about the parasocial and we're both willing to take an excess of liberties about it. We force ourselves into one-sided relationships with people a few rungs above us, the heroes about which we are uneasily ambivalent, in ways that allow us to become the other person or sometimes even self-fulfill into a real, lived connection after we fantabulized it on the page.

Kraus's new book is *After Kathy Acker,* which "may or may not be a biography of Kathy Acker." In quite the same vein as Kraus, I did it with a collection of love and hate mail to the ghost of Andy Warhol, and felt a bit of slippage in my sanity in doing so, which I then inscribed on nearly every copy I signed as a spoiler just in case it saved anybody from going off the deep end: "Beware / congrats — everybody becomes Andy." So I don't really know Chris Kraus and she's surely never heard of me. But I know her because of Eileen Myles. Myles wrote the forward to Kraus's book *I Love Dick.* That's a pretty good recommendation. So I read it and it was the hottest book I'd read in a long time—not because of the sex scenes. It was because *I Love Dick* understood itself. I dig the deliberate and the self-aware, and in reading that book, I admit that I did feel a kinship with Kraus, which in turn means I may owe some kind of debt to Kathy Acker.

How many people would make the list of everyone that Acker has fucked? I'm not on the list. Is Kraus? Acker died when I was sixteen years old. In the most literal sense, my entire body of published work takes place after Kathy Acker and honestly, I feel I absolutely dodged a bullet there—because I would be on her list if we had met, because that's the type of person Acker was. You would just get sucked into the vortex and there was nothing that you could ever do about it. If you said yes to Acker you were unquestionably doomed. You'd have a few days of bliss and then a few months of confusion or misery, but you were ultimately doomed by that decision. And if you said no to Acker? Oh my God, what blasphemy! Who would say no to Kathy Acker?

Who on Earth could deny her anything she ever wanted? That right there is part of the problem—that it was extremely difficult not to enable Acker. This is not only true of the brief amount of time where she was actually famous, but really her whole life people said yes to her—and yet something in her mind made it seem as though people were always saying no to her. That's another thing I don't understand about Acker: it's not just a competitiveness; there's almost a paranoia there. There's this very bipolar "everyone loves me or everyone hates me" extremist, narcissistic, antagonistic viewpoint toward the rest of the world. Everything is a power trip, in the bed and out of it.

Kraus never speculates on whether Acker may have actually been mentally ill. Is it anti-feminist of me to wonder whether Acker maybe could've been much happier had she sought a legitimate biochemical assist? I get it: she's Medusa, she's the ultimate creature of *ecriture feminine*, monstrously profane as an act of political subversion. I do feel a kinship with her on that level. It's just also that she so often seems to do things without deliberation or intention, like she never bothered to grow up or be at all responsible. I stopping messing with people like she messed with them when I was maybe twenty-two or so. Has Kraus stopped? Am I just getting uptight, being happily married and having a steady teaching job, generally embodying the ideal stability of one's late thirties? I'm not trying to stomp on her agency; she just seemed to exist in a feedback loop of misery. You can be highly intelligent and extremely intentional about your work, and still be mentally ill.

I've tried reading Acker's books several different times in several different phases of my life, but I can never get past about page four because the truth is that by page four, you know everything that's going to happen in the book—and I use the word "happen" very loosely because these are not narrative books; they're cut-ups of some of our most belovedly phallogocentric literature combined with random diary entries and collections of Acker's correspondence with all her millions of married lovers, plus pornographic fantasies that she's had and pulp novels that she's slashed to pieces. I've got my own heavily annotated copies of the complete works of the Marquis de Sade, and still couldn't tell you the difference between Acker's *Don Quixote* book and the *Great Expectations* book and the *Pussy, King of the Pirates* book. Every time I try to read them, no matter what phase of life I'm in or how open I try to be to the process of reading Acker, something just stops me dead at about page four and I can't go on because it's boring.

It's occasionally hot, but for a story that never has any plot, ultimately the outcomes are all very predictable—and this is also true of the life of Kathy Acker, that the outcome of it was sort of a foregone conclusion. I don't mean to imply here anything along the lines of "she got what she deserved" or that it was some sort of karmic feedback that was visited upon her, but no matter what stage in her life, no matter how famous or how wealthy or how in tune with her family or with her community she was, ultimately the story of Acker is the same. Or wherever you go—the story of Acker in San Francisco, or in New York, or in London, or the occasional jaunt to Paris or Seattle or Chicago—they all sort of end in the same way, which is always with Acker's self-sabotage, usually immolating herself over the end of a romance with a married man. But more than it's sad, it's just very tedious.

In the bookcase in my office, there is one shelf devoted to authors that I really deeply admire. There are a lot of books that I enjoy but there are very few authors I admire—and out of the number of authors I admire, there are an even smaller percentage of authors who I might like to be. Actually, I have an entire shelf on my bookcase that is writers I admire very deeply as people who nevertheless serve as a kind of counterexample of what not to do—because some of the writers I most admire are very unhappy people. They are pioneers in their work, or even famous in the literary world, but they are not living their best life.

Acker was maybe writing her best books, but at what cost? There's a big part of me that just really enjoys being high school English teacher who is extraordinarily happily married with a normal nine-to-five schedule prohibitive of the type of escapist travel and drug abuse and general romantic melodrama that defined Acker's private life (and I use the word "private" there as loosely as possible). As much as I admire what Acker was able to accomplish in her fifty years on this planet—even if I can't get through a single one of those books myself—and as much as I suppose other people find a lot of her work very pioneering or interesting, I just don't want my life to turn out like her life. I think it's a counter example—a sad, tedious counterexample of how not to be.

Many people reading this review will no doubt think, "how dare Megan Volpert compare herself to Kathy Acker," but the truth is: this is what Acker always did to everyone else. She was a master of parasocial relationships. So no, I never met Acker and of course the trajectory of my career is utterly different from hers—and thank God that it is—but I feel like comparing myself to Acker is something that Acker hoped and expected other women would do. It's unquestionably what Chris Kraus ought to acknowledge she's doing by writing a book that purports to be Acker's biography in the first place, because let's face it: there is an awful lot of overlap there to consider *After Kathy Acker* something that is definitive or critical or objective.

Stated plainly: the specter of Kathy Acker is the other woman in Chris Kraus's marriage to Sylvere Lotringer for the decade that they were together. And now, in order to write a book about Acker, Kraus has to start with the seedling of each of Acker's books by making this very long list of people that Acker has fucked, which includes the man Kraus ultimately married. And yes, Kraus is likewise a master of constructing parasocial relationships. After all, that's a big part of what the entire *I Love Dick* book was about. In a lot of ways, I guess Kraus is actually the perfect person to write Acker's biography. We can even say that Kraus is carrying the torch of Acker—or (less nicely) carrying a torch for Acker—or (with more fanfare) that she is the intellectual heir to Acker's work.

I don't know Chris Kraus either, but there is a lot of big bad voodoo charm in what it is she's trying to do, in the hall of mirrors she's trying to construct, and I really hope for Kraus's own actual sake as a human being that the decisions she makes will work out better for her than they worked out for Kathy Acker. Because it does seem like Kraus is probably entering her imperial phase just now—but it's what comes after the imperial phase that is perhaps more interesting. Ask Bret Easton Ellis about that.

Originally, this essay—that may or may not be a review of *After Kathy Acker*—had about seven-hundred additional words in it that I culled directly from the text. A lot of the quotations were from Acker herself and some were Kraus's analysis. In the end, a greater depth or specificity of detail here seems so far beyond the point as to hinder any reflection on the real implications of the book. Here's what I can say: I read *After Kathy Acker* cover to cover—which is more than I can say of any book written by Acker herself. Acker is one of those writers who will always be more widely discussed than actually widely read. Kraus is so close to this material that it seems a little unfair to think of her as a secondary source. A truly parasocial relationship is in some kind of gray zone between primary and secondary sourcing. It's often said that a biography is just as much about the biographer, and I have never felt this to be more true than of Kraus's stab at Acker. And I use "stab" here very deliberately.

★

Without a Net is a book that should be read quickly. Is there any more undauntedly gripping, more inescapably terrifying, more hauntingly supervillainous character than poverty? No, there is not. These short memoirs, each about ten pages long, will run together no matter how fast or slow one reads them. Despite the different backgrounds of the women who tells these tales—their unique intersections of class with gender, with race, with religion, with sexuality, with rural or urban environments—most of them carry the same hardscrabble cadences, similar easygoing vocabulary, a host of well-known traumas.

They go hungry; they suffer violence. They cope as their parents did—with drugs or alcohol, with violence of their own. They learn to use their bodies as payment. They learn to pass—and to feel disgusted with themselves within the worlds of privilege that they pass into. They learn to keep secrets and tell lies. They feel kinds of shame and embarrassment that congeal into a will to barely survive. They engage in self-sabotage out of a fear of success. They are afraid of what little money they can save, afraid of what rages they might pass on to their own children.

Every single one of these writers makes sure to point out that a lot of people had it worse than they did growing up. At least they had one decent parental figure. At least nobody got killed. At least they had a coat during the winter. At least, at least, at least—always grateful for any crumbs, scattered though these crumbs are across a lifetime of resentment toward broken families, government bureaucracies and unfeeling societies. And each story ends with an awkward dead-stop—the feeling of "whatever is next cannot be very good," the wild-eyed uncertainty of being forced to live one day or one hour at a time and having nowhere to turn for reliable help.

And yet, here are all these women who have piled themselves, somehow still alive and kicking, into the pages of this book. By some miracle, they have been allowed to grow up and to sort of get out of the poverty that defined them as children. But one never really gets out. Sure, you can get a bank account and a college degree and a steady job. You can afford groceries and find a partner who won't beat you. Maybe even buy a house. And yet, how quickly their childhood wounds give fresh blood when picked at just a little, even at a distance of ten or forty years. How easy it is for them to remember the most precise details—the flash of a broken wine bottle, what kind of car it was, whose cousin gave her that dress.

This is not an easy book to read. For some people, it will be hard to read because you can't believe any of it is true—that people have no choice but to live in the ways these stories describe. You'll want to believe these are tales from the Dust Bowl era, or some other inner city planet long since eradicated. For other people, it will be hard to read because every line will call up some fierce, ugly detritus still floating through your own younger years—experiences you have long fought to destroy and disown with physical or financial distance. And yet, in a blink, there is your little girl self alongside all these other little girls, all just trying to keep afloat in a world that either neglects them or targets them. Or is it just me?

If Michelle Tea's achingly powerful collection of storytellers sometimes dips down into the rocky terrain of what Baudrillard called disaster porn, so be it. The first edition of this book debuted in 2003. Fifteen years later, every word rings just as true as it ever did. To be broke and female in America means you have stepped out of time, flattened out into a statistic and a stereotype. These women are not simply simulating scenes of poverty for the reader; they experienced it and now they own it as one constant facet of their diverse identities. They were scattered through my nightmares after reading *Without a Net*.

The happy ending is just that these voices are people who are still alive. You can take the girl up out of poverty, but you cannot take the poverty up out of the girl. That's a figure of rhetoric called "chiasmus," which is a fancy word I learned in graduate school in Louisiana. The most famous example of a chiasmus is JFK's way of asking what we can do for our country. Tell you what we can do: give it a goddamn net.

So Michelle Tea is next. I mean, after whenever Eileen Myles dies—and please for a long time still may they reign—Michelle Tea is going to step in and fill the void. The void: that very lonely captain's chair on the constantly embattled and leaky mothership of queer feminism that one cannot sit in until all the badges have been collected. The badges: survival of a childhood rife with blatant abuses both emotional and financial, survival of a teenage girlhood clouded over by the dampening hands of selfish authorities and reckless consumption of whatever feels intensely good for half a second, survival of a young adulthood with no career prospects and no shoulders strong enough to cry on, survival of a publishing industry that can't look in the eyes of one's unawarded and unmarketable face, survival of envious coattail riders and very public breakups and society's shockingly concentrated and organized disapproval of everything that one radiates.

We, the queer feminist motley crew, can collectively feel who is up next. It's voodoo priestess shit. We can't tell by looking at best seller lists. Myles was over sixty when they finally got handed a Guggenheim. The rest of the world does not look at one of our kind at the precocious, ferocious age of twenty-three and say, "there stands a great American writer." So we just keep standing there, digging our heels into the mainstream D-list—also known as the queer A-list—and running our mouths for decade after decade at top volume until our pile of contributions to the field of the written word is so enormous that whoever was born into the secret society of literary gatekeepers finally has to turn around and say, "oh, I guess this weird little person has been chirping in the background long enough that it will look bad if we don't wave and smile at their relevance pretty soon."

Tea's still totally timely and deeply underrated anthology, *Without a Net: The Female Experience of Growing Up Working Class,* just got the reprint treatment and now we have an awesome compendium of her greatest hits from the past two decades, *Against Memoir: Complaints, Confessions & Criticisms.* It's got some of those *xoJane* pieces about her record collection and some of the stuff she wrote for *Bold Italic.* More evidence of Tea's readiness for the big leagues is how great she is at writing introductions. The book includes her excellently pointy essay on Valerie Solanas published to introduce to the reprint of the *Scum Manifesto,* as well as her background essay for the anthology she did on Sister Spit (and lest we forget: Tea is the one who put together that phenomenon of word warriors in the first place, by which contribution alone she's secured her legacy in our queer history books). There are also some speeches she's given at various forums and universities that even those of us who follow her relatively closely might have missed.

Here too is the very good long-form feature she did on Camp Trans, the protest site across from the Michigan Womyn's Musical Festival, originally published in the *Believer* in 2013. She got there at a crucial point in the conversation about inclusivity, and her quite personal reportage on it is probably the most concise and objective overview of what kinds of penalties our community incurs in the ground game on that. That essay may already be considered an important historical document. The most exciting new piece in *Against Memoir* further develops both the themes and style of the comparatively longish Camp Trans essay, except this time Tea turns her attention to the HAGs. If you have heard of the HAGs, you're no doubt squealing with unparalleled delight right now.

If you haven't heard of the HAGs, Tea is precisely the person you want to tell you about them. They were a female gang of queer punks who roamed the Mission in San Fransisco in the nineties. Their main activities included shooting heroin, beating the shit out of bigots, and arts and crafts (also know as sidewalk chalking and stencil graffiti). Tea was not one of them, but simply another admiring satellite in the outer rings of their orbit. Over a precisely detailed forty-four pages, "HAGS In Your Face" provides an engrossing and beautiful portrait of these intimidating hooligans, rolling out each member one by one with heartrending details about where they came from and how they died. Most of them died in gruesome and tragic ways. The few survivors eventually became healers and life coaches in the suburbs. Tea needs to get to work on the screenplay version of this immediately and Mary Harron should direct it.

Michelle Tea doesn't yet have enough laurels, but she is clearly not resting on what laurels she does have. The new parts of *Against Memoir* demonstrate that she still wants to push herself and explore different avenues in her work. There's a weird three pages on pigeons that reminds us she is still very much a poet. This book is divided into three sections—art and music, love and queerness, writing and life—and yet obviously, everything Tea publishes is infused with all six of these concepts. She knows herself. She reports on herself in a strangely accurate manner that should not necessarily fall easily into the category of memoir. She keeps one finger on the same few threads, no matter what the individual style or substance of any single piece of writing. She is aging well, and for her steadfastness in these matters she will someday be rewarded by a cabal of business people none of us has much cause to respect. She'll have got there not by selling out, but by winning their war of attrition—because attitude is a renewable resource.

"Worlds Apart" / *The Rising* (2002)

It's cold before it storms, weathermen check charts
No ignorance is bliss nor slumber could outsmart
Trust the speed of Eastern winds, pray your wrongs don't reach the stars
No passbook and the grand prize, we'll withstand water's black arts

Inconstant emotions ring baptized in the rain
With all tried and true abruptly lured duty is plain
Another fountain loads prayer and doomsday trolls the parks
Wreathes all our cursed pains while it rains water's black arts

These crimes of youth rust painted rough and no crutch for maritime fists
Wet drowns the proof today, resigned and all dismissed
Let your fins drag on my fin, all our bleeding body parts
Gray forgiving conjoined twins restore the head pair cuss black arts

Regrets flood filled with witch hovered fountains caped by Mars
Trials greet on you on the hitch see levee water's black arts
Spigot this lonely frown a sieve, port of call's nonplussed remarks
Sort of live while it lives, sport sort of lives while it lives

★

Recently, I had a choice of two books to review: Camille Paglia's new collection of reprints and Susan Sontag's early collected work. My editor would have been happy if I had opted to read both of them, but I chose only *Susan Sontag: Essays of the 1960s & 70s*. Why did I do this? For very many years, I wouldn't go near Sontag. Other than myself, the person most to blame for this is undoubtedly Paglia.

As a young feminist possessed of above average academic abilities and a taste for committing offenses in the culture wars, I turned easily to Paglia as an inspirational how-to manual for tearing things down. Her tendency to name big names, to relate everything back to the narrow slice of Greco-Roman history that she studied, to go after the fissures in canonical works of art, to eschew footnotes, to fling campy insults, to give didactic speeches shot through with cutting adjectives—all this appealed to me immensely. A good deal of the voice you encounter from me today was made in the image of a Camille Paglia that I studied for so long.

And Paglia ultimately despised Sontag, perhaps more than any other feminist that preceded her, because Paglia was herself at first easily taken in by Sontag until their supposedly disastrous reading at Bennington. Later, in the 90's, she wrote the "Sontag, Bloody Sontag" essay that appeared in *Vamps and Tramps*. These two writers increasingly diverged in many important ways. Only one of them was really out of the closet. They had different views on warfighting, on French theory, on presidential politics. In my youth, agreeing with Paglia and parroting her style of criticism felt effortless—the raised eyebrows of my peers notwithstanding.

Rounding the bend into middle age, where many facets of my past ideological fashion are beginning to show their juvenile naiveté, I was drawn to *Susan Sontag: Essays of the 1960s & 70s* to see what I'd been missing. Unsurprisingly, it turns out that I was missing a lot. The Library of America has conveniently divided Sontag's life in two, technically by the decades, but also loosely into before and during the lasting influence of her relationship with photographer Annie Leibovitz. There's the early collection including everything from the 60's and 70's, and then *Later Essays* has everything else, from the 80's through her death in 2004. These two volumes contain all nine of Sontag's major works and both were edited by her only child, David Rieff, a foreign policy analyst and former Senior Editor at Farrar, Straus and Giroux.

Her first work was *Against Interpretation*, which won me over immediately on the acknowledgements page, wherein Sontag is happy to admit that she has often said things with which she herself later disagreed. No foolish consistencies here and no unified theory of the field of her own previous works. That alone was so refreshing—imagine Paglia ever earnestly admitting she was wrong about anything. The bulk of this work aims to interpret the works of other artists. Many of these were favorites of mine—Camus, Genet, Artaud. Others were foreign to me—Weil, Ionesco, Norman O. Brown—but I found myself sucked into her engagement with their ideas perhaps even more so than with the essays on those whose works I've read before. Sontag has a way of distilling a work of art into a precise description that needs surprisingly little in the way of textual evidence. She goes by feeling and makes little pretense of historical underpinning, makes no effort to rely upon the scholarship of generations past.

Sontag declares that too many discussions of art now constitute "the intellect's revenge" upon artistry itself. If that's not a description of Paglia, who had barely graduated high school at the time, I don't know what is. This direct approach continues on through *Styles of Radical Will*, originally published in 1969, with additional considerations of particular works of art, but also engagement with broader concepts. In *Against Interpretation*, she'd just begun to touch things categorically, as with "Notes on 'Camp'." *Styles of Radical Will* goes further with "The Aesthetics of Silence" and "The Pornographic Imagination" alongside treatments of Cioran, Bergman, and Goddard among others. By this time, she was facing serious public backlash for an essay in *The Partisan Review* wherein she drew a metaphor that linked white civilization with cancer. Some of her later work, especially *Illness as Metaphor* in 1978, would serve as apologism for those earlier remarks. Imagine Paglia, whose every aspiration is rooted in the pinnacles of Hellenic culture and the good graces of Harold Bloom, ever saying a harsh word against Western civilization.

This book also includes Sontag's *On Photography* from 1977, which was the first of many engagements with the medium. She displays a firm grasp on Warhol and Arbus, for which she won a National Book Critics Circle Award. In 2003, Sontag would revise her sentiments contained in this book with those in *Regarding the Pain of Others*. The same is true for 1989's *AIDS and Its Metaphors* in relation to *Illness as Metaphor*. Sontag has a wide variety of artistic concerns upon which her ideology expands and contracts over the course of her fifty years as a publishing theorist, often repudiating her younger selves in the process.

I don't know when I stopped feeling that it was bold to simply call out the ills of society and the foibles of other writers. I can't recall the first time it felt really good to admit the ridiculousness of something I spouted off a long time ago. What I do know is that I've been struggling to take Camille Paglia seriously while also subbing in a block of salt for the chip on my shoulder regarding my own work. There's this terrific academic legend about their seemingly one-sided rivalry:

Paglia: I'm the Susan Sontag of the 90's.
Sontag: Who is Camille Paglia?

While I may toss my rebellious street cred perilously close to mainstream normativity by declaring it, I'm pretty much ready to put Camille Paglia in my intellectual dustbin next to Ayn Rand. I owe a great debt to both thinkers, and it seems my responsibility now is to get beyond them. In a decade or two, I suppose I am likely to outgrow Susan Sontag as well. But today is not that day. Today, I'm trying not to underline every single passage in *Essays of the 1960s & 70s* because I'm excited to know: Who is Susan Sontag?

★

"Mary's Place" / *The Rising* (2002)

I read severed scriptures for Judas, the province of our young
Of heaven's pained controversy four-leaf clover a foxhole on the run
Fine art smart but surprising, its arsenal of wraith appointees
Get at foxhole wait for Poseidon high gear a choice stalling seas

Hurricane, hurricane, hurricane, hurricane, hurricane, hurricane, hurricane
Groceries just in case, somebody grab Bacardi
Groceries just in case, somebody grab Bacardi
Curacao blue to sail seas uncharted

Shivering traces compounding, after chills despair
Triggering arms race profoundly, disembodied fear
Harbinger floats in a dead march, stupid's unbowed
We scream and sound the alarms and the booze on shelves is allowed

Hurricane, hurricane, hurricane, hurricane, hurricane, hurricane, hurricane
Groceries just in case, somebody grab Bacardi
Groceries just in case, somebody grab Bacardi
Curacao blue to toast our departed

And all those fixtures of youth like a rocket, they speed to keep their head start
Keep their fight winning in darkness, drinking up through this part
Anyways, leavened handles for the widow's biting dismay
Their bravery toward all life disabled, it pops the freedom to say
Hands down at the storm's height, more crumbling shrouds
Sinners stalling so sit tight, slaking from a spout that won't drown

*

Y'all, I hate being told what to do. Raised hell on my parents, then loafed around partying a long while (known as college), then moved to Atlanta to try to rise above my station. Though I spent my first seventeen years in Chicago, adult life has been spent on three years in Louisiana and a dozen in Georgia. As I have no intention of ever moving north of the Mason-Dixon again, we ort consider me a voluntary Southerner. A part of it is: I like living some place where a bunch of folks happen to disagree with me, because I like shooting my mouth off and pushing up against those that would judge me so's I help them broaden their horizons. Which is to say: I am a redneck.

It's an ugly word, though people that would rather die than utter the N-word have no trouble using it in public, similar to its close relative, "hillbilly." First and foremost, being a redneck means you've got white skin, which indeed I do. The second criteria is that you don't have a lot of money, to say the least. These are working class people, like my parents. My public school teacher salary makes me look rich by comparison. Most might say that I can't be a redneck because I'm disqualified by having too much education and too progressive politics. Y'all are wrong and that's what I want to discuss today.

During my life in the South, I have met many intelligent and kind white people what thinks of themselves as card-carrying Republicans and Christians. I wasn't born or bred to be either of those things, but it's weird how after talking to somebody a long while you begin to see how much there is in common between you to agree upon. For example: drinking beers is awesome and so's listening to the sweet sounds of Lynyrd Skynyrd. Everybody in the South can be proud of throwing a good party. We gave Prohibition what for, and on the last day, NASCAR was born. *Skeeeew*, fast cars are real fun.

But in my fourteen years down in the deep and dirty, I'll tell you what: there's a lot of Southern shame, too. Slavery and segregation, y'all. The stars and bars run up high on the pole by some racists peering through some sheets, y'all. We got major prison over-crowding, substance and spousal abuse problems, and the last decade has seen the worst quality country music ever in history. May Dolly Parton never go to meet Dale Earnhardt. And look, nobody ort be hunting with an automatic. Southerners got loads of common sense, except when it comes to voting against their own interests all the time.

Donald Trump is the President of the United States, y'all. I mean, what gives? Everybody's saying that white evangelicals voted him in, that white women fearing for their working class families voted him in. But I know plenty of liberal rednecks who're frothing at the mouth as much as I am about this because the South is full of smart, decent people—as well as a goodly number of folks wanting to get smart and get decent but haven't had much opportunity to do so because of the color of their skin or the contents of their wallet. If only there was a book we could put in the hands of all these interested, capable people to aid them in doing better. Well, there is: *The Liberal Redneck Manifesto* by Trae Crowder, Corey Ryan Forrester and Drew Morgan.

Don't just read it for yourself; be sure to share it around a bunch after church and turn your auntie's book club on to it. Heck, it's written by three comedians, and is plenty funny enough that you could leave it on the toilet tank so's your daddy might pick it up for a minute. Each chapter takes the good with the bad in Southern culture—the pecan pie with the diabetes, if you will. This book celebrates what we do absolutely right, from a killer football tailgate to our fierce loyalties of family. But it also honestly addresses our conflicts and failures, notably rooted in racism and poverty. The South doesn't have a monopoly on discrimination or cash flow problems, by any means, but that's no excuse for not helping to make right what we can make right.

So these three hilarious do-gooders, with plenty of personal experiences running from Tennessee to Alabama and from Georgia to North Carolina, have set out to do what sure as hell needs doing right now. They speak to Southerners about Southerners with their combined Southern voice, making clear and comprehensible arguments about the parts of this heritage that really hit and the parts of it we got to let go. No, nobody is going to come to Jesus about abortion in this book. But it's got many sensible talking points. For example: "Men claiming superiority over women because men make more money than they do is like claiming you're stronger than a lion that you tranquilized and put in a cage. Sure, you're in a better spot now—but how 'bout you unchain the beast and see what happens?"

There's also a bunch of pretty sweet graphics in this book, including *What Wouldn't Jesus Do* and *Rebel Flag Replacements*. The entire thing is in bite-size chunks, as it'll be too much meal for some mamaws and papaws to digest all at once. But look, everybody agrees we ort start talking to each other and finding a way past what seems like insurmountable cultural differences, yet nobody knows how we should proceed to actually talk that talk. So here comes three comedians who luckily have an earnest belief in the progressive side of things already anyway, and *The Liberal Redneck Manifesto* is poised to really put a dent in this mess that landed that creepy moneybag in the White House. That man don't sit right with many a fine Southern figure I've met in my time, and it's high time we heard from some characters who can build an argument and turn a phrase at the same time. No offense to Jeff Foxworthy, but there's a new game in town. *The Liberal Redneck Manifesto* is gonna help us get our healing on, y'all. Talk 'bout rockin' the vote.

★

When I really get to jamming on slide guitar, I'm usually playing old spirituals. Throw some blues in there, some punk rock tempos, all these weird rockabilly noises I discovered in Baton Rouge—that's what sounds good to me. But the lyrics, man! I don't care about all that Jesus stuff. I wish the songs were about something else, some things more relatable to me. That's why the Boss is an easy target for a massive rewrite. There's such excellent pathos, a truly soaring spirit in him. I'll take that juju plus the melody, but season it with my own ethos for word choice and cook it up in my own cast iron. All of the fervency, none of the fever?

★

"The Rising" / *The Rising* (2002)

Won't outrun its confronting bleed
Won't outrun its plumbing up inside
King cake feast day rules are heartless
We won't outrun its glut disdainful of minds free
Glossed black and now war has come
Now war has come, now night is primed
Inside track to Dixie tombstone
Inside older in blink of eye

Tide so high it's surprising
Tide so high pray your land stays dry
Tide so high it's surprising
Tide so high it's surprising in flight

Slaughterhouse forewarning
Mud sliding spilled down there
No repairing the loss of our stalling
The sea's hellfire of foam won't disappear

The limits of love and of kindness
Races put back, lies turning white
Fray ferocious flood blindness
Sword on the land that tore like dynamite

The keys were carried by some warden
And this warden too was drowning died
Wrote only scriptures for civilians
Chancing all the time killed to ride
Some ideal that warms the mystery
Some ideal that flood's fix is fine

The afterlife drums through trees
That cold dish advancing on the thread of our time

Tide of brackish and borrow (the afterlife)
Tide of wave, tide of fears (the afterlife)
Tide of story and madness (the afterlife)
Tide of fury, tide of drear (the afterlife)
Tide of jeopardy and ammo (the afterlife)
Its churning bend spills these harms all night
Tide of warning and rented bliss (the afterlife)
Tide of stillness, tide of afterlife

*

I taught a very nice kid last year, named Madison. She was a bit of a loner, dying her hair a deep red and purple and dating a brown-skinned boy that maybe she could mold into something someday if he had any sense in him. She was often absent and she pulled a steady B, always diligent but not caring overmuch about report cards. Often over the racket being made during group activities in the class, she would look up at me across the crowded room and quietly just smile, kind of thanking me for doing things right and to express her general enjoyment of sharing the space with me. Strong nonverbal cues, street-smart, trustworthy judgment. I don't always have an easy time smiling back at students, but Madison was terrific. We'd have been great pals in high school. Instead, I get to be her teacher, which is likewise an excellent time.

This year, Madison enrolled in my public speaking class. There are several kids in there who aren't big on being chatty, but they loved our sophomore year just so much that they want to squeeze in another semester with me before they graduate. After being pretty quiet and unobtrusive in the classroom vibe as a tenth grader, Madison is now a junior and using her voice much more fearlessly. I'm helping a little bit and the class adores her. They look up to her as a leader, as a future tattooed momma bear. She's given some great speeches to the class, and their favorite was hands down her impromptu speech.

Madison may have had kind of a tough childhood and is possibly still living a bit rough. When she can, she likes to be prepared and control what parts of her life she's able. Most of her speeches were given using extensive notes, but that's not allowed for the impromptu speech. Each kid brings in three items, the class votes, and then the kid has to immediately give a three-minute speech about the object. So you can prepare a little and think about what you might say for each object, but no notes. The objects therefore have to have pretty solid stories attached, and Madison told us a genuine whopper. I don't remember what her other two objects were—she doesn't even remember. She brought in a doll.

Any doll can turn creepy if you just look at it or think about it for long enough. This doll was creepy on its face—its literal face. There were ash and burn marks all over it. The pink dress was kind of torn up and the stiff plastic body was dented in places. The price tag still on the back of its neck was marked with four dollars. Madison bought it at a Goodwill when she was half the age she is now. She didn't have a lot of money and always made her own fun. The doll was weird and she was kind of trying to rescue it from the trash, I guess. Up into the closet shelves it went, never to come down for years. They didn't have any really good times together or anything.

Eventually, in a serious deep cleaning of her closet space, Madison decided the doll would need to move on. She tossed it amongst the miscellaneous ruins of childhood in the junk pile. When she left the room for a moment, she heard a thud. When she went back to her room to investigate, the doll was on the floor very far from its place in the pile on the bed. Nobody else was in the home at the time, and Madison is quite sure the toy was secure on the bed. The class extensively cross-examined her when she finished telling this part of the story.

The doll appears to have moved itself a second time, in this case later that same weekend from the trash bag destined for Goodwill all the way across the bedroom into Madison's closet. Again, nobody else living there can claim to have touched it. So Madison took the hint and returned it to its shelf, not to see the sunlight again until she brought it in to tell the class this story. This is the exact type of story I heard every other day when I lived for three years in Louisiana. I don't know that I believe in ghosts at all, but I do believe in Madison. We've spent an hour together every day for a year and a half, and when I looked into her eyes, I believed that she believed this tall tale she was telling us that day. Her conviction inspired awe in all of us.

It would probably have been one of the most memorable speeches this crop of kids will take away with them after they graduate—until this past Friday, when the doll reappeared in class. This week's speech was focused on ethos, on using your personal brand and charismatic personality to sell us something, real or imagined. Madison offered the doll for sale for twenty-five cents, because of course the joke that we all well knew was that she was desperate to get rid of the haunted doll. She once again gave a terrific speech and when it was finished, many kids laughingly said they'd buy it off of her but nobody actually ponied up. So I came out from behind my big desk reaching for my chain wallet, and slapped a dollar bill into her hand.

She asked me if I was serious and I allowed that I was. I told her to keep the change, grabbed that doll by its scuffed up plastic ankles and marched it out of my classroom in long, determined strides. The kids drew in a sharp collective breath, then squealed as they hurriedly overturned chairs in an effort to follow me out into the hallway. I darted around the corner and drove that haunted doll head first into the nearest trash bin, burying it waist-deep in the detritus of a teenage wasteland. At most, three of four kids running out in front of the pack might have seen where I put it. I herded them all back into class, where Madison greeted me with a face drained of all its color. She wanted to know if I'd thrown it away and I told her it was none of her business.

After a few minutes needed to get their closure and simmer down, they were able to unglue their eyes from one brave and crazy teacher as we continued on with the speeches. I hid it from them pretty good, but my hands were shaking when I came back to my classroom. They were so very worried about whether I'd taken on some kind of curse. I cracked jokes about making sure they would tell my wife I love her and trying to get the yearbook dedicated to me. As the next kid prepared to give the speech, I whispered to Madison that I hoped this weekend she would feel a peace like no other settling upon her. She just smiled at me, still unbelieving that I would assume the debt on her behalf and take it upon myself to incur such bad juju. When the bell rang, the whole bunch wished me a happy weekend with extra shiny eyes.

I had delivered us all from some kind of evil that day. The next two classes wore on, and at one point I had a minute to go back to the spot where I'd dumped the doll. The trash had grown much higher over lunch, but I could still see one little foot sticking out. The doll hadn't moved. I heaved a sigh of relief that I did not know was inside of me, and still sort of half-noted to myself that I might want to check again before leaving the building for the weekend. One thing led to a thousand others, as it usually does for all teachers, and I forgot all about the doll until I was already in the car. At some point as the sun went down on Friday, the night shift custodial staff shepherded that bag, haunted or not, to the dumpster. In a week or so, it'll be at rest in a landfill.

It's been almost twenty-four hours and nothing unusually bad has happened to me. When I see Madison's face on Monday and nothing bad has happened to her either, I'll know my work is done and the loose ends are as tied as they can get. Can't spend my whole life waiting for some haunted doll's other shoe to drop and anyway I taught the children well.

CHAPTER SEVEN

WE WENT TO THE ROCK HALL THREE-FOR-ALL TOUR STOP at Chastain Park Amphitheater: Cheap Trick, Joan Jett and Heart celebrating their mutually belated mainstream recognition. Many moons ago, we'd taken our niece to see Joan Jett and Heart there when she graduated middle school. It rained like hell and she did eventually appreciate it as a formative experience that earned her one of her first punk rock badges. This would be my third go around with the ladies on the billing, so I was actually most psyched to see Cheap Trick.

Cheap Trick could have been the world's best wedding cover band, playing as many shows a year with as many hits as they do today. Instead, they sat around for thirteen years after their original eligibility date and waited with patient sarcasm to be nominated for induction into the Rock Hall of Fame, where they were indeed granted admission upon their first ballot. Being first in the lineup, the band took the stage in front of a sun that had not yet set. Chastain is surrounded by forest and its forest is surrounded by mansions on the hills, the hills themselves surrounded by metro Atlanta. Lovely though our piney seclusion was, it mostly reminded me that seeing a show at Red Rocks in Colorado is one of the few items left on my bucket list.

The band pierced my heart not once, not twice, but thrice. Early in their hour-long set, they covered Lou Reed's "Waiting for My Man." I guess I should say they covered the Velvet Underground, but nobody really covers the Velvets, do they? Cheap Trick does a fair impersonation on the vocals, but the sound is too clean cut to be succeeding at imitation. Cheap Trick is simply too good at playing their instruments to mimic the accidental, instinctual dirty racket that defines Reed's work. But I did find myself with a sudden shortness of breath. I never got to be in the same airspace as Reed; he died before I mobilized to hop on some tickets to see him, so a cover attempt that simply points at the vacancy left by Reed is unfortunately as good as it gets. Then I had a momentary cascade of Bowie-related misgivings and mostly was reminded that it is imperative that I jump on some Iggy Pop tickets. Iggy is the last man standing.

The second thing the band did was bring out one of those insane six-neck guitars. I watched closely; he only played two of them, the second and third necks from the top. I bet he can't even reach the bottom one; I bet it's not even tuned. Doesn't matter though, because parading around with a silly, excessive instrument like this is more about ideology than actualization. Most Cheap Trick songs don't even have enough verses to play one of the six necks per verse. A six-neck guitar is expensive and useless, hilarious in its weight and shape. But it suggests infinite possible worlds. It suggests a cornucopia of choice at one's fingertips, the immediacy of decision-making power. It is fundamentally cynical about the ways rock music goes over the top, yet foundationally optimistic about broadness in the field of music composition.

The third thing was closure with the expected. They played "Surrender" about half way through the set. I knew going in that this song would do it for me. "Surrender" was the other great anthem of my young life, next to the Ramones' "I Wanna Be Sedated." But the Ramones are mostly dead and Cheap Trick is still very much here, kicking ass and caring only slightly if one remembers their names. When I was growing up, I told myself over and over again, "Mommy's alright, daddy's alright; / they just seem a little weird." I seldom convinced myself of the truth of this assessment, but even then I knew that if it was indeed a fiction, the fiction was one worth carrying around. It was a gracious yet dismissive prospect, a hard balance to strike.

Twenty years older now, I still want to say that there is no benchmark for self-evaluation higher than "Surrender, surrender, / but don't give yourself away." Sure, kids, it gets better. But there are always forces beyond your control, people with more power than you could ever possibly want to accumulate. Even when you do get to pick your battles, life is full of waving white flags. Knowing when to pick a fight has not saved my ass nearly as many times as knowing when the time is right to surrender. To relax into a surrender, to allow oneself to be swept up in an occasional tide of ignorant assholes and the grotesquerie of random hardship is the only life skill truly required to be an adult. I'm not talking about diplomacy or compromise now; I'm talking about losing gracefully without giving away those parts of yourself that keep you alive for whatever is next. In short, Cheap Trick offers a clear definition of the soul.

It was some very poignant shit in the moment, but no time for tears because Joan Jett was up next. I was pleased to see the Blackhearts explicitly and repeatedly identifying as a New York band. The Runaways notwithstanding, let me just state what I consider to be fact: there is nothing punk rock about Los Angeles. Saint Joan is exhibiting as much leather-clad crowd control as usual and at some point in the set I see furious bopping around in my right peripheral, so I turn my head in the direction of the action and it's a kid. It's a seven year old kid with a stripy, fleece blanket flung over his head and he is pogoing around like the rapture is upon us, flailing his arms in front of him and thwacking his amused, relatively sober parental units in the legs as he screams the words, "I don't give a damn about my bad reputation."

I lean over to Mindy and jab my chin in the direction of the kid. We both watch him for a minute, then look at each other and smile. I whisper to her that the future is safe. Then I reflect on who all I brought to the show with me, besides my lovely wife, who is a huge Heart fan. Filling in for my niece this go around are two of my former students from my first year as a teacher. They're now old enough to buy their own alcohol. They met in my class, and any other sane teacher would've separated them because they never got any work done. One of them eventually dropped out and got a GED instead. But they had big, bold ideas and they were best friends out to save each other and the world. Over a decade later, they've bought a house together and are basically married.

Despite having helped make that possible, I would never have looked at the two of them at age fourteen and thought that the future is safe. Yet here we are, still together, and someday they will very likely make babies that they will then bring to Joan Jett shows. I went for a walk to cogitate on that, plus take a leak and get another beer. In line for the beer, there was a different mom and her son standing behind me. I turned to her and said that I thought it was great for kids to come to a show like this because it means that our future is safe. She smiled and thanked me, but then pointed at her kid and said it was all his idea. The kid was a bigger Jett fan than the mom; he did all the research on the tickets himself. He said he was eleven years old. When I attempted to fist bump him as a nod to his general excellence, he reluctantly complied with a look that definitively stated he did not give a shit about a stranger's approval. He was there for himself and if we old folks could still get a crank out of a Joan Jett show, good for us, but that wasn't his business.

Then Heart came on and played almost no hits whatsoever in their headlining set. After Cheap Trick running wild with absurdity and Joan Jett exercising an audience's willingness to obey, Heart offered a refreshingly different approach to punk. They played whatever the fuck they wanted, and if we in the audience enjoyed ourselves, good for us, but that wasn't their business. The Wilson sisters are still just doing it for themselves. For the encore, they covered "Stairway to Heaven." Someday, Robert Plant will die and Ann Wilson will be all that's left—her, and wave after wave of little kids in black tee shirts, as long as we keep raising them right by ponying up for their tickets.

★

Since I began holding my wardrobe to a higher standard, I've made far fewer purchases and the ones I do make have been more pricey. This has led rather predictably to dabbling in the various designs of John Varvatos. Making a pilgrimage to his CBGB store is actually a bucket list item for me, as it's all that's left of the historic punk rock venue I was too young to visit. After I bought a pair of Varvatos boots, they put me on the email list. This means I'm getting tiny runway videos in my inbox once or twice a week.

This week, the subject was new spring collection looks. The model is wearing a red bandana around his neck like John Wayne. Sometimes I scroll down through the whole email and look at additional photos, and sometimes I don't. Varvatos is inspired by rock's fashion icons, and at the bottom of this particular email I was greeted by Willie Nelson and Bruce Springsteen. The Boss wore a red bandana on his head through much of his early career. Willie's still doing that, and of course Little Steven is probably a better ambassador for the bandana than his bandleader at this point.

In the photo in the email, Springsteen isn't even wearing a bandana. I feel confident that almost no one thinks of either Willie or Bruce as having good taste in clothes, let alone as being a tastemaker. On the other hand, bandanas that Springsteen has worn in concert go for as much as a thousand bucks online. The Varvatos update goes for ninety-eight bucks, or one-fourth the cost of the boots I bought on super sale. Reflecting on past fashion choices in his memoir, Springsteen said he donned the bandana to look tough to his working class father, who would have worn one out of practical necessity. In retrospect, he does not feel he pulled off the look. Having a uniform is not the same thing as wearing it well, and the passage of time reveals more about such items than the price tag can.

★

"County Fair" / *The Essential Bruce Springsteen* (2003)

Midterm smears a bummer dumbs it down
Pay fetches scammers glossing discreet markdown
Game plan steals trumpin' maddenin' the square
Hell in the White House slipped on Capitol Hill
Began teed up fights cleanin' up routed our battlefield
Breathin' heavy while we count it fair

Count it fair, count it fair
Anybody who votes better care
It runs away, queer showin' round here
Give it a whirl in your strong wronged stare
Wagon for paddies come to handcuff heirs
Shaking down rather count it fair

We'll all be rantin' light as they skid to stop
Where the worn out poser's already propped
Hanging chads, wow the welcome wore out there
First lady eats crow unjust shoved around
Loves a ripe Gorgon for a cherry playground
Shaking down rather count it fair

Plow through the rough trends of the yield, no way to send up fans
So that they can whittle clocks and call hands
With refinancing, snares sprung with uneven care
Tell its flame's tongue on the incumbent sons
Must brew liars, crabby faced and young
Vote blockin' clowns rather count it fair

Always runnin' hate folklore screeds black and brown
Orange vets the Florida steal grin and crown
Can't resist it, banshees are wailin' in prayer
The highway route reveals a miss of the mark
Come again November when our card's shark
Maybe we could count it fair

If you're coming my way we hold fast dreams of laws
That spin at night as our lifeguards
And no pile of dough brings the lofty show
Bag full ballots rose from the start
Panic attack and flare up with the cause
As we endeavor sad to get potent low

★

Colbert says the state bird of New York is the middle finger. I love New York,
and I therefore am in some kind of analogous relationship with middle fingers.

The other day, Abby shrugged at me and stated very matter-of-factly, "if somebody were holding a gun to your head and demanding to know who your pastor was, you'd say it was me." She's absolutely right and there was no need to say so just then. Abby shares a birthday with Hillary Clinton: October 26th. They're also both fervent Methodists. I love methods, but am not a Methodist. However, I did take the United Methodist Church's Spiritual Gifts Assessment, which is freely available online. The results rank your gifts in nineteen categories, giving the most weight to your greatest strengths. Here are my scores:

Wisdom - 9
Servanthood - 8
Leadership - 8
Interpretation - 8
Knowledge - 7
Exhortation - 6
Healing - 5
Tongues - 5
Apostleship - 5
Teaching - 4
Prophecy - 4
Discernment - 4
Administration - 3
Miracles - 3
Shepherding - 3
Giving - 2
Compassion - 2
Faith - 1
Evangelism - 1

★

As a teacher of high school sophomores, I assure you that students almost never read the book that you assign them to read at home. That's one of the reasons why I like to use audio books with my classes. It really teaches them what the words sound like, how to use them together and how to express a complete thought. They like to hear it while they look at it. And I like to see them hearing it while they look at it. That way, I know that even if they are not processing everything that has been read to them, at least they had to physically sit in the room and let the audio book narrator come through their ears and tell them the whole story. As much of it as they can understand is there for them, washing over them.

I do at least know that they were in the room where the audio book happened. When a famous person writes a book, I strongly prefer to listen to the audio book, if it has been narrated by the actual famous person herself. And the reason has to do with pretty much the same thing as giving the sophomores these audio books. I like to know that the famous person who supposedly wrote this book at a bare minimum sat in the recording booth and went through it one entire time for herself, whether she wrote it or not.

When sophomores present a project to me orally, I can tell within the first few minutes whether they have really taken the time to think through and write out these sentiments that they are delivering to me themselves, or whether they had a little or a lot of help from a friend or the Internet. The same is true for a famous person who writes a book. You can tell by the sounds coming out of her mouth whether she has written the book herself. And I promise you this: Hillary Clinton has written *What Happened* herself, because when she reads it, alone in that recording booth, it is so clearly in the sounds of her own, real voice. She is not reading it in a manner that is "selling it" to the listener. She is genuinely expressing her own sentiments.

All audio book narrations begin with an abundance of gusto, but after the first chapter or two, they settle into a more direct vein of the narrator's personality. Some audio book narrators read the book like they assume their audience is a bunch of kindergarteners. Other audio book narrators assume their booth is a stage where everything must be conveyed in the utmost dramatic manner. My favorite nonfiction audio book narrators are those who sound like they're in a darkened bar in the back corner booth with just one audience member. There is a certain kind of intimacy that really good narrators, and some charismatic famous people who have written their own books, are capable of conveying on the audio.

The way she rolls off the names of other politicians that reveals friend or foe, the way she is by turns sad and bitter and sweet and biting. It's all there in the grain of the voice, as Roland Barthes would say. An audio book recording always finds its function through that more intimate sense of smaller, closer audience and this venue is one where Hillary Clinton shines. She is neither reading *What Happened* to us nor performing it for us. It is not spoken in stagey campaign noises, nor poised for didacticism and explanations or excuses. Clinton is alone in the sound booth, reckoning with herself. It won't exactly be private, but it is definitely personal.

Many moons ago, when I called dibs on reviewing the Hillary Clinton memoir, the angle was that she wrote a series of reflections on some quotations that had influenced her life. By the month of the book's release date, the title *What Happened* lent a very different story. I was darned interested in that first book idea though and wondered how much of it would be present in this other book that presumably would re-litigate her loss in the election. Within a week of the release date, the beefs emerged in the form of some leaked pages—harsh words for Bernie, examples of Trump's misogyny. Twenty-four hours before the release date, Clinton went on CBS and said she was not going to be a candidate ever again, but she would remain in politics because it was so important to save our future.

What Happened is not so much any kind of campaign postmortem or declaration of retirement for her as it is a personalization of her public works. Clinton's problem has never been in doing the job. She struggles to do it in front of the camera. Her smile can be uneasy. She can seem wooden even when she is on fire for her cause. When we say someone is unelectable, we're only talking about the pathos of selling the talking points. Clinton is fueled by ethos and logos, and for some reason, America doesn't take the measure of a woman's competency and just marvel, "look at the agility of the intellect on her; she'll do an amazing job on this hard thing that needs doing."

My wife and I have a private joke about running for office together. She says I'm the P and she'll be the VP. I always counter with the suggestion that she can run for the office and I'll hold it after she gets us elected. My wife is iconic. People adore her. Clinton is iconic because she worked her ass off, not because people want to have lunch with her. People want to have lunch with my wife. I'll bet Clinton has metaphorically eaten lunch alone for much of her life, as have I. So we are fit for doing one kind of thing, and other people who are more electable are fit for doing some other type of thing.

Clinton's book tour has fifteen stops, including one where I live. Front row, center is about eight hundred bucks. Nosebleeds are going for eighty. What is it I need to get out of this event? More consistently now, it only matters to me that I'm in the room. Front row is too limited a scene somehow, an intimacy that is senselessly constricted. What good would it do me to be physically close to Clinton? No part of me needs it. Perhaps at best we might make eye contact for a moment. People say that the eyes are the windows to the soul, a cliché with which I do not disagree. But they are not the only windows. I prefer to study the grain of the voice. Perched in the shadows of the third row from the back, high above the speck of pants suit on stage, I will breathe in the sound of Clinton and understand whatever it is I am going there to understand. There's going to be some type of healing it in, some kinds of recognition and a few reversals.

At the same time I was coming to this decision about my relationship to Clinton's book event, I'd unbeknownst to myself crossed a little ways along a spiritual bridge to Patti Smith. My review of her book was quoted at the top of an NPR segment. It provided the fodder for the first two questions in an interview with Smith, who said that she agreed with parts of what I wrote and that I'd written it well. At least for a moment, one of my precious few heroes in this lifetime genuinely knew my name. Her air was waving at me. We were briefly of one airwave, transcending into the ears of an enormous audience.

I know about myself enough to know I shouldn't run for office. Now that Clinton's joined my camp, perhaps someday she will know my name. Some other time. There are so many ways to save the future as a private citizen with a public audience. If you want to influence a crowd, it's difficult to do with a spark in the eye. The signal isn't big enough. Eight hundred bucks can't even bring me close enough. Only a voice casts a vibe that wide.

★

"Devils & Dust" / *Devils & Dust* (2005)

As I might linger it gets bigger
And tomorrow then I must
As that stack begins to rise
In trust double or bust
It's a prolonged day of tomes, sloppy
Tomes go along with school bus
I wield this sturdy pen flowing
Double or bust

They get grades for their time
Some of them striving to delight
The gift of breakthroughs delight
Fills their wings like doves
Cheers an hour's new kings, maybe
One discerns one's part packed cosmic dust
Undertake these grades billed goal
A monolith double or bust

Third eye creams a few alright
With my shield of kids unknown

Those kids madmen can fly
That spell madmen call life
Third eye creams a few alright, maybe
With my shield of words and tone
Our kids madmen can fly

With that spell madmen call life
Memory lemons will beggar lambs
Nirvana stakes lightness freehand
Mind the groove this grade kills
Hand out papers reprimands
As I might linger it gets bigger
Stand in my fate a saint seen tough
What I cook up pricey smarts
In trust double or bust

*

To Whom It May Concern:

    EC is one of my top five best students amongst over a decade of contenders. Furthermore, such was her promise upon our initial interactions that she holds the remarkably singular distinction of being aware of this fact while she was still my student. I met EC three years ago when she enrolled in my Journalism 101 class, and she went on to serve as Assistant Director of Communications for the newspaper. We were preparing to promote her to Director of Communications, the highest honor available to our crew of news nerds, but she wisely made a decision to enroll in online school rather than continue her studies at RHS. When she gave me the news, my heart selfishly sank even though I knew she was absolutely making the right choice.

    The quality of her work in any field will immediately distinguish EC as a cut far above her peers. Running the newspaper meant she faced a ridiculous amount of unusual tasks that all demanded immediate attention. Her grace under pressure, her professionalism in resolving peer conflicts, and her enthusiasm for tackling any challenge made her the go-to girl for every single kid on our staff. EC always thought of it as her honor and pleasure to do the work of newspaper, no matter what that work involved. Her love of communication and its attendant branches of business and design ultimately grew her into the most well-rounded news nerd I've ever mentored.

Our mentorship often also extended to personal matters. EC's dignity in the face of conflict is quite unparalleled for her age, but privately these matters of teenage drama and academic perfection began to shape up into a generalized anxiety that she sometimes sought my help in smoothing. She is literally the only student to whom I have ever given my personal cell phone number before graduation. In the end, by choosing to finish her diploma through online school, she sacrificed her involvement in the thing she most loved in order to protect her mental health. Frankly, I admire her willingness to do it. She knows how to play the long game. Nor did she leave her news crew in the lurch; she was constantly on call to any member of our remaining staff day or night in order to ease their transition to a workplace that was no longer managed by her overwhelming daily competency.

She still keeps in regular contact with me and we sometimes have lunch to check in. As a very driven lone wolf who now works from home, EC has found time to face her fear of driving and also to teach herself basic HTML coding. Separating from the strictures of traditional public schooling has given her so much room to bloom as well as to exercise more choice over the path of her learning. EC knows how to learn. She also knows what she needs to make it happen and she has enough motivation to take joy in the work that she chooses.

Any school would be extremely lucky to have her. I still think about EC two or three times a week, whether she's been in touch or not. The news nerds still sigh about her absence, and it's common for them to remark that various kinds of trouble simply wouldn't be happening if EC were still a daily presence in our office. I can't thank her enough for all she did for our journalism program. Under her leadership, the Georgia Scholastic Press Association awarded us a ranking of Superior—only seven schools in the state were awarded as such and we'd never once achieved this level until EC was at the helm.

Usually in writing these letters, I do not touch a second page to talk about a student and I end by saying that I look forward to knowing what she is doing in ten or twenty years. Not so with EC, because I'm keeping her. I expect to hear about what she is up to—and to continue to help her along in whatever ways I can—for decades to come. Seldom do I adopt a kid in this way, but we know those few special ones when we find them. EC and I were blessed to know the strength of our collaboration while it was still happening, and I have absolute confidence that any institution of higher learning would do well to let EC get started on any type of future she wants.

★

To Whom It May Concern:

KR honestly makes me feel like the future is safe. I've had the absolute delight of supervising her work on the school's newspaper for three years now, during which time she has proven herself a well-rounded and dedicated foot soldier in the war to preserve our humanity. She is expert at many functions of the newspaper, from design to marketing to actually writing articles. Because she is curious and invested in the wider world around her, her byline was equally present on our news, feature, and opinion pages throughout her time on staff. KR also has that keen instinct for clickbait and always knew what her fellow classmates would be most interested to read about in our paper.

Beyond her own articles, she quickly became my go-to girl for just about any major or minor troubleshooting task. When someone else's page layout looked terrible, she was there to fix it. When somebody's headline didn't even contain an active voice verb, KR was there with not only the verb but also a clever pun to spice it up. When somebody failed to make payment on an advertising sale, KR was happy to call and hunt down our money. And above all, she made our team-building a priority.

Any high school newspaper staff is necessarily a kind of dysfunctional family. Well, KR's top goal has always been to keep us as functional as possible. Whether that meant doing a silly personality quiz on a Friday afternoon, or going to a movie together on Saturday night, or celebrating somebody's Sweet Sixteen birthday, or just being a shoulder to cry on, KR has been ever ready to improve the morale and cohesion of our team.

She served two years as Deputy Director of Human Resources, and I don't know how on earth we'll replace her. She never served as Director simply because she has too many irons going on too many fires for us at once to ever devote herself to a single pursuit within the newspaper's organizational structure. She has always been the glue that holds so many of our pieces together. Whenever we need anything, we tag KR and she's up for whatever it is.

Not only is she up for all the things, she's actually good at remarkably many of them. She can be trusted to get the job done quickly and thoroughly, and the few times she's needed help, she speaks up right away to get what she needs. I'm super proud of her for planning to continue her study of journalism after high school, and as she is amongst the top ten percent of students I've ever had the pleasure of teaching, I recommend her most highly for college admissions.

★

To Whom It May Concern:

MG is one of the most professional young people with whom I've ever had the pleasure of running our school's newspaper. She served two years on the staff, and I came to rely upon her steadfast work extensively during that time. Not many kids go two years without missing a single deadline. Not many kids go two years without even one instance of teenage staffer drama or offering up any complaint. In fact, MG is pretty much a category unto herself.

She is probably forty years old inside, an old soul. Any time there was a problem between staff members, I could count on MG to keep her nose out of it and, when prevailed upon to do so, listen to all sides and render judicious criticism for how each aggrieved party could've better avoided the conflict. She was an exceptional peer mediator, extremely fair and objective. During our two years of conversation, I watched her grow this strong sense of social justice from the field of journalism to the field of religious studies to the field of legal studies. There's no doubt in my mind that MG's juridical sensibilities will serve her well no matter the profession she chooses.

Likewise on her projects for the newspaper, she proved to be a well-rounded and open-minded individual, motivated to continually do better and apt at self-directing her own learning. In the newsroom, we've always got a million things going on. Whenever I finally got a moment to swivel around in her direction on any given day, I'd always find her in the same spot, buried in a reference book or engrossed in the desktop screen featuring her newest layout design, working diligently on projects that would inevitably get finished with plenty of surplus energy to help others scramble to meet their deadlines.

About half way through our two years together, I nominated MG for our school's Tom Zachary VIP Award, given to students of exceptional character and academic promise. She's simply one of the most organized, forward-looking, professional teenagers I've had the good fortune to work alongside of on the newspaper. When she had to sacrifice her third year on the paper to squeeze in a few other electives she wanted to try before graduation, the staff was so saddened. MG is very good at setting the tone in a room; she kept us all striving to be our best selves. In her approach to her education she has been a strong role model to her peers. I am grateful for the time we spent together and highly recommend her for college admissions.

P.S. A week after I submitted this letter on her behalf, MG stepped down as the president of our school's chapter of Fellowship of Christian Athletes. They'd asked her to sign a mission statement declaring, among many other things she did believe in, that she believes marriage can only be between one man and one woman. MG is an ally who believes in my right to marry. She wouldn't sign her good name away, giving false testimony just to protect her leadership position. Instead, she started a new Christian group that meets at the same time as the FCA each week. Their ranks are growing stronger all the time. I'm not a Christian and I show up at their meeting every week. Our allyship goes both ways.

*

To Whom It May Concern:

NC knows her business—and there's a fair chance she knows yours, too. I've had the pleasure of her daily company for three years on the school newspaper, during which time she was promoted to Director of Digital. That title is the highest honor accorded to any news nerds, all of whom NC oversees on matters of publicity, marketing and social media. She has a real knack for always knowing what's going on. Often have I approached her to tweet something on behalf of the newspaper only to learn she's scooped me sometimes by several hours. Someday, she'll make a killer publicist.

The main thing I've always admired about NC is her expert evaluations of appropriateness in any given situation. She may break rules, but she knows which ones will bend and which ones will yield consequences. She is careful about weighing consequences, and owns up mightily when the price is worth the reward she's sought. As runner of the newspaper's social media accounts, NC is the only student whose publication work I don't approve in advance. This necessarily requires a kid to keep her head on straight as far as walking the thin line between viral tweets and administrative backlash. If she at all suspects her idea might not go over well, she comes to me to workshop it, rather than asking for forgiveness after the fact.

This kid is a prime mover because of her personality, and she possesses a type of charisma that is somehow easier to reveal in one hundred and forty characters than in high school transcripts. Her grades may definitely showcase the fact that her sibling died and that NC herself overcame cancer, but they don't tell the story of how hard she has worked to keep those traumatic feelings from spilling into facets of her everyday life. No matter what the cause for falling down, NC quickly gets up to dust herself off and keeps moving forward. She carries her baggage with remarkable ease and lightness for someone her age— with confidence and a sense of humor, even. In short, she is a resilient person full of grit and charm.

Through troubling times when most kids would selfishly navel-gaze, NC prefers to direct her attention outwardly for the benefit of the world around her. She not only demonstrates keen awareness of others' feelings, but an active impulse to assist with troubleshooting whether the other kid's problem is personal or professional. She keeps an ear to the ground in our community, a finger on the pulse of the school, and other such clichés for which it is actually rather difficult to find teenage exemplars. I admire her emotional intelligence and the way she wields it through calculations of its appropriateness. NC is born to work in marketing and communications. Any school would be lucky to have her.

★

"Reno" / *Devils & Dust* (2005)

We looked at the clocking
We felt our quickened pace
Our hearts lit candles
We had found our place

"For twelve hundred dollars saved thin
Plus crispy grades in class," I filed with dread
We doubled what was dealt, beat back cold air
Lined in front of me counting heads

I said, "Money now, rat's steal?
Hurry up before train shows?"
Their skies lifted like a fresh dough
As round the subway we go

My belt my compass lightened
The kids studied their why
Priced cool their subtle minds
Exposed to prize

First flight of the news nerd chieftain
Next flight dreaming in their stare
For the doorway to their heroes
We'll all talk college thrilled by care

They woke to hunt for bagels

Clowning all smooth shivers eighteen
They were pure fireworks with that guile drumming up teeth no brats
Enthralled by what I'd seen

From enthralled by what I'd seen
Every other year no bluff to go
So next time, we'll see you, they yearn to grow

We dipped back home to the south
"Corps steady," I led
They'd gone looking for Atlantis
Debts to linger, equipped outsiders
Installed guarantees of godheads

Implored me some other riskings
Thread, "Cheers to our quest old Galahad"
Life raft and prayed their ghosts
Lit doesn't make tests out of launchpads
I was their host

★

I'm not the teacher who holds class outside or throws pizza parties. Yet somehow today I will become the teacher who gets on a plane with a dozen students bound for NYC. #NewsNerdsTakeManhattan

NYC + 12 teenagers, Day 1: naps on flight, taxi through Central Park, rickety hotel elevator (still charming), walked entire length of Broadway till freezing, random pizza, kept Bernadette Peters waiting for 90sec, photos in Times Square, 24hr drugstore snacks, rode the Metro. No incidents. #NewsNerdsTakeManhattan

In the taxi with two girls who have never been to NYC before, Sydney is shouting out the names of iconic streets as we drive past each block and Nikki is taking photos of every dog spotted wearing its tiny winter coat. Cami gets a recommendation for a pizza place and on the way there we discover that she cannot read maps even though she is our graphic designer. The entire gaggle braves a three-mile walk against freezing winds because I ask them to, then runs up three flights of steps to get seated as the house lights come down in the Shubert. They ask permission for bathroom breaks and snacks, and all kinds of little things that they have never bothered to get my input about in our daily lives outside this trip.

NYC + 12 teenagers, Day 2: dragging everyone to coffee and bagels, learning our butts off about digital transmedia / convergence operations, Ethiopian for lunch, more learning, Indian for dinner, shopping on 5th Avenue (them, not me—that'd be cheating on Mindy). 60min worth of tardies for our various check-ins, but no other incidents. #NewsNerdsTakeManhattan

Anna and Ellie seem totally unable to physically move their bodies from place to place on time, even though they have never missed a deadline in the newsroom. Kennedy, who almost never makes deadline, keeps showing up early for everything because she is hopped up on cold medicine. Several kids each declare that they have found the best bagel place in NYC, then we go to some chain place four blocks from the hotel and agree that all bagels are created equal. I tell them they are wasting the trip if they ever eat at the same place twice. They proudly wear their name badges at the conference and take notes about whatever excites them—on laptops with keyboards, on tablets with styluses, on phones with their thumbs, on notebooks with green pens, on loose leaf paper with pencils, on their forearms with Sharpies. They take pictures of everything and treat department stores like free museums.

NYC + 12 teenagers, Day 3: hunting for iconic Greek coffee cups at street vendors, learning about social media optimization all day, touching stuff at the Met when nobody's looking, giant bowls of ramen, Central Park at sunset. Minor shenanigans, no incidents. #NewsNerdsTakeManhattan

Nikki learns that I've never had coffee in the stereotypical NYC cup and brings me two different sizes within a few hours. Ava and Nikki go to the medieval wing of the Met while I go with other kids to other wings. They pose in front of the painting that is on the cover of their history textbook and send it to their teacher. Sydney brings her mother's fancy camera and Cami wants to have a contest about who can touch the most exhibits before we get scolded. We find ramen places using Google Maps and narrow down to the best one using Yelp. My niece meets us there, on the eve of her twenty-first birthday, and mentors the girls by explaining how she ended up in art school in NYC as we slowly walk around the lake. Just as everyone gets tired and cranky, two off-leash Irish setters arrive with a tennis ball to refresh us. The girls are not really missing their parents, but they yearn for their dogs.

NYC + 12 teenagers, Day 4: listened to the Parkland journalism kids with awed solidarity, overstuffed Italian lunch, MoMA or Ground Zero, Greek diner. One lost set of silver earrings, one kid down with a migraine, no other incidents. #NewsNerdsTakeManhattan

The kids ask permission to skip the morning session so they can get good seats for the Parkland session. They sit there listening, thinking about how much gun violence is in their lives and what they can try to do about it—at once bold and terrified. Staff lunch is at the nearest Italian place that can hold all of us on short notice, except for Mary, who's at the hotel sleeping off her headache. Jewel wants to see Ground Zero because her father, who served in the military and recently passed away after a long battle with cancer, always told her how important the site is. His widow is one of the two moms chaperoning the trip. The other one takes some kids thrifting.

On the way to MoMA, we walk by the Ed Sullivan Theater. I wave up at Colbert and thank him for his service. On the way out of coat check, Sydney learns that she got rejected from the same college where Katie got wait-listed. She calls Katie before telling her parents. Back at the hotel, Bridget returns from thrifting to say this trip is the best thing she's done all year and hands me a Colbert t-shirt. Her mom assures me that nobody put her up to it and that she spent her own money. Nikki reports that she has lost a pair of earrings and is afraid that housekeeping stole them. Nobody can find them, but she decides not to complain since whoever did it needs their job more than she wants her earrings back. All the girls want to know what an egg cream is, but none of them will try a sip of mine. We have made all the memories already. They are tired of new adventures and want to get back to work.

NYC + 12 teenagers, Day 5: We're safely back in the warmth and comfort of ATL, now massively better educated and stronger bonded. Turns out, my adulting is convincing. Huzzah! #NewsNerdsTakeManhattan

The kids immediately want to know, so I tell them, yes: we can go on the NYC trip every other year. I no longer have any idea why I had been resisting doing this trip for so many years. Maybe this is a particularly good or special bunch of kids.

★

To Whom It May Concern:

NP is likely to win a Pulitzer Prize. You can't imagine how silly I feel saying that, and yet, there it is. On the first day of Journalism 101, I asked the kids to tell me what brought them to an elective about the news and NP extolled the virtues of Christiane Amanpour for several minutes. I thought she was some kind of mirage—a teacher's hallucination of the ideal newspaper student. Over the course of two years working alongside her on the newspaper, I came to find that NP was very, very real.

171

Her exceptional grades no doubt tell the tale of her scholarly prowess, and with an academic reputation that precedes her, NP has often been misunderstood by her peers and even her teachers as an automaton—but she's actually an autodidact. It's true that she's utterly capable of perfect scores in AP Calculus; she can jump through a hoop like nobody's business. However, the quantity of independent reading she dives into continues to astound me. NP has independently sought to engage me on such wide-ranging matters as the merits of Tolstoy versus Dostoyevsky, strategies of incrementalism in arguments before the Supreme Court, and whether there is such a thing as feminist tone. She's equally invested in fiction and journalism, equally interested in writing and speaking.

She served the production of our newspaper expertly. I found her to be quickly responsive to any challenges as well as possessed of substantial foresight in troubleshooting problems before they start. She was the only staffer to take charge of two sections of the paper for layout—front and news—the two pages most scrutinized for engaging design and most likely to require last-minute changes due to ongoing story developments. She always delivered beautiful work well before deadline with barely any guidance.

At the end of junior year when her enrollment forms for senior year were due, NP and I had a long heart to heart about her future. In the end, we agreed that continuing to enroll in the newspaper elective was not the best use of her time. We'd run out of ways for her to properly grow her skill sets and she was ready to move on to getting her feet wet in the real world of journalism, so I encouraged her to seek an internship that would truly fan her fire, as opposed to staying onboard with our elective just to take the promotion and subsequent resume line she would otherwise get from me as a senior. She continues to write for the newspaper despite not being formally enrolled in the course and her politics column is one of our most-clicked each month.

This applicant is one fierce lone wolf, and I recommend her most highly for college admission. Whichever school is lucky enough to have her will inevitably need to invite her back a few decades hence to give a commencement speech on the secrets of her as yet uncharted but widely predicted immense, international success.

★

To Whom It May Concern:

SK is a delightful person and it has been my honor to supervise her on the school newspaper for the past three years. She came to me as a sophomore with bright blue hair and an equally sunny disposition. Though she's traded the neon ponytail for a nose ring, she remains as positive and uplifting a force on our team as she was the day she first walked into the news office. Whether it's in volunteering to pick up the slack for a fellow overburdened staffer, or in her exemplary cooperation and team-building skills, SK always motivates the rest of the news nerds to succeed by radiating good vibes and optimism.

Also, she's a heck of a journalist and has a keen business sense. SK has written for most sections of the paper during our three year together, and appeared equally on news, feature, and opinion pages of the paper. She is highly dependable at deadline, and when she can't make deadline I always hear about it directly from her first, whereas most kids simply wait for me to notice their work is missing. Writing is actually the easiest part of what we do, and SK is a tremendous asset to the design and fundraising sides of our operation. As a page editor, she has excellent attention to detail and her pages seldom require editing from her director—in fact, the director often asks for her help in editing others' pages. As our Advertising Sales Manager, SK has racked up more dollars for our budget than any other member of the staff. Thanks to her aggressive ad sales, we have field trips and fun sweatshirts all at a reasonable price.

Although her work has always been timely, thoughtful, and interesting, it's really her personality that I will never forget. SK is a buoy in even the stormiest waters. As a staff, we have weathered political crises, football championship headaches, romantic relationship breakups and all manner of other dilemmas that are so typical of life in high school. A newsroom's collective work ethic and attitude tend to lurch toward our lowest common denominator and can easily be pulled off course by one very loudly complaining student. SK is never that student—and thankfully, she's long been my best antidote to that student. She always brings a smile and lends a hand. Her stalwart professionalism in the face of ordinary teenage drama will be sorely missed next year. I recommend SK, very highly and without reservations, for college admissions.

★

To Whom It May Concern:

From the first moment I met VB, she presented herself as an artist. VB has been taking a variety of classes with me for the past three years, beginning with 10th grade Literature & Composition. During the first week of school I gave some kind of short writing assignment and began circulating around the room to check on the students' progress. VB had finished her work early and promptly began silently amusing herself in her sketchbook. By the time I came around to look over her shoulder, she was halfway through creating a formidable looking female super hero. She tried to hide it, either because it wasn't on task or because it was too much exposure of her inner life.

Indeed, in many ways over the past several years, I've watch VB grow into this very image that she'd been drawing when I first took notice of her. Eventually, she began to volunteer the sketchbook for me to flip through and came to see her doodling as more of a professional asset and proper career path than simply a mindless hobby. For a while, the sketchbook also served as an excuse not to socialize, as a retreat from all the mundane evils of daily life in high school. When our time in Sophomore Lit expired, VB agreed to look up from her pages and begin expressing her thoughts aloud by enrolling in my Public Speaking class.

It was in Speech class her junior year that she and I both were floored to discover VB was as gifted with her words as with her images. She has a knack for impromptu, bolstered by a willingness to be honest and to share her worldview with others. VB regularly garnered the students' vote for "best overall" shout-outs at the end of each performance in our class. She always had boldness and vision, and by the time that elective was over, she had really found her voice and her confidence in using these strategically.

During her senior year, I recruited her to do illustrations for the paper, which necessitated my permission to leapfrog over the Journalism 101 training usually required to work on the school newspaper. VB has certainly proven her mettle in our fast-paced newsroom, always asking around to see how she can be of help and delivering quality imagery to accompany many of the articles we've published this year. She is highly reliable when it comes to meeting strict deadlines, and her positive energy brings a smile to everybody when we're stressed about publication timelines.

She is a good human—informed and interested, talented and judicious, possessed of strong potential. She knows herself well, and I have known VB well enough to say that all along, I expected her to eventually enroll in art school. She will unquestionably succeed in art school, and I recommend her highly for college admissions.

★

"Long Time Comin'" / *Devils & Dust* (2005)

In here the geeks learn callow but handy
My classroom cups brimmin' bouquet of scars

That kid in the back seat runs gushin' out of her hightops
Skates away from harms

We're guidin' guards ferryin' day to day supposes
With the next tricks that we trade
Alright we wanna get earth sacred and carry their mind mold
A chance to be brave

This is the song I'm singin', you hear
This is the song I'm singin', how do you hear
How do you hear

In this abbey we're all tossed with danger
Walking on eggshells like clowns
Hell when we're on the skids it hurts everybody
Nobody can steal our crown

Bell rings start the show no killin' them with work
Cause Heaven forbid their mind's blown
It's not a petri dish for these grades mistaken pearls, bids
For to see that our sweepstakes carry backbone
Yeah our wins carry backbone

Underneath charms of teacher soothsayer
When the word of their buy-in peaks
Turn key of truth, poses, tacklin' with tossed pliers
For their teethin' and critique

Bell flares up the art of my church spire deft earning
Few bids on a steep price tag denied
We preach and breathe alert, lesson plans our cross to carry
To reel in anyone fixin' to hide
Our restraint like a truck pick-up sublime

★

My best friend of many years recently began to study at divinity school. Many
of the women to whom she provides pastoral care can feel their frustration
bubbling up, but they do not know its cause. The cause has something do to

with their womanhood. It has something to do with the gaze of male eyes resting malevolently on their endeavors. Many of them have been touched in a way they did not solicit. Many of them have been made to feel small by their husbands, by their bosses, even by strangers who sensed instinctively that these women lacked whatever power might be needed to protect themselves. They simply feel besieged by the lives they have cobbled together.

These are Southern Baptist ladies, Republican ladies, traditional and conservative ladies. They do not even like the word "feminism," having been made wary by the steady drip of fearfulness in their lives. My friend slips them books to help them step into their own light. A lot of Christian books are garbage, either very poorly written or simply badly argued in order to deepen the subservience of women in religious culture. They need words from those writers who stand apart from the white picket fencing to which they are accustomed, but these women do not know where to look. They look to my comparatively extremely liberated friend and they take her suggestions.

She will soon be slipping them Chimamanda Ngozi Adichie's *Dear Ijeawele, or A Feminist Manifesto in Fifteen Suggestions.* It's a small book, good for hiding inside a fat Bible. They can take the dust jacket off so nobody will shoot an evil eye at all the bad words in the title—*feminist, manifesto, suggestions.* They can say vaguely that they are reading about African girls, which has a sort of implied missionary goodness to it that will put an end to any scrutiny. Despite what they view as reactionary titling, they should be able to hide the book in plain sight with relative ease.

It's only sixty-three double-spaced pages. Its sentences are short and its word choice is clear. They needn't have gone to college to be able to understand it. They can read it three minutes at a time, suggestion by suggestion, in between the chores and the kids and the job and the sleep. The suggestions do not seem hard, nor are they expensive. Adichie is sometimes funny and is always realistic. All of this stacks up to a heap of possibilities. *Dear Ijeawele* is the perfect wedge. It can open the doors of these women that have slammed themselves shut for reasons of safety or bitterness or confusion.

But are they the ones to whom this book is addressed? Who is Ijeawele? She's a dear childhood friend of Adichie's who has a new baby girl. So this book is not about how one becomes a feminist, but more how one teaches feminism to others. We mostly learn by example, but many mothers are not themselves able to be those examples, either casually or explicitly. Adichie is undertaking the daunting task of listing principles by which we may consciously raise the next generation of women to be empowered. "It's not enough to say you want to raise a daughter who can tell you anything," she counsels. "You have to give her the language to talk to you."

Many women lack this language, even for themselves. *Dear Ijeawele* is a shockingly lucid, surprisingly simple road map to living a more feminist daily life so that our daughters may do better for themselves than we did. We should be more authentic and not worry so much about likeability. We should not think of marriage as a prize to be won. We should value our own work and treat each other as equals. We should question the assumptions of gender roles and the assumptions of language. We should be deliberate when we talk about our appearances and our careers. We should have a sense of cultural identity and we should be full people.

The fifth suggestion is one of the best: be sure to read. Indeed, many people need to start by reading Adichie. We cannot break free of systems unless we know how we have been trapped inside of them. As she quite rightly concludes about where our brightest future lies, "I cannot overstate the power of alternatives." *Dear Ijeawele* offers a comprehensive and comprehensible alternative to patriarchy without ever using words like "patriarchy." The author doesn't water down any concepts; she just speaks to them plainly. Even for those of us who went to graduate school and have wiggled our way past feminism to humanism, Adichie's adept essay is a refreshing reminder of our first principles and a handy checklist for when we inevitably sometimes lose our way. It's a real shot in the arm and it doesn't hurt at all. You can finish it in less time than it takes to drain a bottle of wine.

★

As a kid, I was obsessed with astronaut ice cream for two reasons. Firstly, it is obviously its own thing that is only barely parallel to actual ice cream—a thing that is a weird, flavorful form unto itself. Secondly, why couldn't astronauts just eat regular ice cream? Oh, because gravity—because when your job involves being in space, there are some circumstances beyond your control that impact what and how you can eat. Mom was always just putting a plate in front of me a couple times a day; kids don't have to think about the logistics too often. As an adult, of course, I think with extreme regularity about what and how I eat, and the how often radically restricts the what.

Most people don't have time to cook a big, fresh breakfast for their family every morning. We're all trying to get out the door in a timely manner without having to wake up too long before sunrise. Once we get to work, the challenge of a proper lunch sometimes feels insurmountable. We give in to take-out, or the bleakness of frozen cafeteria foods even though at sixteen we promised ourselves we would leave behind that thin, square, cardboard pizza after graduation. There's also the guy constantly stubbing his toe on the sad wholesale brick of soup cans hiding under his cubicle desk, and the lady who is perpetually toting either a protein bar or a meal replacement diet shake.

We go to great lengths to feed ourselves at some point in the rush of our workday. Unless we're schmoozing the clients in a white tablecloth scene, most of us are looking to maximize our efficiency at lunchtime so we can leave the office at a reasonable time where maybe we can lead the rush hour charge instead of idling endlessly at the back of traffic watching sunset from the highway. I'm a teacher, and lunch poses a big problem for teachers. Nationwide, the absolute best case scenario is that a teacher has one hour for lunch. Personally, at my public high school in Atlanta, I get twenty-five minutes. I usually eat lunch in ten minutes while also doing other things on my laptop.

My colleagues think I am superhuman. They can't imagine how I sustain productivity during lunch time without burning myself out. They use lunch to treat themselves to leftovers or a frozen dinner that is aligned with their most recent dieting plan or they rush out to the nearest fast food place to bring back something half-cold that they will scarf down as their next batch of students is arriving. Most of my colleagues have seen it, and reactions range from disbelief to affectionate dismissal: Aww, isn't that food for babies? I started teaching with ninety thousand dollars in student loan debt, and bringing lunch to work is a great way to cut costs. I'm debt-free after a decade, but am still bringing my lunch to work because I've found enough side benefit to doing so as far as this banner of extreme efficiency under which most of us labor each day.

First of all, the lunch has got to be viable at room temperature. The fridge in the office has its ebb and flow of disgustingness, and besides, it's not on my hallway. I'm not going to burn two extra minutes walking to and from the office, nor up to seven minutes to nuke my lunch and then paradoxically wait for it to cool down again so I can eat it. I also am not going to be the guy leaving weird food odors that linger in the office for days (we hate this guy only marginally more than the guy who taunts us all with burnt popcorn smell at 3:35pm each afternoon). My lunch can't be cold either, because then I've still got to make the trip to the fridge. I stash my lunch in a desk drawer, where it can be dumped out on my desk in seven seconds.

For most of the colleagues who've inquired about my system, what gets them is the squeezy fruits, but this is for real the most important part. We need to eat lots of servings of fruit and veggies every day, right? What are your options? One: you can bring actual whole fruits and veggies. Challenges: finding grocery store time, cost of fresh produce, fresh produce becomes rotten produce, takes a long time to eat, watch that cap on your tooth, re-apply your lip stuff before students march back in.

The second tier option is fruit cups. This is the way I went for many years. You can get an entire truckload of applesauce cups for about the same price as one tree full of fresh apples. Truly, for under $150, you can buy enough applesauce cups to last through the entire school year. If you like it cold, put them in the freezer and let it melt until lunchtime. Or fine, by all means, go put it in the yucky office fridge. The efficiency problem with fruit cups is rooted in the fact that it takes two hands to eat them—one for the cup and one for the utensil. This also requires hand-eye coordination, so my lunchtime serving of fruit or veggie was not only occupying my hands, it was taking up the use of my eyes. Can't read the news and eat a fruit cup at the same time; either the news intake or the fruit intake is going to get slowed down by dividing your attention between them. With both activities taking longer, I was officially wasting my time.

Enter the squeezy fruit pouch. It's true that these were invented to solve problems about babies. Babies make a mess with cups and they don't tend to finish their food. The pouches are resealable and better for traveling around in overstuffed diaper bags. Because squeezy pouches were meant for babies, it's pretty easy to find variety of flavor and nutrients in them. You can find ones with protein, superfoods, fancy pulp or pulp-free, organic, gluten-free, no sugar added, et cetera. They're great for many kinds of dietary needs. Now that the market has caught on to adults eating them, you can also get more interesting flavors or somewhat bigger sizes. The cost of a variety pack of squeezy pouches is a little higher than the applesauce cups, but the variety is worth the added expense, especially when the other two items in my lunch never change. I can have carrot-apple-pumpkin on Monday, apple-cranberry on Tuesday, mango-banana on Wednesday, apple-orange-kale on Thursday, and blueberry-pomegranate on Friday.

If you knock on my door during lunchtime, expect to find me with a squeezy fruit pouch dangling hands-free from my mouth while my hands are furiously working their way through my email inbox or the latest headlines on my laptop. If we're stuck in a lunch meeting together, I will have better manners and at least hold the pouch to my mouth with one hand so that you don't think I'm an animal. But I am an animal—one with only twenty-five minutes to herself every day, and dang, I'm gonna make the most of it! Is it a well-balanced, perfectly healthy lunch? I'd rather have a well-balanced mind and heroic time management skills. Have you seen what soldiers eat during wartime?

★

"The Hitter" / *Devils & Dust* (2005)

Call you to floor, Pa, this crosstalk for shame
I grew up laughin' at you with most thought to my pain
The stuntin' still haunts, stuntin' overfeeds your play
Cussed debts that try clown for a smile but then agree you will pay

It was cold war where we lived your foot leaned always on my spleen
All that malice round my neck turned breath acetylene
Hell I longed for a churchyard and in my studies was saved
And that light was my own and words were my blade

Subterfuge, water cooler, and suffragette crown
While you fed me cartoons, Pa, I blocked them all out
While some kids will be kids, I grew up speedily
Thanks to your show Pa, complaint
And thirsty still sometimes linger set free

I've wrought scorpions hacked goblins for their shields in cold blood
Disdain for the scent of outlandish affixed to your bud
In your hell I gripped the rungs clovers with four-leaf laws
I was grounded and bawdy home brewing cure
Swelled the hell fang for fang with will I pressed on
I melt harder than feathers clip teens of sin and home

For those lemons and the honey breakfast, in the ways I pay back
Those lemons bled, that honey lean, as my classroom wisecracked
I taught with cayenne at the grassroots to break down regrets
So I spook no nightmares, Pa, but you still do I bet

I book this gig at a great public school bigwig on the prowl
And it's late in these chapters to notch every scowl
Where I'm praised for charm, intellect fixed it but the why still grows back
I crushed your flag with my hood honey, Pa, where it cannot rook jack

So I stand, in my win, Pa, not all dads are the same
Had to grow some less ignorant to sleep and reclaim
Hell Pa, with my choice now you call me a prize
If you must hit the doorknob shook your brilliant disguise

I pass by your stuntin', swing and miss by a mile
You've broken a score of debts that try clown for a smile

How my classroom keeps callin' and my sing writing's sung
Now in battlefields with allies I'll shake all you've done
I'm not a fettered man you see when I rep for what's mine
Grow my own honey and geek out on rhymes
Stuntin' will haunt, Pa, stuntin' overfeeds your play
Cussed debts that try clown for a smile but then agree you will pay

It's alright I'm a lifeguard I can cross the world with converts
The groove in my classroom will your standoff subverts
Still bloody kids in their ruts, their stars, their brains
Your crimes won't debase
I recover your thefts in my students' workspace

★

Sometimes when I am talking about my experience of life as a queer person, whoever is in earshot will just simmer down and turn to me to quietly soak up whatever that day's LGBT-related challenge is. I have a lot of straight friends. Some of them are Republicans but all of them love and support me. They are doing their best to be allies, but privately I sometimes reflect that their efforts are hilariously not good enough. They know not what they do.

So I become their queer friend, a person in their lives to whom they feel they can turn for answers to life's big gay mysteries, a safe space to experiment with bettering themselves. Katie Couric just did that National Geographic documentary called *Gender Revolution*, where she basically rounded up a gaggle of trans people to help her understand. My wife and I have a fair number of trans friends, but we often feel like our efforts are hilariously not good enough. We know not what we do. And hey, we cried like twelve times during Couric's interviewing—bless our hearts.

The public high school where I teach has about three hundred adults in the building, at least a dozen of which are queers, and I'm the only teacher who's out amongst the kids. One openly queer teacher divided by the attention of three hundred well-meaning colleagues who have questions that should get answers. So I become their expert on anything gay, even though I can only speak for myself. Mostly I coach them into a field of greater acceptability by using statements about my thoughts, feelings and wishes, rather than using any language of correction or right and wrong. I'm not policing or picking fights with anybody, but how can I turn away when they ask me stuff in all their good heartedness so much of the time?

This kid is crying about how his boyfriend just broke up with him—can you spare five minutes? The mom says she's supporting the kid's transition and she's happy to sue us—so do you know what's the best policy for sending this kid to a bathroom? This kid needs a book on how gender roles are oppressive for her research paper for my class—can you recommend some things? He goes by Sean—but isn't it still Hannah in our online grade book? I can't stand all that kissing they do in the hallways—were you like that in high school? Did you hear they nominated her for Prom King—is that even legal? Can you just go in and get that other paperwork—in the girls' locker room? How come you never ever ever wear a skirt to work? Would you wear a skirt to work if the kids raised thousands of dollars for charity and you wearing a skirt is their prize? Is she your wife, or partner, or what? Why don't you and Mindy ever come to our football games? What time is the Gay-Straight Alliance meeting again?

I jumped at the chance to read Ben Passmore's *Your Black Friend* because I suspected that being someone's black friend is roughly equivalent to being someone's queer friend. The content will all be different, but the forms will be much the same. At the Women's March a couple months ago, one of my favorite signs was "same struggle, different difference" being carried around by a black woman who was about my age. She had on a cool outfit, too, over which she and my wife bonded. At work, I have two black friends. One of them is a librarian and one of them teaches career skills. The teacher's son was in my class a few years back, and from the way he engaged with me in class discussions I knew his mom was talking to him thoroughly about blackness when they sat down at home for dinner.

It's good to have people to talk to me thoroughly about blackness. I loaned them Passmore's eleven-page comic and once all three of us read it, we had a little bit of a book club going about it. Sometimes they related to Passmore's feelings about a given stereotypical scenario and found his commentary hilarious. Other times they thought they might be too old to get into that situation or they identified with the situation but not Passmore's feelings about it. Neither of them found anything in the book offensive. They found it mildly funny and mildly informative, but neither said they would think to pass it along to others, whether those others were black or white.

They liked that I thought to share it with them and they both patted me on the head for trying another try. They seem to be keeping it as real with me as they can and I appreciate it so much, hoping that they don't ultimately feel like

I'm an annoying idiot—even though I know they must because of the way I feel about my own ambivalent burden of being other people's queer friend. My naïveté and casual lapses while carrying the ally banner probably aren't as lovingly forgivable as Katie Couric's. Kudos to Passmore for gladly suffering to depict the fools in *Your Black Friend*.

★

The only people who should be writing memoirs about their time in the White House are the speechwriters. Most of the time when people are reading books about the presidency, they are looking for interesting tidbits and facts. Speechwriters actually have access to almost no useful or new facts about the White House. What they do know is what it's like to grind away as a public servant day in and day out. Probably ninety percent of everything said by every president ever was actually written by speechwriters. They are the great unsung heroes of American politics. Rather than mining these type of memoirs for facts, we should be expecting the memoirist to be a competent writer. The main thing about speechwriters is, well, they know how to write.

Amongst the speechwriters, there are a few different species. One of them is the head speechwriter, which is the Rob Lowe character from Aaron Sorkin's beloved Democratic fairy tale, *The West Wing*. Then there's the guy in charge of providing spirited poetry, those couple of lines that ring throughout history. Then there's the guy who is capable of processing very large amounts of boring infrastructure research into digestible pieces on an exceedingly short timeline. Then there's the rhetorical handyman, brushing up a stump speech template by changing out Ohio for Michigan and putting an extra comma in the right place before a speech gets loaded into the teleprompter. And then there's the guy who writes the jokes, and that's David Litt. If you want to read a White House memoir, I simply can't think of a better person to do the writing than down to earth funnyman Litt.

He calls *Thanks, Obama: My Hopey, Changey White House Years* a speechwriter's memoir, but really it is far more broadly about life as a public servant. Litt used to work at *The Onion*, and then one day on a long flight he watched Obama give a speech on television. From then he was hooked, and after working on the election campaign he ended up as a low-level speechwriter. By the end of Obama's second term, he had gained significantly more footing in the food chain and this gave him insight into, among other things, why you must not tell the president that his hair is about to literally catch on fire and why you must tell the president that he looks like Hitler in a particular photograph. So there are some very funny and totally great anecdotes in here that are sort of worthless if you're trying to gather actual information behind the policymaking and leadership conundrums of presidential politics.

But Litt applies a sense of humor to his own life as much as he applies it to dealing with the president, and this is *Thanks, Obama's* greatest asset as a memoir. Litt knows that ultimately he is nonessential personnel, as a government shut down once so pointedly reminded him. There is no shortage of people waiting in line to become presidential speechwriters. Obama did not even know Litt's name until most of the way through his first term, because that's the nature of each of their jobs. But of course Litt isn't doing it for a slap on the back from the president. *Thanks, Obama* is exemplary of the attitude one should have as a public servant:

"This, I was realizing, is what it really means to work at the White House. Ping-ponging between emotional extremes, I had finally arrived at my inner common ground. I was in paradise and limbo. Indispensable and disposable. Defined by process and purpose. Washington was in the grip of unbreakable fever, yet there was nowhere I'd rather be. Was my job as wonderful as I'd imagined when I'd first walked through the gates? Of course not. But it was also more than enough."

Substitute "a public high school" for "the White House," and that's exactly the sentiment most veteran teachers express. As a high school English teacher who could've very well ended up taking a totally different course in life and becoming a high school History teacher, I often day dream about a parallel universe where instead my career took an even stranger path and landed me in the shoes of David Litt, in the Oval Office as a speechwriter to a Democratic president. I went into *Thanks, Obama* to use it as a sort of test case for whether or not my dream of being a speechwriter was actually viable and furthermore still desirable, and what I learned from David Litt—which genuinely shocked me—is the things that I would love about being a speechwriter are already the things I love about being a high school English teacher. That sense of accomplishment, that calling to public service, that ability to make big differences based on little things I do throughout my day and the way they aggregate for my audience over time—Litt and I are already barking up the same tree. I've often thought that being a high school teacher has the same type of pacing or vibe as working in an emergency room, or in a firehouse, and now I know that actually working in a high school is also kind of the same as working in the White House.

Public service is a frantic beast. The particulars of any given day often suck. After having suffered an especially nasty diatribe by phone from a Hollywood big shot in response to an issue over which Litt had no actual decision-making power, Litt reflects:

"Time that might have been spent on issues that truly mattered was spent emailing publicists instead. Where did that place me on the scale of moral flabitude? Was putting all that effort into pleasing one powerful person really the right thing to do? But what if I looked at it a different way? Were a few hours of my time worth placating someone who paid the salaries of organizers in Florida, Pennsylvania, and Ohio? What if those organizers swung an election? What if that election got Zoe Lihn her heart surgery? What if that surgery saved her life? This, I had begun to realize, was politics. Sometimes the answer depends entirely on the questions being asked."

Look, only a few dozen people can truly identify with Barack Obama's position in this world. As for the rest of us? Call me hopey and changey, but I'm picking up what David Litt is laying down. This "merely funny memoir of an unknown speechwriter" is a profound call to any type of public service. Just know that if you're going to do it, you've got to do it with a sense of humor.

★

My father is a Christian and my mother is a Jew, but both are only believers just in case (of flood, of sudden accidental death, et cetera). When I was younger they went to church or temple on their respective holy days, and never bothered their four children about picking a faith. We were encouraged to be religious to whatever extent that it interested us as a cultural phenomenon, as a series of social groups. Putting up the Christmas tree was an excuse to get together with friends; same with lighting the menorah. In my family, we gravitated less toward these actual practices than to the objects they required. Primarily they justified social functions, but we felt that we were made religious by these objects because these objects were religious and they orbited our familial world. My mother told me shortly before I went away to college that I should try to find a temple near to campus. Though she did not go to one very often herself, she said that being in close proximity to one was often enough of a comfort. Her awareness of its presence and of its location was enough to keep her feeling Jewish.

I grew up on the north shore of Chicago, where there is no shortage of Jews and consequently no shortage of kosher foods. Matzo ball soup has always been a comfort to me. My mother made it when I was sick. Now that I am grown and moved away to Baton Rouge, I'm responsible for making the soup myself when I need it.

There are not a lot of Jews in Louisiana, and there are an even fewer number who do their grocery shopping at my local Winn-Dixie. My matzo ball mix is elusive for this reason. When the store carries it at all, I invariably stumble into it—not in the soup isle, but in the foreign foods section wedged in between taco shells and soy sauce. My Jewish friend Rob moved to Baton Rouge from somewhere in Texas, which is why he is quite used to buying Campbell's instead of Manischewitz.

I dated a girl who had never heard of matzo ball soup. Once I made it for her, she loved it. You don't have to be Jewish to eat matzo ball soup; you just have to live near a supermarket that carries it.

★

I've often thought of Bruce Springsteen and Billy Joel in the same breath. The King of New Jersey and the King of Long Island have a lot in common, musically and personally. They both write about working class problems with a dark realism that ultimately hinges the merits of life upon a sense of hope. They are both wordy storytellers who love to hold forth with some sense of humor. They are both widely associated with their religions in a way that most superstars outside the purview of county music generally are not. They both struggle with personal demons, though in strangely opposite ways. Springsteen's depressive fear of intimacy causes him to stick close to Patti Scialfa and surround himself with a giant ensemble band. Joel's four wives have watched him suffer through substance abuse behind the scenes and while sitting alone on stage.

One of their most substantial commonalities is motorcycles. Springsteen rides them and Joel actually builds them. In fact, one of those he built for Springsteen was the bike that failed on him last year. It stopped dead somewhere outside of Freehold, and a couple bikers coming back from a Veteran's Day celebration tried to help him get it started again. Two months later, Billy Joel is on Colbert waving around the new part needed to resurrect the bike. He was on *The Late Show* to promote the upcoming tour, which is slated to roll through my city at some point.

When it was announced, I was super psyched to see Billy Joel. That's pretty close to a bucket list thing. I was doubly psyched because this show will be the inaugural use of our city's new ballpark. We'd planned to just get cheap seats, as I blew past my annual ticket budget many moons ago. The day before tickets went on sale, something about the show date was sticking in my craw, so I look at the calendar and it turns out that Billy Joel is coming to Atlanta the day after Tom Petty.

And you know I got amazing tickets to that Heartbreakers show; it's their fortieth anniversary tour. So we're not going to Billy Joel. On the one hand, what an amazing and historical weekend of concerts that would be. On the other hand, which is the hand I'm shaking, ain't nothing going to step on my buzz from joining Petty in doing his thing. It will be glorious. It will kick off my summer by restoring my soul at the end of a long, hard semester of teachering.

No way can I check a bucket list box by slapping the Piano Man on the back end of what is going to be one of the best shows I've ever seen—even if Joel's concert is going to be equally great, and perhaps especially if it's going to be equally great. When you've got something so righteous going on, you've got to savor that as best you can. It seems like middle age is in part about not feeling tempted to double down on every chance that comes my way. There's only so much shit I can get serious about at one time.

CHAPTER EIGHT

I TOOK TWO DAYS OFF WORK AND FLEW TWO HOURS to do a seven minute gig at a local bar so that I could hang out with Gina in Philly all weekend. My wife loves it when I visit the City of Brotherly Love without her; she calls it my working class vacation. Gina and I play a bunch of skee ball and drink full-fat Budweiser at Lucky 13, a good little townie bar that used to be fourteen blocks from her apartment. She moved and now the bar is three blocks away, a superior commute. The bar is managed by a bald guy named Clark who looks like J.K. Simmons in the face but kinder in the eyes. He has an excellent playlist for weekends, mostly old school punk music. The first time I visited, he gave me the link and I find myself hitting up his Spotify playlist regularly on weekends in Atlanta.

He recognized me when I came in last night and I gave him a copy of my new book. Clark might not be much of a reader of books that aren't about sports, but he can hold forth on his own opinion on a variety of pop culture topics and he never lets our bottles of Bud empty out before turning an inquiring eye in Gina's direction. In fact, when Gina walks in, he sets down two bottles unasked. Other regulars can tell whether Gina has been in based on how many Buds are visible in the cooler.

When I arrived this time on Thursday evening shortly before the gig, Gina announced she'd taken Friday off work. I never ask Gina if she's taking off work because I don't want to guilt her into taking extra days off, so this was a good surprise. My previous Friday plan had been to sleep late, go to the Melrose Diner around the corner for brunch and camp there with a stack of books until Gina gets off work. She declared that we would be taking a field trip—to Asbury Park, hallelujah.

I haven't researched where Springsteen grew up. I mean, I've read a variety of biographical, autobiographical and interview material in the course of working on this book, but I had planned no field trips. So extensive was my aversion to making treks on his behalf that six months ago when he came through Atlanta on the River redux tour, I instinctively chose not to get tickets. I have been to only one Springsteen concert in my life, one of the first few dates he did after Clarence died. In thinking about and planning this book, I simply did not find it necessary to make the pilgrimage.

But here was Gina offering me skee ball in an exciting new locale just under two hours outside of town. So we gassed up, loaded the car with Motown albums and began to make our merry way to who knows what. We put the Stone Pony in the GPS and headed out. We crossed the Walt Whitman Bridge to get out of the city. This was in late October and the leaves along the highway had begun to turn red. The trees gave way to brick houses and the turnpike gave way to the boardwalk. It was overcast and drizzling, literalizing my attitude toward visiting a place from which the Boss worked so hard to escape. If I ever get fantastically famous, please know for the record that there is no reason to visit the Park Lane house.

We went in reverse chronological order, parking at the bar but beginning our unprepared and aimless investigation at the boardwalk. More than half of it was empty or under construction, and nearly everything was closed at lunchtime on a Friday afternoon. Our first stop was the pinball museum, where we paid $7.50 for a half hour of access. The cashier gave us neon green wristbands and wrote the expiration time on them with a black Sharpie. He gave us a full hour, instead of the half for which we'd paid. Through the turnstile we went, back in time eighty years to the first wooden pinball machines, up through the advent of Pong and Pac Man, toward the back where we did indeed indulge in a whole bunch of skee ball.

Skee ball was one of the first redemption games. The higher the scores, the more tickets the machine would spit out and then you'd trade the tickets for some useless tchotchkes at the cashier. I didn't know these were called redemption games. The top scoring point holes were more narrow than I was used to and the well for a mere ten points was crooked enough that players often ended up with zero no matter how low they were willing to aim. Many of the older pinball machines were not quite rigged, but severely slanted with short flippers and dented gutters intentionally designed to stack the odds for the house.

The machines were somewhat arranged by company and in sections sometimes by themes; nothing was chronological. The first machine I bothered to play after skee ball was a pinball machine called Super Star, from 1978. It has a rock and roll theme so it just felt appropriate. I haven't played pinball in years, so I sucked at it and lost all three balls pretty quickly. Then Gina pointed down at the instruction window near the right flipper. Someone had scribbled on it. I looked closer and it was a signature in black Sharpie: Vinny Maddog Lopez, 2011, E. St. Band.

When you play pinball, there are only four places to touch and you must touch all four to play. You press the start button to load the ball; you pull the spring lever to release the ball; you push the right and left side buttons to move the flippers; that's it. My fingers had been in four places that Vinny's had most definitely, unconditionally been. I noted that he didn't make the high score board perched on top of the game, and I noted that the board was divided by age and also by gender. To get his signature on the bit of plastic near the right flipper, they'd have to unscrew the plexiglass cover off the entire field of play. His photo wasn't on the wall with the other famous visitors. By famous, I mean Chris Christie, Ivanka Trump, and Paul Shaffer. Springsteen wasn't up there either.

In another aisle, I found a machine explicitly labelled as an E Street artifact, the Big Star game that appeared in the background of the "Girls in their Summer Clothes" video filmed on Ocean Grove Beach in 2008. I don't even know this song or this video. There was a photo of the beached machine attached to one corner and I played it simply because Big Star was a great band and I was there at the museum with unlimited play for thirty-five more minutes. We left with thirty minutes to spare because we were hungry. I almost bought a tee shirt, but recently promised myself that I would stop wearing tee shirts that aren't made of good cotton that drapes nicely.

On our way to find lunch, we ran into Madam Marie's. I don't know why I thought the "madam" moniker was poetic license. There was her tiny shack on the boardwalk, promising psychic services and offering availability for party rentals. I guess once the Boss drops your name into a famous song, you don't need to practice or preach a damn thing. He likely enabled her early retirement without ever actually giving her a single cent. On the other hand, I wonder how often young Springsteen visited Marie and what she might have prophesied for him, if any part of his perseverance was rooted in the faith she quacked at him in those early days.

After one of the best shrimp quesadillas I've truly ever had, we approached the Stone Pony. It was not yet open for business, but with the door swinging wide open, Gina and I marched in. Just a bunch of roadies loading in some gear, a lone box office manager asking if we wanted to buy tickets for that night. Pennywise. We did not. I once again thought about buying a tee shirt, but something inside of me screamed that this tee shirt was no longer sacred, like seeing the massive proliferation of CBGB tee shirts on people who haven't earned them. Don't know if I've earned a Stone Pony tee shirt, but I didn't walk out with one that day.

We climbed back in the car as the sun was finally coming back out and headed fifteen miles onward to Freehold. Springsteen's house was knocked down to expand the parking lot for St. Rose of Lima Catholic Church. This is a gross irony, as his whole young life revolved around that church. He spent Sundays there at services as a crap under-qualified altar boy, spent weekdays at the Catholic school, spent Friday or Saturday nights at the local socials and dances, lived right across the street from there for far longer than he could really stand. All the doors were locked. I touched all the handles and probably he did, too.

Then we drove two miles to the cemetery. You can't approach it in a quiet and respectful manner. Heading down Throckmorton, the street is paved in a segmented way that bumps up the suspension on any car every few seconds, making a big bass noise like you can find on some of the shittier highways all across America. It is throbbing, rhythmic, gently wounding. The St. Rose of Lima cemetery gates are flung wide open and the space is surprisingly sprawling, representing generations of townies who were born here and stayed here until death. Some, like Springsteen's father, finally got out alive and still came back as a corpse.

A lot of the cemetery is packed with headstones, but there is a comparative spaciousness on either side of Douglas Frederick Springsteen, 1924-1998. It's a double-wide stone, with room for his wife. There seems to be room for Bruce and Patti, plus Virginia and her husband. I wonder if that's the plan, if one day people will be making this pilgrimage to the tombstone of the Boss. There's no map around the place, because it's a damned townie cemetery and nobody famous is buried here. But it's a vast and haphazardly arranged place. Gina and I wander by car and on foot for fifteen minutes. We spotted two groundskeepers idling near their pickup truck, and resolved to be those city-slick bastard looky-loos in search of Boss trivia—which indeed we were, unironically and with totally undisgusted self-awareness of our quest.

Just as we began to head in their direction, I caught the headstone in my peripherals. It was like the pictures, dark gray with a cross and some calla lilies engraved into the top of it, an American flag on the left side, a votive holder in the center, a little white statue of a sitting dog on the right. I'd like to know what the dog is all about; I saw more than a dozen of them as we walked the rows in search of this grave.

I stood on the ground covering the bones of the father of the Boss, looking down at my boots and envisioning how far beneath me the remains were. Then I threw my jacket over a corner of the headstone, got behind the thing and tossed my phone to Gina so she could take some pictures of me. The wind picked up and the drizzle came back on. I began thinking about how I will someday eulogize my own father, how much forgiveness is in the cards and who owes an ask to whom on that score.

At no point did I feel a sentiment that could be characterized as paying my respects. As we left, I turned back toward the headstone and said, "OK, Doug,

I hope it works out for you." And I really do. I hope it works out for everybody, even sons of bitches who treat their kids meanly because they were themselves never raised to know better and the ones who did it because they were poisoned by mental illness such that they simply couldn't do better and the ones who knew full well that they should've done better but selfishly, simply didn't. Good for the Springsteens for making what peace they could.

And good for the Boss for getting the fuck out of Freehold, where I believe he felt the hold far more often than he ever felt free. There's a giant cemetery near where I grew up. My mom's mother, who often raised me when my parents couldn't totally handle it, was a charmingly superstitious Jew who counseled me to hold my breath when we drove past this cemetery. It was two blocks long and there was a stop light at the end of it. You'd have to hold your breath for at least a minute and she never really gave me a reason why we ought to do it, but I often participated in her ritual all the same, even when it was mild torture. She wasn't buried there and I won't be either.

Life is full of enough circles; I think it's naive to manufacture extra ones. If Bruce ends up buried in Freehold, I will likely consider it a weakness in him. Whether that weakness will be effectively symbolic and further endear him to me, whether it will teach me a lesson I have enough age and experience to properly appreciate, only time will tell.

*

"Livin' in the Future" / *Magic* (2007)

The debtor strums mandolin
His mortal sins bail out deeds with tune
Human bein' my brother amen
Jump cut and cue bad blood
Dumb luck refs the flood
Mic grins with hiss
Lays waste with mud in his lungs

So hurry starling, won't have to pay your debts
You're sittin' in an armchair
Where some of us are spared regrets

King's cup rejection says
Lies are over and laid to praise

Bequeath their thirty sons
This missal of crimes unpaid
Justice has been gunned down
Hokum dockin' in crown
Dispute feels stickin' spikes
Your peril in a fist full winnin' sound

This birth paved the way
For he chose chords that stun
And hoping we could start anew
We rot all damaged and unsung
The sick family tree failed to sway
In its study made of poison
That grim reaper loaded his rates
Sunset exiled loved ones

Headstones deter me now
The cost of joy in ghost towns
Play that funky new pastiche
Plot my queer new horse around
These weights adorn girl wonder
Banshee quizzed no knucklin' under
For must we thinkin' hound
Lest hummin' Midas knowin' plunder

*

On Inauguration Day, I got a tattoo on my inner right ankle—of Hillary Clinton's campaign logo. When I announced my intentions to do this, the internet yelled at me. Also, my mom's response: "No! No! No! No!" Several members of my family voted for Bernie Sanders in their state's primary, but such is their distaste for Clinton that they voted for Donald Trump in the general election. Even amongst fans of Clinton, I found that people were very reluctant to get psyched for my ink job. The prospect of this tattoo was generally viewed as an exercise in fanaticism and the presumption was that I would soon regret it.

My mother has a couple of tattoos, including one we both have that reads, "shake the dust." We both graduated from the same public high school in the north suburbs of Chicago, Maine Township High School East, in Park Ridge. Clinton also went to Maine East for three years. It was always a huge school.

In her senior year, the district opened Maine South to alleviate the overcrowding and she was transferred there alongside many of her peers. She was on the newspaper and served as Vice President of the Junior Class, but she lost her bid for Senior Class President.

Harrison Ford also graduated from Maine East. He founded the A/V Club. Like most public schools, the building has one long main hallway with ancillary hallways that branch off of it. Toward one end of this spine of the school, near the stairs to the English Department where I spent most of my time, there was a tiny wall of famous alumni with just two pictures posted there behind the plexiglass, Ford and Clinton. I attended Maine East from 1994 to 1999, the last class of the millennium. Bill Clinton was inaugurated in January of 1993, so his wife was serving as First Lady of the United States throughout my time in high school.

I walked by that photo of her no fewer than twelve times a day, five days a week for four years. The idea that somebody who went to my high school could work in the White House was a very powerful prospect. It wasn't that she was a woman, or that her politics aligned with mine. I was too busy trying to keep my queer closet doors from swinging open and actually I identified as a Libertarian in high school, bandying about my dog-eared copy of Ayn Rand's *The Fountainhead*. My admiration was based on our mutual location. This person grew up where I grew up, and she had gone so far in life. My family was struggling to exchange their blue collars for white ones, and Clinton's image in the hallway offered me a great deal of hope that I could make something of myself, that I could get beyond the circumstances into which I was born.

My interest in the details of her life began shortly before I graduated, as her husband faced impeachment proceedings. I heard expressions of pity for her that she had to suffer such public embarrassment for her husband's misdeeds. I heard outrage that she was forced by politics to stick with her troubled marriage, skepticism that the marriage was anything but a sham for the sake of ambition, vicious rumors that she drove him to it and that she was a lesbian. That last bit certainly struck a newly raw nerve for me, for at the ripe old age of seventeen, the label of "lesbian" was a terrifying means of slander.

But I was always an unabashed feminist, believing in my own equality with men and willing to speak up to root out unjust, unequal treatment of my kind. "My kind" would grow broader with time, as I became comfortable in my sexuality and eventually outspoken about it as another facet of the mission for equality. I closely observed Clinton's effort to pass universal healthcare legislation, a massive effort and subsequent failure on her part that unquestionably paved the way twenty years later for one of the foundational measures of Obama's legacy. I listened to many of her speeches expressing utmost care for the needs and dreams of women and children. As I traded Ayn Rand for bell hooks, there were more frequent points of common sense agreement between Clinton's goals and my own.

She went to the Senate and I went to college. We were both coming into our own, and watching how she operated provided ample material to assist me in more closely considering the line between pragmatism and politicking. I had been a punk who never saw virtue in reaching across the aisle. Then I moved to Baton Rouge for graduate school and got the same shock to the system that Clinton no doubt got when she made her way to Little Rock. Six months after I finished school and moved to Atlanta to settle into building a home with my beloved new wife, Clinton announced her exploratory committee for the 2008 presidential race. We were both finally arriving, both working to maximize our adulthood and fiercely female independence.

Carl Bernstein's excellent, thorough biography, *A Woman in Charge*, ends where the presidential race begins. I picked it up recently to reacquaint myself with all the ways my life and Clinton's seem to intersect. Working on her behalf was the most natural thing in the world to me, as Bernstein's fine portrait reminded me that I too have often been given the message that my ambition is inappropriate, that my strengths of voice and moral character ought to be dialed back, that I have an attitude problem and that the stars I reach for don't exist. So that moment on Election Day 2016 when I had the incredible opportunity to vote for Hillary Clinton for President of the United States was just the cherry on top of a gorgeously satisfying rocky road sundae that I've been building since I was fourteen.

I would have gotten my tattoo whether she had won or lost the White House, because, newsflash: it's not whether you win or lose; it's how you play the game. Clinton often gets stepped on for pushing us forward as a nation. She takes infinite heat for her willingness to get down in the muck of what is too casually considered a man's game and score very many points in that game. She may have a bleeding heart, but she can also cut throats. I admire many of the qualities that get her into regular trouble and I consider her a role model. Though I would have loved to be there and see her take the oath of office, I am neither much surprised nor particularly possessed of sour grapes over the fact that this round was a swing and a miss.

Win or lose, before Election Day, I was already making clear to my wife that the logo tattoo was coming on Inauguration Day. Getting it done on that day just hits. I'm glad that the campaign happened, since it generated the artwork that could represent some small part of these feelings I have about my spiritual connection to Clinton. My cousin called me out for slapping a permanent logo on myself, sure as he is that I'll feel silly about my decision when we do eventually get some other female president. Well, I've also got ink incorporating the logos of Elvis and the City of New Orleans. Those are far gone things for me too, but their symbols have not at all faded in personal importance to me.

He ought to have credited me with the courage of my convictions, instead of laughing at me under the condescending assumption I have no thought for long-term consequences. I'm a grown woman and I'm celebrating a lifetime of feminist activism—Clinton's and mine—with regret that we each have but one life to give to this country. It'll be excellent to look down at my right ankle every morning and be reminded of how powerful I can be when I put my ideals into action. That swollen sting radiating from inside my boot definitely made the next day's Atlanta March for Social Justice and Women exercise all the more painfully poignant. Sure, sometimes we will lose. No matter who is in the White House, there is so much good work to do.

★

"Working on a Dream" / *Magic* (2007)

It's queer some rights are wrong, we pray scars holy
We blink a new grand mind running down a theme

How the farthest pawns handcuff bands, quarrelin'
Cut Satan no slack grand mind running down a theme

Mind running down a theme
Throw hard rhymes that peel memoir pathway
Mind running down a theme
Just now Gainesville in time betrayed

Pain roarin' round, we climb that ladder
Woman enough drum running down a theme

Mind running down a theme
Thought bubble motorbike sincere mystery
Mind running down a theme
Sort of erase that bubble history

Mind running down a theme
The vote repeals owed holiday
Mind running down a theme
Cash bar of thrills steering wheel ready

Baptized scum, no time no matter
A few say wakes grand mind running down a theme

*

Getting in to see Stephen Colbert is not unlike trying to get in to see the Pope. The process is shrouded in mystery. Nobody has concrete strategies for best positioning to make it happen. When do you queue up for tickets? How do they decide who gets what seats? How truly cold is it inside the Ed Sullivan Theater? These questions haunted me as I fantasized about my pilgrimage to the Church of Colbert. What was I hoping to find there? What did I need out of the experience?

I found the 1iota website and put my name in the hat for two tickets. The fine print said we'd be notified a few weeks before the show as to whether or not we'd get in. Three weeks before the show, I got an email notifying me that I had priority tickets. There were a lot of instructions about what we could bring, when we should arrive, what we could wear. The dress code was particularly worrisome because my wife is a visual activist. That means she wears clothes— loudly. Mindy wears gender non-conforming outfits that are coordinated to draw attention, most of which is positive but some of which is negative, and we were now faced with the force multiplier of Jon Batiste, whose wardrobe is a subject of much study in our household. Jon and Mindy are kindred spirits of the cloth, constantly bringing new meaning to the concept of "sharp dressed."

After reading the fine print about the dress code, we attempted to translate what "nice casual" might mean for Mindy on the big night. Was it even possible that we might be denied entry if her outfit truly blasphemed the fine print on our tickets? And if it wasn't loud enough, would she still succeed in making that meaningful eye contact with Batiste? That's all she wanted. As he shimmied his way toward wherever our seats were going to be, working that melodica up and down the aisles on commercial break, would he be drawn in firmly enough by her outfit choice to give her a little head nod of acknowledgement? People with fashion sense like to affirm each other. Mindy wanted Batiste to know she was approving of what all he has going on, and she dreamed of one iota of reciprocity.

It was this wish that she made known to Lauren, one of very many stage hands in big red CBS coats corralling everyone into the appropriate parts of different lines as we waited to go in. Lauren liked Mindy's coat. The coat looked like Willy Wonka had a baby with my grandmother's drapes. Lauren even said that she thought Jon would totally dig Mindy's style. Well, that was at least half of the one iota of recognition that my lovely wife was seeking.

I don't know what I was seeking. I suppose it was simply to set foot inside the Ed Sullivan Theater—spiritual launch pad of Elvis, the Beatles, Letterman—and breathe within the same airspace as Stephen Colbert. Call me a transcendentalist. Of course I was hoping to get in the front row, calculating the non-zero chance of getting that sideways high five as he sweeps across the edge of the stage upon entry for the standing monologue.

When we finally got inside the theater, we shuffled single file down the aisle and it appeared like we'd gotten in line soon enough to score the fifth row. Every seat is a good seat in such a small house with a capacity of about three hundred and fifty, of course, so we were very excited. It was looking like we'd be in front of the band, so maybe Mindy's dream would be realized after all. But at the end of the aisle, we were pulled out of line by Lauren, who had unbeknownst to us been waiting for us to make our way in. She said she very much wanted Jon to see what Mindy had on, so she saved us two seats up front. What could be more up front than fifth row? The two seats, all by themselves, directly in front of the actual first row, so close to the band that we would be able to reach out and touch some of the brass players if security looked the other way for a moment.

We squealed with delight, hugged Lauren and thanked her profusely, then took our seats in awe of our good fortune. After about five minutes, Lauren came back down the aisle and said we were being moved to the other side. At first we were nervous about whether we'd lost our amazing seats, but she simply moved us to the same island of two seats on the other side of the stage. We would now be directly in Jon's eye line inside of somewhere beneath his Steinway, and we were ten paces from the guest chair where Ewan McGregor would soon be sitting. We were directly in front of Colbert's desk. Without even stretching, I could put my feet up on the stage's first step. Mindy and I just stared at each other with saucer eyes, grinning from ear to ear.

Before the taping begins, there is a warm up featuring a comedian and a little music from Stay Human. Paul Mecurio was going to call up audience members and improvise with them a bit. It wasn't a stand-up routine at all, nor did he take volunteers. He immediately called upon me and Mindy. Her outfit got his attention. Our hand-holding got his attention. Our screaming energy and applause got his attention. He picked us first. There was no scanning the crowd for better options. He bet on us. We bounded onto the stage, hand in hand.

We stood right where Colbert does the standing monologue. It was exactly the right spot because at some point in the couple of minutes we were talking to Paul, I had the presence of mind to look down and see the big red dot on the floor. Colbert has to hit that mark before he begins whatever is in the teleprompter. As Paul was talking, I slid my boot on top of that big red dot and felt all of pop culture history surge up through my veins, granting me a preternatural focus on the simple fact of just being there in that moment.

He asked our names. We said we'd been together almost twelve years and the audience exploded with applause. When he asked what Mindy did for a living, she said she was a visual activist. He wanted to know more, so Mindy began to preach on it. And the audience exploded with applause. While Paul searched for a punchy retort, I helpfully translated, "she wears clothes." The audience exploded with laughter. When he asked what I did for a living, I said I was a high school English teacher. And the audience exploded with applause. I gave a little salute and they gave a little laugh. Paul asked how we met, and when Mindy grinned and shrugged, he exclaimed that he knew it would be a good story. I helpfully translated, "it was a one night stand that lasted forever." More laughter and applause.

The audience was speaking in our tongue. They understood us. Three hundred and fifty people, plus fifty more show biz people that should have been more jaded, lit us up with the overwhelming strength of their unequivocal validation. Our love was good. They were rewarding our love, our living out loud, our living loudly. Paul took pictures of us and posted them online. There are absolutely no phones or cameras allowed inside the theater for any reason, unless you're the guy warming up the crowd. So we have a one of a kind document of this miracle moment, our shining faces reflecting back all this love as we stood in the spotlight together at the Ed Sullivan Theater in the very spot where Colbert himself stands every night. Never in a million years did we imagine such a miracle. It would have been more than enough, and the show had not even really begun.

Up next was the band. Would Jon see Mindy—really see her? Yes, he would! He danced right over in front of us even before the improvised breakdown in the middle of the first song, and gave her a strong, clear nod, pursing his lips around the melodica in as much of a smile as he could without losing the note. Mindy squealed and clapped so hard that her wedding ring left a huge bruise on the inside of her right palm, a rock and roll stigmata. It served as a kind of proof that she had made it to the land she had promised herself was real.

The rest of the band dug it also and appreciated the extra energy it was giving to Jon. As the band marched past us down the aisle, the drummer held out his tambourine and Mindy smacked it with all her might, right in time to keep the back beat. One song later, he would run up the stair next to the drum kit and play that tambourine from the catwalk, eventually striking it so hard on the railing that it shattered into a dozen pieces, raining little silver cymbals down upon the band and the stage. Stage hands scurried in from nowhere to pick up the pieces as the band played on.

Then, without fanfare or introduction or warning of any kind, Stephen Colbert ran out from the side of the stage. He swept across the front row for a series of high fives just as I'd seen him do a hundred times on television. He was beginning to round back toward the desk but something drew him to us and he extended his sweep just a little further than could fit into the band's wrapping up music. Mindy and I each stretched out a hand, but we did not quite connect. If I had put my foot up on the first of the two and a half stairs to the stage, Colbert's hand would have made contact with mine. But I did not want to literally overstep. Our fingertips were four or five inches apart and it was absolutely good enough. We made eye contact. I was screaming like we were coached to do and he was smiling like he was coached to do, and it was a totally perfect moment where each of us achieved a private satisfaction while simultaneously delivering what we had promised by entering that building.

We were chanting, "Stephen, Stephen, Stephen," and the echo of it in my mind rang as, "amen, amen, amen." We were all there because we believed in something—roughly the same something, as I'd just realized when I'd stood on that stage myself. Before the taping begins, Colbert always takes a few questions from the audience. Most of the questions were political in nature. One person asked what Broadway role Colbert would most like to take on, if gender and range and such were not at issue. He immediately replied, "Judas in *Jesus Christ Superstar*." The band immediately began to play and Colbert belted out three verses on the spot with perfect timing and perfect pitch.

He confessed to having been asked that question before and I began to think about how often Colbert might be performing *Jesus Christ Superstar* before the show. There was a strong possibility that he might have begun to think of it as a ritual. After we'd been seated, I'd asked the nearest stagehand who chooses the music that pipes in for a half hour or so before the show. She said she'd been working there for seven months, and it was exactly the same playlist in the same order every night the entire time she'd been there. Whoever is in charge of that in the control room apparently added Michael Jackson's "Black or White" shortly after Trump's inauguration, and all the stagehands were thrilled both for the messaging and the newness.

When the taping began, Colbert sang some more. There was a standing monologue bit about Trump junior's recent comments on the blind trust, that he hadn't spoken to his father in almost a month. Colbert sang a sad, hilarious rewrite of Harry Chapin's "Cat's in the Cradle," finishing on the image of a golden toilet bowl. The audience went nuts for it, but Colbert wasn't happy. He paused the show, they rewound the teleprompter, and he did the entire bit again. He sang it much better the second time, fuller in the throat and maybe a half step higher in his register.

Then we got to boo the weekend's various Trumpian conundrums and Colbert stuck his head inside a microwave next to a Hot Pocket, from which he'd taken several bites. The desk monologue went perfectly the first time through. Ewan McGregor got a standing ovation when he made his entrance. He was wearing all black, including a pair of serious combat boots, and sporting an eighth of an inch of stubble on his scalp. He was promoting *Trainspotting 2* and told some sad stories about researching heroin addiction without ever trying the drug himself.

He was also promoting the live action *Beauty and the Beast* film, in which he plays Lumiere, and admitted to still never having seen the animated version despite having raised four daughters. I always thought the French candlestick character was fairly gay, but the new movie has given the gayness to LeFou, sidekick of the antagonist Gaston. Sure, LeFou works as a sidekick to Gaston in part because he feels some vagary of romantic love for him. Disney's publicists have really been talking up the character's gay identity as revolutionary, the first of its kind in a kids' movie. McGregor dismissed Colbert's inquiry out of hand, saying that it was 2017 and what on earth is the big deal about showing children a gay character. The audience was screaming with approval. I wondered if he'd been watching the pre-show warm-up. He concluded with his favorite Scottish saying, "if you're gonna get hung for stealing a sheep, you might as well fuck it as well." When it airs on television they'll bleep out the curse word, but we were there and we heard him say it with a smile.

The second guest is Finn Wittrock, who has the honor of starring opposite Sally Field in *The Glass Menagerie* this month. Field was on a few weeks ago and when she kissed Colbert on the mouth, he turned red, wilted and fell under the desk. Who wouldn't? Wittrock tells Colbert that Field said to give Colbert a kiss for her, but he then appears to demure from the actuality of the joke. This is his late night debut, after all. Making out is probably best left to more famous or important guests. Colbert leaps into the gap left by Wittrock's polite hesitancy and unfurls his right arm toward the back of Wittrock's neck.

The crowd went wild with anticipation, with preemptive approval noises rather than risqué censorship noises. Neither of them has looked at Mindy and I directly during this segment, but as Colbert leans over the desk to unabashedly peck Wittrock's nervous lips, he does look out into the darkness of the crowd at the far end of his side of the stage, between the two cameras where he knows that Mindy and I are perched. Courage, comrades! Colbert is happy for a chance to remind us that he numbers among us, a proud ally who need not make too big of a deal about being a man that will kiss another man.

Wittrock went to Juilliard with Jon Batiste. When they cut to commercial, Stay Human once again paraded down the aisles. This time Jon looked very pointedly at Mindy, paused on the step right in front of us and leaned down to her. He had the melodica in his face, crooning away on it, but his body language invited Mindy to approach. It was like watching Harry Potter approach Buckbeak when the formidable mythical hippogriff bowed to him. Mindy stood next to him on the step, put her arm around his back and staged whispered into his ear, "I love you." Then she kissed his shoulder as he rested his right temple against her left temple and they just stood there for one forever-long second, Jon holding the note on his mouth piano before picking up the tempo and moving on down the aisle. Mindy's face was toward the stage, but when she turned back to me she had tears in her eyes. She had done it. She had made her connection to its fullest possible extent. And Jon had, too. I watched his face as they touched—he'd closed his eyes and soaked up her energy, both of them instantly somehow even more vitalized.

As they played through the crowd, the first row was ushered out of their seats by quickly-moving stagehands. As it turned out, we should never have wanted the first row proper because as The Shins set up for their upcoming song, it became clear that the front row must be vacated in order for the folks operating the cameras to stand there and get all the sweeping shots they need of the musicians. The second row became the new first row, much to their delight. Colbert was waiting for The Shins to be ready, standing off toward the wing with their album in hand. Well before he needed to move back to center stage, he began casually drifting toward us. He landed fewer than ten paces from us, and when he once again made eye contact, Mindy blew him a kiss. He smile broadly, then I gave him a toothy, cheesy grin back and waved floppily like a fourth grader. He chuckled silently and gave me back the same wave, looking me right in the eye for several seconds. It was a magic I'd forgotten I possess, the directness of our non-verbals and how we built a tiny, ephemeral home in them together.

He introduced the band and The Shins played the excellent and timely "Name for You." This is the end of the first verse and beginning of the chorus: "Somebody with an antique notion / Comes along to tighten the line / They're just afraid of you speaking your mind // They've got a name for you girls / what's in a name?" I have a profound affection for Sub Pop bands, like everyone who graduated in the Class of '99 of course, and was very glad to hear these affirmations. We bopped joyously. We yelled raucously. We held hands and we kissed and it was not at all difficult to be in the moment. Everything was in very sharp focus and yet everything was giving way to the next amazing thing in a way that was not exactly rushed but still gathering momentum. We knew the show was coming to an end but we searched for a sadness that was not there. The entire experience was fleeting, but we knew we were going to stay human.

Stay Human once again made the rounds through the audience and Colbert was waiting to do his exit. As he waited, he came down the stair into the aisle and stood directly in front of us. I could have straightened his tie. We looked at each other and smiled. He reached out his hand to me. I reached out my hand to him. We shook. Both of us had warm hands somehow, despite the freezing temperature in the theater. Then he turned to Mindy and shook her hand also. He took her in and said, "I like your jacket." Earlier that morning, at the hotel, Mindy had laid out two jackets on the bed and deliberated over which one was right. Her decision was validated and we both beamed. Actually, all three of us beamed.

Then the music died down a bit and Colbert turned around, stepping just slightly in front of us. He looked into the camera and said who the guests were for tomorrow, with Mindy and I directly behind his left shoulder. Colbert always makes this announcement from this spot. The show runners collectively conspired to put us in the two seats where they could be absolutely certain that not only would we be most able to interact with everyone on stage—they knew the show's parting shot would broadcast this image of two loud, loving, happy, human queers all across America and to the entire world. The Church of Colbert affirms Mindy and affirms me—it lifted us up and it wants us to be seen.

When I say I believe in the power of a live show to conjure a religious experience, this is what I mean. Mindy and I have been doing our best all along, but lately we've been tired and have sometimes felt our best was not going to cut it. Call it Trumpian Affect Disorder. Throughout the pre-show, every person coaching us through it emphasized that the audience is what makes the show great and possible. As *The Late Show with Stephen Colbert* has finally achieved top dog status in late night, I am thinking deeply about how my kind is the majority. We have contact info for several people with whom we waited in the line. We had great talks full of laughter and commiseration, vigorous nodding of heads and sharing of perspectives.

After the show, back outside on the street, many people approached us as we all waited at a red light. They complimented Mindy's outfit. They thanked us for being so publicly out. They admired me for being a teacher. They said we did well, were funny, were nice, wanted to hug us. I am reflecting on how all of us in that audience were collectively traveling the same path, looking at each other and really seeing our sameness, our agreement, our potential for connection and the unbowed, unblinking security of our happiness. What is a church if it is not this?

★

"One Way Street" / *The Promise* (2010)

Felt stiff this fun could crawl endlessly with sorrow
Name in vain wrings the fear from you guys time could bare cures borrowed
From your dumb show, we make our grief
Your reign jaws long, we deign claws meet
Spare me your talking all these bromides, this whole town is bittersweet

Win the fight, we bleed lonely buyers of the prize
This warning slight sings to bulldoze you fun-sized
Now your exchange is numb and gray
Once roared your songs now there is shade
You blur talking all these bromides, this whole town is bittersweet

In worshipping we trust, but trust it less
No man above, yet we are blessed humans progressed
Your sanctified must burn away
Cavemen burn yet talk all day
Pause me your talking all these bromides, this whole town is bittersweet
Au revoir
World, mere talking all these bromides, this whole town is bittersweet

★

Jason Diamond and I passed like two sinking ships in the night. At basically the same age and location during the 80s and 90s on the North Shore of Chicago, we each grew up suffering the indignity of abusive parental units and a constant feeling of genuinely not belonging amongst our peers. We experimented with being bad—or what passed for bad in the suburbs. Like Diamond, I sought refuge among punks. Like Diamond, I was deeply interested in the fact that John Hughes, writer and director of several of the unarguably best and most timeless teen movies ever made, lived among us. You might run into him at the Jewel-

Osco. He might be getting gas at the 7-Eleven. But I never searched for him.

Searching for John Hughes is the supremely excellent result of Diamond's quest to hold on to his own optimism. He failed spectacularly for many years at writing a proper biography of Hughes. That first manuscript was ultimately "wedged somewhere between cultural criticism, essay, and a manifesto." Diamond failed for many reasons and in many ways—personal, chemical, professional, circumstantial, and surreal. Some of the manuscript's failures were swift and self-evident, others were agonizingly slow and grew multi-faceted over weeks or months or years. These failures ultimately came at great cost to the author's life. "I had a book that I'd been working on for a few years, one that I'd spent money I didn't have on, lost jobs chasing interviews I didn't end up getting, moved halfway across the country, all because I'd told myself it would all be worth it in the end."

"How many more times could I tell myself there'd be a happy ending?" Indeed, Diamond always finds a way to take one more stab at his homage to Hughes, both for Hughes and for himself. "I kept getting on a plane to O'Hare because I'd wanted to see if things could work out. I'd wanted to see if there was any possible way of having the life I thought I could lead when I was young. [...] Despite everything, I'm an eternal optimist. It's both a strength and weakness." Through his work on the book, Diamond revealed to himself a variety of connections with Hughes' oeuvre. "And the more I drove around his suburbs, the more it dawned on me that I was driving around the places where my own memories were born, how his life and mine, although thirty years apart in age, shared a similar geography. [...] I was looking for John Hughes, but subconsciously I was starting to understand why I felt such a deep connection to his film, and also why I'd decided writing this book was my destiny: I wanted to live in a John Hughes film."

It wasn't only that the author found himself intertwined with the filmmaker's work, as he had been since his teens. He also found himself increasingly woven into the fabric of the filmmaker's own life. "When Hughes was toiling somewhat fruitlessly at the ad agency in Chicago he was in his twenties. When I was writing about him and that job and his climbing the ladder in that city that had raised us both, I was also twenty-five, just another young person looking to write chapters and chapters full of triumphs—either his or mine." But the biography never quite gelled. Diamond simply didn't have the connections needed for such an enormous undertaking. "Like Hughes, I had all these ideas, but they were useless without all the little things I was trying to find out, like if his father served in the military and whether Hughes was a good student. Those details that I just didn't have the resources to get were so crucial. Those were the things that made a biography.."

It's so easy to see the runaway train of oncoming failure, to hear it screeching in the near distance, yet Diamond can hardly stop himself from one last gasp and one more try on every page. What's harder to understand is why he dove into the project in the first place. "Faith had never really played a part in my life, yet there I was, over a decade later, sitting in a bar and telling my friend that I wanted to become a holy man. [...] There was no vision of Moses in my toast, no sudden and inexplicable interest in ancient Jewish texts; I just wanted to be a rabbi. It sounded like an admirable profession, like how some people wake up and decide they don't want to be a stockbroker or some other shady profession, that instead they'd rather do something good."

Diamond is in search of salvation by almost any means, returning to the root of Hughes as a primary cultural influence. And he's also bluffing his way through a confidence game with some successful jackasses with whom he went to high school. "'I'm writing the unauthorized biography of John Hughes,' I said with the kind of authority I didn't even know I possessed. [..] That sounds really cool, I thought, the lie turning into an actual plan right there on the spot. Really cool. I would write the John Hughes biography that nobody else had ever attempted. I would pay the highest tribute to a man whose work had such a huge impact on me, whose vision I had basically based my world view on. This was my big idea, the one I came up with while drunk and lying."

What begins as tribute naturally transforms into something more grounded and therefore necessarily more critical. "I found myself disliking a lot of things about the guy who was supposed to be my hero. [...] It felt as though the belief system I'd built for myself, the idea of a better life that I wanted, all hinged on me figuring out what really happened, why he either sold out or just faded away." Diamond is slowly but steadily killing his darling, walking that complex, fine line between homage and homicide in engaging one of America's foremost cultural icons. "My relationship with Hughes was more complicated than I had thought when I started out, and I liked that. I liked that I found fault in his work and in the man himself. [...] My feelings on Hughes and his work went from obsessive fan to obsessive critic, but I still felt an undeniable link to him and his movies. They had helped shape me."

Though it had helped keep him alive when he was younger, there are a pile of signs that it had begun stunting his growth. "I had wasted half a decade. I was sitting there with that untouched plate of food in front of me, in a town I didn't know, jobless and close to being broke, and I was stalking the guy who played Jake Ryan even though my book was about the life of John Hughes. I'd been going about things the wrong way, I thought. I'd become a total creep, and to be honest, I wasn't even sure I wanted to keep doing this anymore." And there's a terrific breed of irony imbedded in that complexity, too, in the ways this book project threads through his life as a grown man. "All told, my John Hughes biography was the best and longest relationship I'd had as an adult, and thinking about that made me queasy. We spent long nights together, sometimes I'd confess to it through my writing, letting parts that were supposed to be about Hughes become more about me, my own views, my own thoughts, my own fears."

Diamond anointed himself chosen for this work. He needed it and felt it needed him, and yet, "when the one agent I did talk to at a 'Meet Publishing Insiders' event I paid fifty dollars to go to, which had been moved from a larger venue to a smaller bar with a faux French bistro vibe, asked me why I was the person who should write a biography on such a famous and beloved director, I was taken off guard for some reason." He was simply called to it, unambiguously but without concrete reasons. Many times he was challenged by this work, facing one defeat after another and often losing his resolve. "To think I had come so close to giving up! I was one step closer to John Hughes, one step closer to making my biography a reality. [...] And then I got a flat tire just outside of Jersey City, surrounded by smokestacks, like a living Bruce Springsteen song."

Searching for John Hughes is among the finest tragedies in the brave new genre of memoir wherein the author's own life is reflected in the undertaking of a biography fail, in the process of describing why some other book about some more important person did not materialize. As with all such books—Geoff Dyer's *Out of Sheer Rage*, or Alina Simone's *Madonnaland*, for example—the human succeeds where the book project fails. And on the human scale by which Diamond gauges his success, "Andie [of *Pretty in Pink*] was the first John Hughes character I wanted to be. Getting through all the crap and coming out awesome, to me, was the coolest thing anybody could do."

Did Jason Diamond get through all the crap and come out awesome? Yes. Yes, he did. "I was becoming an adult and it didn't feel as though my heart was dying. I'd spent years failing, but I realized I had basically failed upward." We cannot ask for more. We all define ourselves through popular culture. Jason Diamond is just like me, but it isn't because we're of the same generation or because we grew up in the same suburbs, or even because we have a similar cultural frame of reference. The process of referencing—this searching labor of love, how it fails us and why we need it anyway—is itself universal. For better and for worse, we are married to the icons given us in our youth. Diamond is keeping the faith.

★

Ah, the notorious RBG—as affectionate and cool a nickname as any Supreme Court Justice will ever have. But for what exactly is Ruth Bader Ginsburg so notorious and what is the actual source of our affection for her? With the help of her longstanding biographers, Mary Hartnett and Wendy W. Williams, Justice Ginsburg will herself attempt to answer these questions in *My Own Words*. A bombshell tell-all this book is not, with a few warm jabs at her dear friend, the late Antonin Scalia, notwithstanding. Ginsburg is a sitting Justice on the highest court in America, and perhaps the only one of the three branches of our government still trying to maintain a sense of decorum. Plus, she's a lawyer—a very personable one, but still, the bulk of her own words have always adhered to a certain juridical standard. Her memoir, if we can call it that, is no exception.

Is *My Own Words* a memoir? Of sorts. I'd say it's closer to a collection of greatest hits, though many of the hits were previously only performed for a small, exclusive crowd. The contents are both chronological and themed. There are very few new words here beyond the short introductions to each chapter; most of the book is a lightly edited and expertly arranged series of things she has previously published as decisions or has spoken as a guest at various luncheons and awards ceremonies. The biographers say, "Striking to us is the way the Justice would give a speech, adapt it to other occasions, use its various points in different contexts, and, in one or more iterations, add footnotes and usher it into print. [...] A similar process was evident in the briefs lawyer Ginsburg wrote for the gender equality cases she brought to the Supreme Court in the 1970s, briefs that organically grew or shrank, changed in emphasis, or altered in their details over the course of years."

Taken together, these fragments serve as an excellent reminder of why we hold RBG so very dear—and picked apart, we still have a long way to go for equal dignity under the law that Ginsburg kept a steady eye on long before her nomination to the Court in 1993. She wrote in 1971 that "the attention to feminist organizations and activities is not misplaced, however, for in the current decade a less submissive majority seems certain to develop." Of her work as a professor and advocate at the ACLU, she says, "work progressed on three fronts: we sought to advance, simultaneously, public understanding, legislative change, and change in judicial doctrine." This three-pronged strategy, which Ginsburg helped to pioneer and then proliferate through all three means, is still the basis for progressive activism today.

Progress toward female equality has hardly been swift. Instead of counseling patience, Ginsburg relies upon incrementalism and her funny bone. She counsels that "a sense of humor is helpful for those who would advance social change." Of the Supreme Court figure she most admired before her own career there, she reflects, "Justice Benjamin Cardozo said, 'Justice is not to be taken by storm. She is to be wooed by slow advances'." Indeed, seldom do the real heroes of progressivism fathom themselves as such. Of her work on the landmark equal protection case *Reed v. Reed*, she notes that "Sally Reed was not a sophisticated woman. [...] She probably did not think of herself as a feminist, but she had the strong sense that her state's law was unjust, and faith that the judiciary could redress her grievance."

Faith in the judiciary is above all the theme of *My Own Words*. This is not to be conflated with Ginsburg's faith in herself. She is neither a braggart nor a grandstander, despite the fact that she could lay uncontested claim to having personally done more to advance the equal protection of women under the law than any other figure in American history, as a lawyer, professor, ACLU activist, judge, and ultimately Supreme Court Justice. Her husband Marty says, "All in all, great achievements from [the Moritz] tax case with an amount in controversy that totaled exactly $296.70." From these small potatoes came immense changes in the lives of women, but Ginsburg never got bogged down by big feelings or historical tides, especially after she was seated on the Court. Of her nomination, she said, "What has become of me could happen only in America." Of her early work there, she recalls, "I sought Justice O'Connor's advice [on writing my first opinion]. It was simple. 'Just do it,' she said. [...] That advice typifies Justice O'Connor's approach to all things. Waste no time on anger, regret, or resentment, just get the job done."

And yet, the wellspring of her feelings is clearly quite deep. With over two decades on the Court under her belt now, she clings to a particular high water mark. "I had the heady experience once of writing a dissent for myself and just one other Justice; in time, it became the opinion of the Court from which only three of my colleagues dissented. Whenever I write in dissent, I aim for a repeat of that experience. Much more often than not, the conference vote holds, but hope springs eternal!" The biographers say, "To Justice Ginsburg, history teaches that the Court should avoid either impeding, or leaping too far ahead of, the political process, instead engaging in a 'temperate brand of decisionmaking' that proceeds incrementally, ordinarily deciding what is required by the case before it and leaving further development to later cases." Americans have come to view dissent as a radical immediacy, but in fact, Ginsburg makes an argument for dissent that more closely approaches a pragmatic incrementalism.

The overall effect of *My Own Words* is a sense that Justice Ginsberg remains a cogent and agile mind devoted to a singular life-long mission. As a history of her good deeds and right thinking, this book showcases in stunningly precise detail how the hard work of equality has been moved forward under Ginsburg's judicious hand. What she told the Senate Judiciary Committee as they prepared to question her before confirmation feels like the perfect way to endorse this book: "[My complete body of published material] is the most tangible, reliable indicator of my attitude, outlook, approach, and style. I hope [the committee] will judge my qualifications principally on that written record." Yes, *My Own Words* proves the notorious RBG qualified for her prime place in American history.

★

"Wrong Side of the Street" / *The Promise* (2010)

World on the ledge strippin' scoffs at camp
Some fences won't mend, snarling, in their friendless fight
We girls have big dick energy
Prayer, tight strung orbit fans the plight of our race
No overlooking scores of mothers in bold face
You see, big dick energy

We, leap queening shady with our fiery stings manned world
It shows no gladness that our minds can sing, so blue
While they just beat their meat, strut crushing shrews?

We, true to our coterie land our accrued pearls
Unwind the gate sides with grace for our daughters' world
Prayer, we girls have big dick energy
Prayer, we write the books that shift from stone to pearls
Restored, high turnout where hands pray slaying as we learn
Maybe, it's big dick energy

We, sure fire as alpha rays slinging our game as the true
Young mouths cooking with outraged blue flames
We witty tunes at the door not whores neither bores

So, it's a game changer when we fire up and sing
Stand and show the greatness of our minds
Gaining with our creed greater than their doom or their deeds
We win when these men go crazy and scoff at camp
Some fences won't mend, snarling, in their friendless fight
Girls with big dick energy

Prayer plans alpha rays, we, we must sling our game
Young mouths are cooking with their mother's aging flame
Girls with big dick energy
We, burning fires with their weak illusions
We'll talk and slay when, no free rides or collusions
Our creed, no room for lies just free, world

★

Am I cool? This has long been our preoccupation, the essential question of American life. To properly answer, we should turn to the work of Joel Dinerstein. He curated the Smithsonian's exhibit on cool and wrote a history of New York cool. His new book, *The Origins of Cool in Postwar America*, is articulate, thorough, and oddly reassuring. Dinerstein approaches the notion of coolness as a theorist, historian and lover of popular culture to produce a book that synthesizes the best of all three domains. Our interpretation of cool may be emptying out, may be changing with each new generation's cultural output, but a close examination of the roots of coolness shows that as a fundamental way of being in the world, little about cool has changed.

As an ontology, cool is primarily about resistance in subjection. The word itself did not proliferate until the end of World War II, when it became attached to certain elite practitioners of particular forms of art. Cool has always been the label we slap on cultural products, the most admirable compositions of music, film, and so on. But as a composition itself, Dinerstein demonstrates that cool hinges on specific values. The first half of the book traces these values from the end of the war through 1952 and the second half goes from 1953 to about 1960. He examines archetypes of cool in several genres of popular culture with an emphasis on where these diverse practitioners intersect.

Dinerstein begins with Lester Young on saxophone and heads toward the movies of Humphrey Bogart. Taking jazz and noir film together, he then proceeds to define their convergence in terms of existentialism. Camus in particular highlights how the practitioners of jazz and noir film are embodying a mode of resistance to the problem of collapsed empires. World War II is a kind of trauma, a failure of many systems of Western civilization. Colonialism and fascism began to fizzle out and existentialism rushed in to fill the vacuum, along with a politics of identity. A long history of shutdowns based on racism and sexism was coming to the forefront of American consciousness, which would eventually give birth to the civil rights movement.

Meanwhile, there were intellectuals like Billie Holiday or Simone de Beauvoir to channel the newfound well of resistance into art. To be cool meant to give violent social systems the skeptical cold shoulder, to retain a stoic attitude of composure despite the daily lived encounters with oppressors. To be cool meant to be inventive, witty, and creative in the face of political endangerment. This was not only a mode of defense against the subjection of women and black people; it also found footing among the working class. Dinerstein analyzes white rebels including Marlon Brando, James Dean, and Frank Sinatra.

To be cool is to interrogate the social norms that hold us down. It is a form of rebellion that doesn't let cards show to police or politicians. It is the product of an anxiety about the systems whose justifications are collapsing all around us. Cool is the means by which we can cope with our lived experiences of injustice, a means of enacting hope that after these injustices are unmasked as such, there will be something better on the other side. To be individualist, to be aloof, to be cynical, turns out to be the most optimistic position available as well as a historically sound one. Dinerstein posits that what looks like quiet, icy hope for the revolution is actually itself the revolution.

This is why Miles Davis stays with us. This is why Jack Kerouac or Lorraine Hansberry or James Baldwin or Elvis Presley stays with us. Their timelessness is rooted in the cool, in their oppositional stance toward their own anxieties about the reformation of Western values after World War II. They rode the wave of a seismic shift in culture, surfing along the edge of it with art products that insulated them from the despair so often left in its wake. The arc of history is long and slow, but when that pendulum begins to swing back the other way after a period of nervous almost-entropy, it's cool that keeps us safe.

If you want to be cool, you've got to make art. It's as true now as it was then. In the crumbling of Judeo-Christian values, in the confusion of a know-nothing president and the crisis of escalating geopolitical tensions, in the collapse of pretexts for oppression and the reckoning with what American citizenship really means, cool is what saves. Dinerstein's cogent analysis stops at the assassination of John F. Kennedy, but I'll be damned if it isn't awfully resonant in the world of today and tomorrow. This isn't about whether Taylor Swift and the Kardashians can preserve this notion of cool. It's about how Paul Newman's films might still be our best road to salvation, how Ralph Ellison's novels are still completely right on the money. Cool is that self-confident and emotionally understated mode of rebellion that made America what it was in a time of unprecedented anxiety—and what it will be again.

★

"Land of Hope and Dreams" / *Wrecking Ball* (2012)

Start the pickets state our truth case, mother's pulling out comebacks
Hell, let's all reap what they're sowing plowed, our ammo is in the black
Fell, sparkling, as we cheery, slay their dead from out this breast
She'll break ground as librarian, heart-sleeves for our best

Roller heels bowl crew with shields and airtight seams
Defeating a clan of vague extremes

Solidified by truth fertile band certified
Please read this hood champion vow taken to heart with pride
Tell, recommend words borrowed, bet the weight in your glass
Spells, on my row steadily headline man mauled by sharpened sass

Hell, dis brain marries paints with thinners
Dis brain buries users with dinners
Dis brain parries doors with ramblers
Dis brain varies patrols

Ahead, dis brain's team cannot be distorted
Dis brain, wakes your will transported
Dis brain, we're the real deal swinging
Dis brain, spells a heathen stinging

Ahead, dis brain ferries cross uncharted
Dis brain, grieves and loopholes guarded
Dis brain fairies' schools with wings grown
Dis brain, a boss broad

Read some dis brain
Steeple so heavy
Don't you kneel for kicking
Soul grew strength renewed this
Must bet boss broad
Boss broad dis brain
Steeple so heavy
Don't you feel it pricking
Don't you hear it ticking

Who must bet boss broad
Who must bank these gods

★

Something delightful about Patti Smith is that she frequently agrees to do unusual gigs. Most of the time it's a charitable endeavor, because Smith has never cared about making money. She just makes whatever kind of art she wants and freely gives it to interested parties, especially those backed by a good cause. For a long time now, I have been waiting for Smith to say something new—something identifiably and strikingly different from other things she's said. So I often pick up tiny bootlegs or monographs from her more obscure happenings in hopes that the ones done under less general scrutiny offer her a place to experiment. In this manner, I consistently set myself up for disappointment.

Patti Smith does not experiment. She has oddball moments or works in differing genres, or includes some kind of artwork, sure. But the content of Smith's voice—her actual modes of thinking, her romantic trademarks, and the conclusions she draws about how we should live—have remained steadfast and consistent for more than forty years. Across her body of work there is a very particular attitude. This is despite tonal shifts; she can be confrontational, rhetorical, melancholic, or ecstatic in tone, but the attitude sliding around under everything she does has a constancy to it that seems impossible. It was hard to find in someone so young when she was young, and it still seems untenable to maintain in someone so experienced enough to know better.

She's an unquenchable optimist. Not the glass half full, turn the other cheek kind of naive person who goes on smiling as morons let slip their dogs of war. Smith's optimism is a type of soldiering on—one that can wade through grief, one that can expect an upside to be revealed in the flames of failure, and one that can absorb anger to transubstantiate it into good deeds. It's this last quality that shines most clearly in the pages of her newest obscure thing: *The New Jerusalem*, a long prose poem just published by The Nexus Institute in the Netherlands.

The mission of *The Nexus Institute* is to study European cultural heritage in an artistic and philosophical manner. Its founder and president, Rob Riemen, is the author of two books on nobility and fascism. Other thinkers in the Nexus series include luminaries such as Jonathan Sacks and Sonia Gandhi. Riemen's introductory essay to Smith's poem makes explicit the fact that artists engage in a religious activity when they make their art. For Smith, the purpose of imagination has always been as a rudder for the ship of her conscience—she uses art to envision a better world.

Well, don't we all? Yeah, exactly—but you may have noticed that since Trump took office, there has never been more art with less optimism. News journalism has fallen into a state of sarcasm rife with editorializing adjectives. Street art has devolved into little more than trolling three billboards at a time. And, wow, the poets are very, very angry. It is no great leap to assume Patti Smith is not supportive of Trump. As *The New Jerusalem* is her first official product both written and published during the Trump presidency, I was keen to know what she's doing with the anger and anxiety she no doubt feels to the same extent as the rest of us. I'd been waiting for her work to take some kind of new turn, but it's the times that have turned—and now I'm damned grateful for Smith's unerring constancy.

The New Jerusalem is a prose poem of fourteen pages broken into seven sections with a handful of accompanying images. The sections: a matter of time, what manner of herald flies over, triumph and deceit, the alchemical sovereign, prophecy's lullaby, the cup, and a time of gifts. The images: three photos of her handwritten manuscript in progress, one photo of the bombed out skeleton of the South Tower of the World Trade Center that she took in 2001, and Leonardo da Vinci's oil on wood *Salvator Mundi* painting. Is this teensy volume worth twenty euros and an hour of your time?

The opening sections depict a new era presided over by "controllers, cultivators and mercenary priests." Anyone bloody but unbowed has fled. The resistance is led by "girls in purple rain coats" who "infiltrate the forbidden zone," asserting their existence and "eluding virtual crucifixion." "Triumph and Deceit" depicts the brutal ceremonial slaughter of one hundred oxen that, to my thinking, unquestionably constitutes Smith's portrait of Trump's inauguration. It's a moment when "the rabbits scurry and know they are called rabbits."

Leonardo's portrait of Jesus, "right hand raised in benediction, the left holding the orb of the world," still sees "the holy city within us" as "salvation scavengers" try to recover the artistry and history that has lived inside humanity from the sixth day until this new era. In place of anger, Smith delivers "Prophecy's Lullaby." She moves from present tense, where we are keepers of the flame, to future tense, where we are the New Jerusalem realized. In the final two sections, "we" becomes "I" as Smith takes her own lullaby to heart. She relates a dream where she receives the gift of a communion cup and then extends such a "Time of Gifts" to everyone.

Though Smith has always been easily identified as "a tribe of one," *The New Jerusalem* cultivates her sense of being in the army of tribes of one, of being a slice of "the voice of the sixth day." Her goodness proves inexhaustible, and art is the method of its dissemination. Smith's is a voice that has never depleted.

Her buoyancy remains as staunchly resilient as ever. Whatever anger has landed on her heart in the jungles of Trumplandia, she consistently performs the miracle of putting it down.

The New Jerusalem should prove as timeless as her other works of art—but because it is gifted to us at precisely this moment in the Age of Trump, it arrives as a salve like no other. For a few minutes at least, I was able to put my own anger down. Though we are radically uncertain of how long our present future will last and deadly sure that it must end, it feels very good to bridge that anxious gap with faith in the prophecy of Patti Smith. Really, you can listen to any of her albums or pick up the memoirs and find this same energy. Similar to *Devotion*, Smith is spending more time thinking explicitly about how and why she uses her voice.

This beautiful, dutiful, reassuring constancy notwithstanding, I still find it completely unfair to compare *Devotion* to her previous two non-fiction books, *Just Kids* and *M Train*. *Just Kids* and *M Train* are memoirs. While *Devotion* purports to be non-fiction, it is not strictly speaking a memoir. *Devotion* is actually the title of a short story, which takes up most of the scant hundred pages in this book. It opens and closes with Smith's reflection on how the short story of "Devotion" came to be written. What we really have is the first piece of fiction by Patti Smith, and her accompanying thoughts on how it was made. She knows there's no great secret to this work: "I push aside my computer and cast a ruling upon the uneven plaster ceiling: we pillage, we embrace, we know not." Yet it is still the greatest of mysteries, how writers transcend to their writing space: "I linger, content to be with the ghosts of writers who have passed into this same perimeter."

In the short fiction of "Devotion," she sometimes inserts a cliché. Smith knows she's inserting a cliché and favors them because of her profound love of detective stories. In detective stories, you can always find clichés because the truth is that often times it's enough to say "the man sat down in the chair." We don't always need to know what kind of man nor do we need to know what kind of chair, or how he sat. At other times, the telling detail is a more psychological one that paints no proper image at all: "He was a solitary man, in his late thirties, of unusual control, hardy and virile, yet uniquely sensitive, having already negotiated the spectrum of academics, risk, art, and excess." This is likewise an apt description of Smith, though she is twice as old as her character.

Sometimes it is enough to know it was a dark and stormy night. Great American literature is riddled with dark and stormy nights, so why shouldn't Smith take advantage of those same telling, clichéd psychological details? Her story, "Devotion," contains: a promising ice skater, the aforementioned mysterious man, a frozen lake, a small cabin in the woods, some trains and passports, and a good deal of feeling. Feelings include: surprise, gratitude, lust, and death wish. Smith is telling it her way, but also in the ancient way. It is recognizable to readers for its mythic proportion, accessible to all kinds of people for its brevity and intensity—and yet, it is still distinctly Patti Smith.

Of her effort to write about the writing, we might say that Smith ends up saying what a lot of writers who write about writing might say: that it is a calling, that it is done out of necessity, that it aims to improve the world, that it aims to show the best of its author, that it is hard, that it is joyous, that it is under the influence of everything in the author's life, and that it is an influence on everything in the author's life.

Patti Smith is some messed up kind of a saint. On the one hand, she is shrouded in the darkness of Gotham, hard boiled and sharp shooting. She loves her trains and her camera and her coffee. On the other hand, she glides along the clouds of lapsed Jehovah's Witnessing, innocent and ethereal. And honestly, I'm uncertain about whether we should refer to her as lapsed. Because the fact is Patti Smith seems both closer to herself and to her God than most mere mortals. Her influences are so clear, so near: "Initially I wondered what prompted me to write such an obscure, unhappy tale. I did not wish to dissect with a surgeon pen, but as I reread I was struck by how many passing reflections and occurrences had inspired or permeated it. Even the most insignificant reference I saw clearly as if highlighted."

There is a dash of Paul Auster about her: "Theirs was a story that could not resolve, only unravel. [...] One that turned in on itself, leaving only a transparency. [...] When does it cease to be something beautiful, a faithful aspect of the heart, to become off-center, slightly off the axis, and then hurled into an obsessional void?" There is a spoonful of Walter Benjamin: "Most often the alchemy that produces a poem or a work of fiction is hidden within the work itself, if not embedded in the coiling ridges of the mind. [...] I can examine how, but not why, I wrote what I did, or why I had so perversely deviated from my original path. Can one, tracking and successfully collaring a criminal, truly comprehend the criminal mind? Can we truly separate the how and the why?" And there is the spirit of Edna St. Vincent Millay: "We must write, engaging in a myriad of struggles, as of breaking in a willful foal. We must write, but not without consistent effort and a measure of sacrifice: to channel the future, to revisit childhood, and to rein in the follies and horrors of the imagination for a pulsating race of readers."

In *Devotion* in particular, Smith repeatedly returns to those tensions of paradox found in more flattened form in Camus: "She experienced in horror the potential bliss of unrequited desire. [...] They were at once dogs and gods." One of her characters is reading *The Myth of Sisyphus* and has a violent reaction that expresses Smith's admiration for the human predicament: "The text posed a philosophic examination of the question of suicide—'Is life worth living?' He had written in the margin that perhaps there existed a deeper question—Am I worthy of living? Five words that shook her entire being." A psychological cliché is no more or less than a symptom of the human condition.

Perhaps what *Devotion* teaches us most easily is the cool virtue of hubris: "But slowly I discerned a familiar shift in my concentration. That compulsion that prohibits me from completely surrendering to a work of art, drawing me from the halls of a favored museum to my own drafting table. [...] That is the decisive power of a singular work: a call to action. And I, time and again, am overcome with the hubris to believe I can answer that call." It is hubris to write a short story in answer to the call in one's heart. It is hubris moreover to analyze one's own short story for signs of the writerly. Of course, as the critic, to comment on her commentary about her own story is a feat that takes place at a dizzying distance. And in our human folly, we realize we have hardly any choice—for the world is right there around us, and how dare we not respond to it?

We write because we respond because we dare because we dream: "What is the dream? To write something fine, that would be better than I am, and that would justify my trials and indiscretions. To offer proof, through a scramble of words, that God exists." The writer steers the wheel when she can: "Fate has a hand but is not the hand. I was looking for something and found something else, the trailer of a film. Moved by a sonorous though alien voice, words poured." And we must imagine that she is happy. Isn't this what Camus taught us?

Pushing the rock up the hill is a writer's work: "Having no past we have only present and future. We would all like to believe that we came from nowhere but ourselves, every gesture is our own. But then we find we belong to the history and fate of a long line of beings that also may have wished to be free." Readers of any writer may recognize a certain rock or a particular hill, but *Devotion* is the certain rock and particular hill that belongs to Patti Smith. *Devotion* is at its root an expression of ownership of the rock and hill that comprises any life: "That is my final conclusion, one that is absolutely meaningless." Hers is an existential glory served straight up, no chaser.

She believes she is doing God's work, and the question of any agreement about her actual religion notwithstanding, I am inclined to approve simply by echoing Smith's gratitude toward her own influences: "One could not help but thank the gods for apportioning Camus with a righteous and judicious pen."

SAINTS & PLAYERS

END NOTES

Chapter Two

"He didn't want to rejigger…" ~ Gaar, Gillian. *Boss*, Minneapolis: Voyageur Press, 2016, page 27.
"There was an awkward start…" ~ Gaar, page 77.
"(In 2000, the compilation Badlands…" ~ Gaar, page 83.
"Side note: race car driver…" ~ Gaar, page 71.
"The Max's show also generated…" ~ Gaar, page 39.
"There would also be a…" ~ Gaar, page 88.
"Springsteen's relationship with Julianna Phillips…" ~ Gaar, page 94.
"At a few shows, Springsteen…" ~ Gaar, page 73.
"the piece ultimately became best…" ~ Gaar, page 49.
"it's not so easy writing…" ~ Smith, Patti. *M Train,* New York: Knopf, 2015, page 1.
"I followed whatever train I…" ~ Smith, page 72.
"Not all dreams need to…" ~ Smith, page 86.
"always hated loose ends. Dangling…" ~ Smith, page 96.
"the visualization detective" ~ Smith, page 65.
"ninety-seven clues but nothing solved…" ~ Smith, page 31.
"One proceeds by uttering an…" ~ Smith, page 107.
"Without noticing, I slip into…" ~ Smith, page 25.
"[Portals of the world] float…" ~ Smith, page 68.

Chapter Four

"Most of the songs were…" ~ Springsteen, Bruce. *Born to Run*, New York: Simon & Schuster, 2016, page 177.
"Most of my writing is…" ~ Springsteen, page 267.
"It is my nature to 'dissemble'…" ~ Springsteen, page 391.
"In this house, due to…" ~ Springsteen, page 10.
"The grinding hypnotic power of…" ~ Springsteen, page 11.
"He was exciting, scary, theatrical…" ~ Springsteen, page 21-22.
"At the first sound of…" ~ Springsteen, page 26.
"that sought to reap damage…" ~ Springsteen, page 357.
"I can't lay it all…" ~ Springsteen, page 413.

"to move forward, we'd have…" ~ Springsteen, page 209.

"CITIZENS OF LOS ANGELES: EVAN…" ~ Springsteen, page 368.

"mayor, judge, jury and sheriff" ~ Springsteen, page 199.

"I needed disciples […] This would…" ~ Springsteen, page 253.

"I nearly drowned in a…" ~ Springsteen, page 148.

"As funny as it sounds…" ~ Springsteen, page 17.

"I came to ruefully and…" ~ Springsteen, page 17.

"Along with (when necessary) supreme…" ~ Springsteen, page 427.

"Let the service begin" ~ Springsteen, page 7.

"A 'man' did this. A…" ~ Springsteen, page 41.

"I determined that there on…" ~ Springsteen, page 266-267.

"Each record was a statement…" ~ Springsteen, page 277.

"it was less of a…" ~ Springsteen, page 476.

"I never had the frontline…" ~ Springsteen, page 328.

"A lot of what the…" ~ Springsteen, page 453.

"[The E Street Band is] more than…" ~ Springsteen, page 217.

"It's a life-giving, joyful, sweat-drenched…" ~ Springsteen, page 186-187.

"Something that before the faithful…" ~ Springsteen, page xii.

"The shows were real, always…" ~ Springsteen, page 226.

"By the end of the…" ~ Springsteen, page 294.

"As my success increased, there…" ~ Springsteen, page 399.

"When people wanted a dialogue…" ~ Springsteen, page 443.

"Rock 'n' roll music, in…" ~ Springsteen, page 454.

"One plus one equals two…" ~ Springsteen, page 236.

"There is something to be…" ~ Springsteen, page 213.

"Songwriters with their own voice…" ~ Springsteen, page 167.

"You have to make thoughtful…" ~ Springsteen, page 79.

"What makes something great may…" ~ Springsteen, page 222.

"Rock 'n' roll is a…" ~ Springsteen, page 353.

"All I know is that…" ~ Springsteen, page 306.

"It's a common malady, a…" ~ Springsteen, page 271.

"There is but one life…" ~ Springsteen, page 274.

"My pal Bonnie Raitt, upon…" ~ Springsteen, page 285.

"The theory of relativity holds…" ~ Springsteen, page 464.

"Your blessings and your curses…" ~ Springsteen, page 495.

"I know how it works…" ~ Springsteen, page 227.

"The Sphinx spoke! My dad…" ~ Springsteen, page 409.

"Soul man, soul man, soul…" ~ Springsteen, page 481.

Chapter Five

"What an absurd question. I..." ~ Bruce, Lenny. *How to Talk Dirty and Influence People*, Boston: Da Capo Press, 2016, page 188.

"It is impossible to label..." ~ Bruce, page 97.

"Every man reading this has..." ~ Bruce, page 174.

"Of course I disagree with..." ~ Bruce, page 72.

"The what-should-be never did exist..." ~ Bruce, page 187.

"How can I ever get..." ~ Bruce, page 92.

"As a child I loved..." ~ Bruce, page 21.

"Believe it or not [...] I..." ~ Bruce, page 164.

"Well, I want to know..." ~ Bruce, page 152.

"It is because of newspapers..." ~ Bruce, page 160.

"Of course, there are some..." ~ Bruce, page 82.

"it is never popular to..." ~ Bruce, page 150.

"I felt—and still do..." ~ Bruce, page 53.

"Constant, abrasive irritation produces..." ~ Bruce, page xi.

"a tightrope walker between morality..." ~ Bruce, page ix.

"a career out of expressing..." ~ Bruce, page vii.

"I don't think about changing..." ~ Bruce, page vii.

"seldom funny without an ulterior..." ~ Bruce, page ix.

"Bruce has the heart of..." ~ Bruce, page x.

"Bruce was no preacher, telling..." ~ Bruce, page xv.

"Perhaps thinking about Bruce as..." ~ Bruce, page xvii.

"What doth God require of..." ~ Lamott, Anne. *Hallelujah Anyway*, New York: Riverhead Books, 2017, page 4.

"kindness, compassion, forgiveness" ~ Lamott, page 5.

"Polite inclusion is the gateway..." ~ Lamott, page 82.

"God doesn't give us answers..." ~ Lamott, page 104.

"I desperately want to stop..." ~ Lamott, page 126-127.

"I hate this, but in..." ~ Lamott, page 129.

"over and over, in spite..." ~ Lamott, page 138.

"a blend of damage, obsessiveness..." ~ Lamott, page 137.

Chapter Six

"may or may not be..." ~ Kraus, Chris. *After Kathy Acker*, Cambridge, MA: Semiotext(e), 2017, page 14.

"Men claiming superiority over..." ~ Crowder, Trae et al. *The Liberal Redneck*

Manifesto, New York: Atria Books, 2016, page 229.

Chapter Seven

"It's not enough to say..." ~ Adichie, Chimamanda Ngozi. *Dear Ijeawele*, New York: Knopf, 2017, page 52.
"I cannot overstate the power..." ~ Adichie, page 48.
"This, I was realizing, is..." ~ Litt, David. *Thanks, Obama*, New York: Ecco, 2017, page 206.
"Time that might have been..." ~ Litt, page 146.

Chapter Eight

"wedged somewhere between cultural criticism..." ~ Diamond, Jason. *Searching for John Hughes*, New York: William Morrow Paperbacks, 2016, page 126.
"I had a book that..." ~ Diamond, page 226.
"How many more times could..." ~ Diamond, page 82.
"I kept getting on a..." ~ Diamond, page 267.
"And the more I drove..." ~ Diamond, page 183.
"When Hughes was toiling somewhat..." ~ Diamond, page 146.
"Like Hughes, I had all..." ~ Diamond, page 157.
"Faith had never really played..." ~ Diamond, page 201.
"I'm writing the unauthorized biography..." ~ Diamond, page 120.
"I found myself disliking a..." ~ Diamond, page 215.
"My relationship with Hughes was..." ~ Diamond, page 248-249.
"I had wasted half a..." ~ Diamond, page 233-234.
"All told, my John Hughes..." ~ Diamond, page 243.
"when the one agent I..." ~ Diamond, page 155.
"To think I had come..." ~ Diamond, page 228.
"Andie [of Pretty in Pink] was..." ~ Diamond, page 40-41.
"I was becoming an adult..." ~ Diamond, page 275.
"Striking to us is the..." ~ Ginsburg, Ruth Bader. *In My Own Words*, New York: Simon & Schuster, 2016, page 193.
"the attention to feminist organizations..." ~ Ginsburg, page 124.
"work progressed on three fronts..." ~ Ginsburg, page 155.
"a sense of humor is..." ~ Ginsburg, page 71.
"Justice Benjamin Cardozo said, 'Justice..." ~ Ginsburg, page 184.
"Sally Reed was not a..." ~ Ginsburg, page 159.
"All in all, great achievements..." ~ Ginsburg, page 129.

"What has become of me…" ~ Ginsburg, page 182.

"I sought Justice O'Connor's advice…" ~ Ginsburg, page 90.

"I had the heady experience…" ~ Ginsburg, page 282.

"To Justice Ginsburg, history teaches…" ~ Ginsburg, page 196.

"[My complete body of published material] is the most…" ~ Ginsburg, page 185.

"controllers, cultivators and mercenary priests" ~ Smith, Patti. *The New Jerusalem*, Netherlands: Nexus Institute, 2017, page 25.

"girls in purple rain coats…" ~ Smith, page 27.

"the rabbits scurry and know…" ~ Smith, page 29.

"right hand raised in benediction…" ~ Smith, page 31-32.

"the voice of the sixth…" ~ Smith, page 39.

"I push aside my computer…" ~ Smith, Patti. *Devotion*, New Haven, CT: Yale University Press, 2017, page 6.

"I linger, content to be…" ~ Smith, page 14.

"He was a solitary man…" ~ Smith, page 45.

"Initially I wondered what prompted…" ~ Smith, page 24.

"Theirs was a story that…" ~ Smith, page 59.

"Most often the alchemy that…" ~ Smith, page 27-28.

"We must write, engaging in…" ~ Smith, page 87.

"She experienced in horror the…" ~ Smith, page 69.

"The text posed a philosophic…" ~ Smith, page 73.

"But slowly I discerned a…" ~ Smith, page 92.

"What is the dream? To…" ~ Smith, page 93.

"Fate has a hand but…" ~ Smith, page 27.

"Having no past we have…" ~ Smith, page 74.

"That is my final conclusion…" ~ Smith, page 28.

"One could not help but…" ~ Smith, page 91.

APPENDIX

THIS IS A COMPLETE LIST OF THE SONGS in the Springsteen catalog that appear to be addressing a female listener. One might suppose that "darling" or "you" are gender-neutral, and there is some decent evidence for that at least in the case of *The Rising*. Yet on the whole of almost fifty years, we can safely presume the heteronormativity of this songwriter's vision and thus also his diction. So this is the complete list from which I cherry-picked forty pieces for translating.

In choosing which poems to work on, there were a variety of factors. I established a constraint based on chronology and then secondarily based on type of address—so everything in chapter 1 is proper names, chapter 2 is nothing but "girl," followed by a long string of "baby," etc. Beyond that, I freely chose my favorite songs, ones that I thought would serve particularly good reversals, or ones that caught my poetic faculties in some other interesting way.

It seems to me this list stands alone as an object worthy of contemplation. And of course, it demonstrates there is plenty of room for two or three more such sets of translation, should you wish to try your own hand at it.

Greetings from Asbury Park, N.J. (1973)

Mary: Mary Queen of Arkansas / Chapter One
honey: For You
mama: It's Hard to be a Saint in the City

The Wild, the Innocent, and the E Street Shuffle (1973)

Sandy: 4th of July, Asbury Park (Sandy) / Chapter One
Rosie: Rosalita (Come Out Tonight) / Chapter One

Born to Run (1975)

Mary: Thunder Road / Chapter One
Wendy: Born to Run / Chapter One

Darkness on the Edge of Town (1978)

girl: Badlands / Chapter Two
girl: Streets of Fire / Chapter Two
baby: Prove it all Night

The River (1980)

baby: The Ties that Bind
Sherry: Sherry Darling
girl: Jackson Cage / Chapter Two
baby: Out in the Street
baby: I Wanna Marry You
darlin': Point Blank
baby: I'm a Rocker
girl: Fade Away / Chapter Two
dolly: Ramrod
girl: The Price You Pay / Chapter Two
honey: Drive All Night

Nebraska (1982)

baby: Atlantic City / Chapter Three

Born in the U.S.A. (1984)

baby: Cover Me / Chapter Three
girl: Darlington County
girl: I'm on Fire
Bobby Jean: Bobby Jean / Chapter Three
baby: I'm Goin' Down
baby: Dancing in the Dark / Chapter Three

Tunnel of Love (1987)

baby: Ain't Got You
honey: Tougher than the Rest
angel: Tunnel of Love
baby: Brilliant Disguise / Chapter Three

baby: One Step Up
honey: When You're Alone
baby: Valentine's Day

Human Touch (1992)

girl: Human Touch
baby: Soul Driver
baby: Cross My Heart
Gloria: Gloria's Eyes
baby: Roll of the Dice / Chapter Four
baby: Real World / Chapter Four
child: All or Nothin' at All
darlin' : Man's Job
baby: I Wish I Were Blind / Chapter Four
baby: Real Man

Lucky Town (1992)

baby: Better Days
baby: If I Should Fall Behind / Chapter Four
baby: Leap of Faith
baby: Living Proof / Chapter Four
baby: Book of Dreams

The Ghost of Tom Joad (1995)

Jenny: Youngstown / Chapter Five
dear: Across the Border
baby: My Best was Never Good Enough

Blood Brothers (1996)

darling: Without You

Tracks (1998)

girl: Seaside Bar Song
girl: Rendezvous

baby: Iceman
baby: Bring on the Night
girl: Hearts of Stone
darling: Don't Look Back
little one: Restless Nights
girl: Dollhouse
girl: Where the Bands Are
baby: Loose Ends
baby: Wages of Sin
baby: Take 'Em as They Come
baby: be true
you: I Wanna be with You
Mary Lou: Mary Lou / Chapter Five
Cynthia: Cynthia / Chapter Five
darling: My Love Will Not Let You Down
Frankie: Frankie
friend: Lion's Den
Catherine: Car Wash
baby: Pink Cadillac
honey: Two for the Road
Janey: Janey, Don't You Lose Heart / Chapter Five
Ma: The Wish / Chapter Five
sister: Leavin' Train
you: Seven Angels
baby: Sad Eyes
I: My Lover Man
baby: Over the Rise
baby: Trouble in Paradise
darling: Happy
honey: Back in Your Arms

18 Tracks (1999)

baby: The Fever

The Rising (2002)

you: Into the Fire / Chapter Six
girl: Waitin' on a Sunny Day

darlin': Nothing Man
darlin': Countin' on a Miracle
you: Empty Sky / Chapter Six
you: Worlds Apart / Chapter Six
baby: Let's be Friends (Skin to Skin)
baby: The Fuse
you: Mary's Place / Chapter Six
you: You're Missing
Mary: The Rising / Chapter Six
you: Paradise

The Essential Bruce Springsteen (2003)

baby: None but the Brave
baby: Missing
darling: Lift Me Up
Carol: County Fair / Chapter Seven
baby: Code of Silence

Devils & Dust (2005)

Bobbie: Devils & Dust / Chapter Seven
baby: All the Way Home
Maria: Reno / Chapter Seven
Rosie: Long Time Comin' / Chapter Seven
Ma: The Hitter / Chapter Seven
baby: All I'm Thinkin' About
darling: Matamoros Banks

Magic (2007)

baby: You'll be Comin' Down
darlin' : Livin' in the Future / Chapter Eight
Theresa: I'll Work for your Love
darlin': Last to Die
darling: Long Walk Home

Working on a Dream (2009)

honey: My Lucky Day
darlin': Working on a Dream / Chapter Eight
darlin': What Love Can Do
you: This Life
darlin': Good Eye
dear: Tomorrow Never Knows
baby: Life Itself
darling: Kingdom of Days
Billy: The Last Carnival

The Promise (2010)

girl: Gotta Get that Feeling
babe: Outside Looking In
you: Someday (We'll be Together)
darling: One Way Street / Chapter Eight
baby: Because the Night
darling: Wrong Side of the Street / Chapter Eight
darling: The Brokenhearted
darling: Save My Love
darling: Ain't Good Enough for You
girl: Fire
Christine: Spanish Eyes
girl: It's a Shame
baby: Come On (Let's Go Tonight)
girl: Talk to Me

Wrecking Ball (2012)

baby: This Depression
baby: You've Got It
darlin': Land of Hope and Dreams / Chapter Eight

High Hopes (2014)

honey: Hunter of Invisible Game
baby: Dream Baby Dream

ACKNOWLEDGMENTS

I OWE THIS BOOK to publisher Bryan Borland's never-ending faith in what I might do. This project was interrupted several times and his enthusiasm for it helped keep me in motion. Also infinite gratitude to Karen Zarker, my editor at *PopMatters*, where many of these essays first appeared. A few of the poems were previously published in *Coldfront Magazine*, *Shock of the Femme*, or *WUSSY Magazine*, as well as in the anthology *Reading Queer: Poetry in a Time of Chaos*.

My thanks to some of the main subjects of this book, most of whom I have never met: Hillary Clinton, Stephen Colbert, Patti Smith, and Bruce Springsteen. Your sense of humor is greatly appreciated and I love each of you in my way.

Then there are all the girls in the band, helping me make so much noise: Abby Norman, Gina Myers, Ellie Black, Claire Dixon-Wilson, Nicole Volpert, and the news nerds at Roswell High School, for starters.

Mindy Dawn Friedman, no words can do justice to what we are to each other. I love you, wife.

To my thousands of nieces and gayish nephews: please take what you can from me and leave the rest. If some of the ideas in this book are already behind you, thank you for leading the way. None of us is getting any younger and there is a lot to do.

ABOUT THE AUTHOR

Megan Volpert is the author of a bunch of books on popular culture, including two Lambda Literary Award finalists and an American Library Association honoree. She has been teaching high school English in Atlanta for over a decade and was 2014 Teacher of the Year. She writes for *PopMatters* and has edited anthologies of philosophical essays on Tom Petty and *RuPaul's Drag Race*. More info can predictably be found at www.meganvolpert.com.

Other Sibling Rivalry Press books by this author

Sonics in Warholia (2011)
Only Ride (2014)
1976 (2016)

editor, *This assignment is so gay: LGBTIQ Poets on the Art of Teaching* (2013)

ABOUT THE PUBLISHER

Sibling Rivalry Press is an independent press based in Little Rock, Arkansas. It is a sponsored project of Fractured Atlas, a nonprofit arts service organization. Contributions to support the operations of Sibling Rivalry Press are tax-deductible to the extent permitted by law, and your donations will directly assist in the publication of work that disturbs and enraptures. To contribute to the publication of more books like this one, please visit our website and click *donate*.

Sibling Rivalry Press gratefully acknowledges the following donors, without whom this book would not be possible:

Tony Taylor

Mollie Lacy

Karline Tierney

Maureen Seaton

Travis Lau

Michael Broder & Indolent Books

Robert Petersen

Jennifer Armour

Alana Smoot

Paul Romero

Julie R. Enszer

Clayton Blackstock

Tess Wilmans-Higgins & Jeff Higgins

Sarah Browning

Tina Bradley

Kai Coggin

Queer Arts Arkansas

Jim Cory

Craig Cotter

Hugh Tipping

Mark Ward

Russell Bunge

Joe Pan & Brooklyn Arts Press

Carl Lavigne

Karen Hayes

J. Andrew Goodman

Diane Greene

W. Stephen Breedlove

Ed Madden

Rob Jacques

Erik Schuckers

Sugar le Fae

John Bateman

Elizabeth Ahl

Risa Denenberg

Ron Mohring & Seven Kitchens Press

Guy Choate & Argenta Reading Series

Guy Traiber

Don Cellini

John Bateman

Gustavo Hernandez

Anonymous (12)

CPSIA information can be obtained
at www.ICGtesting.com
Printed in the USA
FFHW022233060519
52328999-57677FF